Craig,

authors—

Good reading. Excellent

Ken Hains

NO GOD BUT GOD

OS GUINNESS
& JOHN SEEL

EDITORS

MOODY PRESS

CHICAGO

Deo Optimo Maximo

and to Billy Graham and Carl F. H. Henry,
giants in their time
who leave us inspired, challenged, and without excuse
in our time.

© 1992 by
Os Guinness
and John Seel

ISBN: 0-8024-6337-1

3 5 7 9 10 8 6 4 2

Printed in the United States of America

CONTENTS

ACKNOWLEDGMENTS

Special acknowledgment and appreciation go to Amy Boucher, who with a passion for the ideas and a dedication to the project that equaled any of the writers, served as project manager, in-house editor, and friend to the eight contributors. Rarely have writers been served so selflessly.

Our thanks as well to Jim Bell, who represented Moody Press with enthusiasm, professionalism, and patience. In a day of market-driven, mission-deficient publishing, he consistently demonstrated a better way.

Editors

Os Guinness is a writer living in McLean, Virginia. Born in China and educated in England (D.Phil., Oxford University), he has lived in the United States since 1984. He was a visiting fellow at the Brookings Institution and the executive director of the Williamsburg Charter Foundation. He is the author of several books, including *The Gravedigger File* and *The American Hour.*

John Seel is the son of medical missionaries in Korea. He has an M.Div. from Covenant Theological Seminary and is a doctoral candidate in American Studies at the University of Maryland. He was formerly the administrative director of the Williamsburg Charter Foundation and was cofounder of First Liberty Institute at George Mason University. He is presently writing *Wars of Position: Evangelicals and Cultural Tactics.*

Contributors

Michael Cromartie is a research fellow in Protestant Studies and director of the Evangelical Studies Project at the Ethics and Public Policy Center in Washington, D.C. He is the editor of five books, including *No Longer Exiles: The Religious New Right and American Politics*, and coeditor with Richard John Neuhaus, of *Piety and Politcs: Evangelicals and Fundamentalists Confront the World.*

Richard Keyes is the director of L'Abri Fellowship in Southborough, Massachusetts, which he and his wife started in 1979 after working at the L'Abri Fellowship in both Switzerland and England. A graduate of Harvard University and Westminster Theological Seminary, he is the author of *Beyond Identity* and is completing a book on heroism.

Alonzo L. McDonald is the chairman and CEO of Avenir® Group, Inc. He has four decades of management experience in professional firms, government, academia, the media, and in large and small businesses. He is a former U. S. ambassador, White House Staff Director, president of the Bendix Corporation, managing director (CEO-worldwide) of McKinsey & Company, Inc., and a member of the faculty of Harvard Business School. He now divides his time between serving as chairman of Avenir® Group, Inc., a private development bank, and a group of Christ-centered activities and foundations.

Thomas C. Oden is Henry Anson Buttz Professor of Theology at Drew University. He is an ordained Methodist minister and the author of many books, including *After Modernity-. . . What?*, *Pastoral Theology*, and a three-volume systematic theology: volume one, *The Living God*; volume two, *The Word of Life*; and volume three, *Life in the Spirit*. Most recently, he wrote *Two Worlds: Notes on the Death of Modernity in America and Russia.*

Paul C. Vitz is professor of psychology at New York University. He is the author of several books, including *Psychology as Religion: The Cult of Self-Worship; Sigmund Freud's Christian Unconscious*; and *Censorship: Evidence of Bias in Our Children's Textbooks*. He is currently writing and publishing on the relationship of the Christian faith to psychological theory in the context of psychotherapy and counseling, with respect to moral development.

David F. Wells is the Andrew Mutch Distinguished Professor of Historical and Systematic Theology at Gordon-Conwell Theological Seminary in South Hamilton, Massachusetts, and an ordained Congregational minister. He is the author and editor of many books, including *Turning to God* and *The Evangelicals: What They Believe, Who They Are, and Where They Are Changing*. He is a member of the American Theological Society and the Lausanne Committee for World Evangelization.

PREFACE FOR READERS
OUTSIDE NORTH AMERICA

*N*o *God But God* is written primarily for American evangelicals, but it deserves a far wider audience for a simple reason: The problems addressed stem directly from modernization, and modernization is a global force that shapes the lives of Christians on all five continents. Where the problems are American, other people can afford to attend to their own business. But wherever the problems are modern, they will become other people's business sooner or later, in one form or another.

Put differently, those who are not Americans tend to make two equal and opposite errors about America in the modern world. (It is perhaps worth saying that one of the editors of this book is a European born in China and the other, though an American, was raised in Korea.) Some resign themselves, either with delight or despair, to the prospect that modernization is inevitably Americanization (or "Coca-Colanization"). Others reject Americanization altogether and believe that they can as easily reject modernization.

The fact is that, as this book demonstrates, many of the church's problems in the modern world stem from modernization, not from America. Often America displays these problems in a particularly sharp form only because it is at the leading edge of modernization in the twentieth century, as Britain was in the nineteenth.

Thoughtful Christians would therefore do well to ponder the impact of modernization on the churches in the United States, asking themselves if and how the same trends and developments will touch their countries in the long run. Although experience is an excellent teacher, its lessons are often costly—especially when they come late. Christians in other countries have the opportunity to learn now from the challenges that modernity presents to followers of Christ in America. Consider the following ten propositions:

1. Modernity is the central fact of human life today: Modernity, or the character and system of the world produced by the forces of development and modernization, especially capitalism, industrialized technology, and telecommunications, is the first truly global culture in the world and the most powerful culture in history so far. In short, modernity is a counterfeit of the kingdom of God. Extensively, it encircles the planet; intensively, it encompasses more and more of each individual's life.

2. Modernity is double-edged for human beings: Modernity simultaneously represents the greatest human advances in history—in such benefits as health, speed, power, and convenience—and the greatest assaults on humanness in history—in such areas as the crisis of identity and the crisis of the family.

3. Modernity is double-edged for followers of Christ: Modernity represents the crux of the contemporary challenge to the gospel because it is the greatest single opportunity and the greatest single challenge the church has faced since the apostles. In the first case, it is equivalent of Roman roads in the first century and printing presses in the sixteenth. In the second, it is our equivalent of the challenges of persecution and gnosticism rolled into one.

4. Modernity is foundational for the character and identity of both Americans and American evangelicals: Both America and American evangelicalism have prospered at the growing edge of modernity. But this is a disadvantage in a double sense: those most blessed by modernity are most blind to it, and those first hit by modernity are often the worst hurt by modernity. This is one reason why non-Westerners in relation to Americans, and Roman Catholics and Orthodox in relation to evangelicals, consider themselves superior to, and immune from, either the crises facing America or American evangelicals.

5. Modernity is a monumental paradox to the everyday practice of faith: Modernity simultaneously makes evangelism easier—more people at more times in their lives are more open to the gospel—yet makes discipleship harder, because practicing the lordship of Christ runs counter to the fragmentation and specialization of modern life.

6. Modernity pressures the church toward polarized responses: Ever since the early days of modernity in the eighteenth century, a pattern of response to modernity has grown strong. Liberals have generally tended to surrender to modernity without criticizing it; conservatives have tended to defy modernity without understanding it. This tendency has been reversed in the last generation as evangelical "progressive conservatives" now court the "affluent consumers" of the gospel just as liberals once courted the "cultured despisers" of the gospel. The two main American examples today are the megachurch leaders marrying managerial technique and the Christian publishers romancing therapeutic solutions.

7. Modernity's challenge cannot be escaped by the common responses to which Christians typically resort: Those who recognize the deficiencies of the extreme liberal and conservative responses often go on to two further deficient responses. One is a resort to premodernism—looking to the Third World to refresh the West, not realizing that Third World Christians have yet to face the inevitable challenge of modernization. This is true too of our brothers and sisters in Eastern Europe and Russia, who face a greater challenge from modernity than they previously faced from Marxism. The other is the resort to postmodernism—failing to see that though modernism as a set of ideas built on the Enlightenment has collapsed, modernity, as the fruit of capitalism and industrialized technology, is stronger than ever.

8. Modernity represents a special challenge to the church: The three strongest national challenges to the gospel in the modern world are Japan, Europe, and the United States. Japan has never been won to Christ; Europe has been won twice and lost twice; and America, though having the strongest and wealthiest churches, is now experiencing the severest crisis. Thus America represents the clearest test case of Christian responses to modernity.

9. Modernity represents a special challenge to reformation: The reason for this special challenge is its central dismissal of the place of words. On the one hand, the overwhelming thrust of modernity has been to replace words with images and reading with viewing. On the other hand, the words that remain have generally become technical, specialized, and abstract to most people. At the same time, postmodernism further devalues words by using them to create a pastiche of effect regardless of their original meaning.

10. Modernity represents a special challenge to revival: Quite simply, the church of Christ has not experienced revival under the conditions of advanced modernity. On the one hand, modernity undercuts true dependence on God's sovereign awakening by fostering the notion that we can effect revival by human means. On the other hand, modernity makes many people satisfied with privatized, individualistic, and subjective experiences that are pale counterfeits of true revival. While many Christians no longer have a practical expectation of revival, those who count on God's sovereignty over modernity have every reason to look to God for revival once again.

No God But God is written for all who are prepared to wrestle with the opportunities and challenges of modernity. More importantly, it is written for all whose hope for revival and reformation is in the hands of the One who is sovereign over modernity as He is over all of life and time.

Preamble
A SERIOUS CALL TO EVANGELICALS IN AMERICA

It is time once again to hammer theses on the door of the church. As on the occasion of Martin Luther's ninety-five theses in the sixteenth century and Søren Kierkegaard's single thesis in the nineteenth century, Christendom is becoming a betrayal of the Christian faith of the New Testament. To pretend otherwise is either to be blind or to appear to be making a fool of God.

The main burden of this book is a direct challenge to the modern idols within evangelicalism. But this idolatry is only one part of the wider cultural captivity of evangelical churches in America. We therefore begin by looking beyond idolatry to the broader need for revival and reformation within evangelicalism. Our greatest need is for a third Great Awakening.

THE AMERICAN HOUR

The American republic is nearing the climax of a generation-long crisis of cultural authority that calls into question its very character and strength. The problem is not simply "out there"—in either such obvious problems as drugs and crime or such common explanations as the influence of family breakdown, moral relativism, secularism, neo-paganism, and the New Age movement. Nor is the crisis of cultural authority simply a matter of the "culture wars," deep and serious though they are. Instead, American beliefs, ideals, and traditions—civic as well as religious—are losing their compelling power to shape and restrain lives in both the private and the public spheres. This loss of power is evident in scores of recent developments.

Moreover, effective remedies are not a simple matter. Cultural change has gone too far. Political change can do too little to resolve the problems.

The present moment is one of those great times of reckoning on which the future of the nation will hinge. At the very least, the United States is experiencing a time of testing in which the myriad questions of faith and public life have come center stage and cannot long be evaded. More important, the present *kairos* moment is a critical period in the American century —the American hour.

It is therefore time, and past time, for Americans to face the challenge of faith to the character, ideals, and institutions of our nation. More important still, it is time for our church to examine the integrity and effectiveness of its character and witness and its own response to the above questions. For if the nation's crisis is largely because of the decreasing influence of faith on American culture, the church's crisis is largely because of the increasing influence of American culture on the Christian faith.

The overwhelming majority of Americans—more than 85 percent— still identify themselves as Christians. But if the statistical indicators of faith are up, the social influence is down and the reasons are becoming plain. There has been a carelessness about Christian orthodoxy, a corruption of Christian obedience, a vacuum of Christian leadership, and a disarray among many of the public initiatives in which Christians have recently placed their confidence. Much of the public face of "American Christianity" is a stunning testament to the power of religion without God. Much of the private face is an act of indifference to history and human society that borders on disobedience and a gross negligence. The United States has become the storm front of the battle between the gospel and modernity.

The Evangelical Moment

We as American evangelicals face our own moment of unprecedented challenge and opportunity. Criticism of evangelicalism is widespread: "Evangelical is not enough," "The term evangelical has lost all usefulness," "There is no longer any identifiable evangelical community," "We can do without evangelicalism," "The label evangelical has its roots, not in the churches, but in the power politics of the neo-evangelicals after World War II," and so on. Behind such caustic dismissals and the celebrated defections to which they sometimes lead are quieter, deeper concerns about the state of evangelicalism in the 1990s—concerns that are far more serious than the well-publicized scandals of the television evangelists.

For all the undoubted growth and achievements of the past fifty years, many of the hopes of the evangelical leaders of the forties and fifties have not been fulfilled. Much of the promise of the so-called Year of the Evangelical in 1976 has not materialized. A great deal of the "family resemblance" between evangelicals in scores of different denominations has become unrecognizable. Commentators on evangelicalism now reach routinely for such terms as mosaic, kaleidoscope, umbrella, and even "twelve-ring circus of evangelical faith." As the last of these labels suggests, part of the chaotic appearance of evangelicalism is the fruit of a genuinely burgeoning diversity. Too much, however, can be attributed only to disarray—in theology, in discipleship, and in numerous ventures in both private and public life.

Yet the opportunities we have in front of us are equally immense—opportunities for the renewal of a vital orthodoxy, participation in public and professional life, and partnership in worldwide mission.

Today the evangelical movement is often compared unfavorably with other traditions of the church, the Catholic and the Orthodox. Many complain that evangelicalism is hard to define. Others doubt whether evangelicalism has a future. But such fears are unwarranted. There is no question that concern for the church's living, consensual truth, as in the Orthodox tradition, and for worldwide universality, as in the Catholic tradition, is vital. But no defining concern of any of the traditions comes closer to the heart of the gospel than that which seeks to be loyal to the gospel (*evangelion*) itself. So long as the gospel remains the gospel and the church the church, and so long as the church is in need of reformation, the world of mission, and one last person of salvation, there will always be a future for evangelicals—those who seek to define themselves and their lives by the gospel of Jesus Christ.

The present crisis of evangelicalism is thrown into sharp relief by a series of wider considerations: the remarkable story of evangelical contributions to American life and worldwide missions in the past, the seriousness of the national crisis of cultural authority, the menace of the worldwide challenge to faith posed by modernity, and the varying responses to modernity by other religions, ideologies, and other traditions within the church of Christ.

At this momentous chapter in the ongoing story of the Christian church and the modern world, one of America's greatest spiritual movements is in danger of losing its way or missing its moment. To be a nominal evangelical is a contradiction in terms; therefore to be Christian and evangelical in America at the close of the second millennium is a high privilege and a solemn responsibility. To be evangelical is not to be part of a subculture, nor to have a subjective experience, nor to belong to a fraternity of special-issue organizations. It is to participate in the life of the church and the

13

world with all the perspectives, powers, and passion of the truth and life of the gospel itself.

God's Part and Ours

We who write these essays acknowledge that privilege and assume that responsibility. We therefore join with all who recognize this critical moment and reaffirm the historic call to "Let God be God" and to "Let the church be the church—and free." And, to that end, we also join with all followers of Christ in this land, of whatever tradition, denomination, church, and calling, to commit ourselves to seek and pray for revival and reformation—reminding ourselves that who we are comes before what we do, that faith comes before works, that worship and contemplation come before action, that citizenship in the city of God comes before citizenship in the city of man, and that as in the past the church can only be freed from its cultural captivity today by the free Word of a free God.

We recognize that some matters must be left to God alone and acknowledge openly that a spiritual and theological awakening within evangelicalism is our greatest need, but it is not ours to predict, initiate, or effect. Such an awakening is a matter of divine sovereignty, not human engineering or historical cycles. Yet we know too the perils of fatalism, of a passive, private devotion to God, and of presuming that praying well is the best revenge for the loss of cultural influence.

We therefore call for a humble dependence on God that is matched by vigorous rededication to doing what is ours to do. In particular, we call for a rediscovery of the gospel in the church; a renewal of the integrity and effectiveness of Christians in society, beginning with a serious examination of both the theoretical and practical assumptions that shape the life of the church and society; and a systematic recovery of the first things of the gospel—those forgotten truths and neglected requirements that are vital to reformation, revival, and mission.

Specifically, we believe that faithfulness to Christ requires that we evangelicals respond to the present moment with prayer, discussion, and action on eight issues. These themes are vital to the renewal and redirection of evangelicalism. This book will focus specifically on the second theme, confronting idolatry in the church.

1. Recognition that the opportunity is in the crisis

How can Christians engage the modern world with both realism and hope? Many believers confuse the answer to this question with psychology, being either optimistic or pessimistic by nature. Others confuse the answer with social and economic conditions, depending on either the openness of society or the bullishness or bearishness of economic prospects. All such grounds, apart from faith, are inadequate.

At another level, evangelicals have responded to the present crisis in two common ways. One has been to seek, as with the Christian Right, to prevail by a forceful assertion of Christian strengths, such as numbers and organization. The second has been, as with the megachurch movement, to prevail by a forceful appeal to the world's felt needs, such as with the baby boomers. But all too often both strategies have failed. The first has led to an unsuccessful confrontation with culture, because the presumed "Christian strengths" were neither Christian nor strengths. The second has led to an unsuccessful accommodation to culture, because becoming "all things to all people" has been a process of massive adjustment and compromise.

A better way for constructive engagement is to follow the prophetic dynamic of the gospel itself—law before gospel, judgment before grace, repentance before regeneration, and the disproof of Baal before the demonstration of Yahweh. We must require prophetic confrontation before personal and social transformation. The radical demands of the gospel will then be fulfilled with the demonstration that conversion, once begun, can never stop. Having touched a part of our lives, conversion must transform the whole.

With this constructive engagement underway, America's crisis of cultural authority could be the greatest opportunity for the American church in the last 150 years. Followers of Christ may be weak and their influence on society only marginal. But with the devastation of the alternative faiths and the depth and urgency of the issues raised, the crisis is a momentous opportunity. Both America and Americans are at a rebound point—a pigsty moment of recognition when the course of prodigal choices and their consequences are plain. At such a moment, even the humblest and most weak can point the road home. As Aleksandr Solzhenitsyn has reminded us, just as a shout in the mountains can start an avalanche, so a word or stand for truth that does God's work in God's way in God's time can have an incalculable effect.

2. Radical confrontation with sin, heresy, worldliness, and idolatry

The charge of sin, heresy, worldliness, and idolatry has lost plausibility for many American evangelicals. They act as if loss of self-esteem outweighs sin and being un-American were far more serious than being heretical. They seem to believe that worldliness by definition is a problem for other traditions in the church just as idolatry is a problem for other religions and cultures in the world. Yet these believers close their eyes to the biblical teaching that our hearts, and specifically the sinful imagination of our hearts, are the supreme idol-making factory. They also ignore the current evidence that evangelicalism appears to be vastly careless about orthodoxy as well as being the worldliest tradition in the contemporary church and productive in idol-making.

To be more specific, the idolatry in question is the idolatry of good and useful things from our modern world that, in the form of powerful modern myths, have been allowed to become distortions of the gospel and substitutes for faith in God. For, contrary to popular misconceptions, the idols against which the Bible warns are not simply the concerns of others (those "pagans") and the obvious crudity of their objects of worship (their "gods of wood and stone"). In the biblical view, anything created—anything at all that is less than God, and most especially the gifts of God—can become idolatrous if it is relied upon inordinately until it becomes a full-blown substitute for God and, thus, an idol. The first duty of believers is to say yes to God; the second is to say no to idols.

Such idolatry is a problem for contemporary evangelicals because evangelicals have uncritically bought into the insights, tools, and general blessings of modernity. Thus a radical confrontation with heresy, worldliness, and idolatry is part and parcel of a serious examination of the theoretical and practical assumptions that shape the life of the church in modern society. We are under the searching demand of the truth at the heart of the gospel: There is one God, there is no god but God, and there is no rest for any people who rely on any god but God.

3. Recovery of forgotten first things

Typically, today's search for greater Christian power in culture becomes a search for improved management internally and improved mobilization and communications externally. Our real need, however, is simultaneously simpler, more biblical, and more effective than programs and methodologies. Our real need is a recovery of the forgotten first things of the gospel of Jesus.

Today's ultimate battle is the battle for the gospel—its supernatural realities, ethical imperatives, and disorienting simplicity as well as its doctrinal distinctives. Are we disciples as Jesus called disciples, or Christians for whom discipleship is an optional part of a larger program of religious observances and practices? The first things of the gospel are fundamental to the restoration of Christian integrity and effectiveness, and to Christian reformation and mission in the modern world.

For evangelicals, five of the most important forgotten fundamentals are these: the kingdom of God as God's here-and-now rule that orders and reorders our life's priorities and perspectives; discipleship as a lifetime apprenticeship under Jesus that teaches us to live as He would live if He were us; calling as the compelling source of vision, discipline, and accountability for every sphere and stage of life; Christ-centered thinking as the fruit of the imparting of the mind of Christ; and persuasion in all forms of Christian communication as the natural expression of Christ's message and heart. No one who has pondered these five fundamentals can deny either their weakness or absence in the evangelical movement, and the serious theoretical and practical consequences.

4. Revitalization of the laity

Despite commendable talk of thawing "God's frozen people" and "solving the church's unemployment problem" by putting Christians to work, the general outcome has been a massive harnessing of lay people to only two spheres of service: spiritual ministries within the church or service ministries of crisis relief outside. Yet the greater part of life, including the world of work, has been overlooked.

Even when the discussion comes to the sphere of work, and goes beyond evangelism in the workplace, people frequently suggest that the main problem is that Christians are not where they should be—and that in such fields as the academic world and the media Christians have been excluded unfairly.

Again, the real problem is overlooked. Our problem is not that Christians are not where they should be, but that they are not what they should be right where they are. In such fields as business or in such professions as law and medicine Christians are plentiful in numbers, but are ineffectual in discipleship, vision, and influence. Parallel to the priesthood and ministry of all believers, the calling of all believers is vital to the reformation of evangelicalism. Clerical dominance is a fatal handicap in secular, modern life. But the modern world has yet to see the power of lay Christian leadership exerted strategically across the multiple spheres of secular life.

5. Reexertion of leadership

Just as modernity has turned "crisis" into a cliché, so it has made "crisis of leadership" into a standard lament. Yet there is unquestionably a serious dearth of genuine leaders in the evangelical community as there is in the wider church and the contemporary world.

Explanations abound. Some point to reasons purely within evangelicalism—for example, the fact that the great postwar leaders were such giants that few were able to grow in their shade. Others point to wider historical reasons—above all to the authority-sapping effect of the 1960s on the generation now in their forties and fifties. Still others cite sociological reasons—the same dislocations that cause breakdowns within families also cause breaks between the generations.

Whatever the reasons for the crisis, the reformation of evangelicalism requires a fresh exertion of godly leadership. The rampant individual egotism that is common today must be dissolved for the wider concerns of the kingdom. Parochial shortsightedness must be transcended to strategic vision. Superstar authority must be humbled in servant ministry. Unacknowledged, ghost-written communications and other forms of ventriloquist inauthenticity must be renounced. Approval-seeking caution must be abandoned for courageous action. And our chronic evangelical proneness to entrepreneurial individualism and endless fragmentation must be confessed and healed as we shoulder the yoke of discipline under the Master as well as the responsibilities of membership in the worldwide church.

6. Reintegration of truth and theology

Contemporary evangelicals are no longer people of truth. Only rarely are they serious about theology. Both problems are a tragedy beyond belief. A solid sense of truth is foundering in America at large. Vaporized by critical theories, obscured by clouds of euphemism and jargon, outpaced by rumor and hype, overlooked for style and image, and eroded by advertising, truth in America is anything but marching on.

With magnificent exceptions, evangelicals reflect this truth-decay and reinforce it for their own variety of reasons for discounting theology. Repelled by "seminary theology" that is specialized, professionalized, and dry, evangelicals are attracted by movements that have replaced theology with emphases that are relational, therapeutic, charismatic, and managerial (as in church growth). Whatever their virtues, none of these emphases gives truth and theology the place they require in the life and thought of a true disciple.

The crisis of truth and theology has been highlighted by the recent dissolution of distinctive differences between denominations and by the forlorn quests periodically undertaken to find a single-issue "watershed" behind which some purported last stand can be made. Worse still, the

Protestant principle of *sola Scriptura* is no longer operative in much of evangelicalism. Adherence to formal orthodoxy is still strong, but such modern sources of authority as politics, psychology, and management theory routinely eclipse biblical authority in practice. The combined effect is to render unthinkable the notion of an evangelical community that is defined by truth, united by truth, and guided by truth.

Yet truth and theology are the royal road to knowing God. No one can love God and not be a theologian. No one can follow Christ and not be committed to taking truth seriously. Probably only the restoration of the notion of covenant will provide bonds strong enough to bind the free and diverse evangelical peoples to God and to each other—securing our unity while recognizing our diversity and holding us to live a certain way as well as believe certain truths. Unquestionably, however, the reintegration of truth and theology in all that evangelicals are, as well as all that they think and do, will be one crucial measure of how evangelical evangelicalism remains.

7. Recovery of the past

For a Christian who appreciates the importance that remembering our past has on faith, the past must never be blank or a matter of nostalgia and historical reverie. The latter are false ways of seeking access to the past without allowing the tradition of the past to gain authority over the present. Tradition as the living faith of the dead and traditionalism as the dead faith of the living are two very distinct things. Remembering the past is the key to identity, faith, wisdom, renewal, and dynamism.

Most evangelicals, however, suffer from historical amnesia. Like Rip Van Winkle's return from sleep, they act as if there were no jump from the last chapter of the book of Revelation to the first pages of the story of modern times. For American evangelicals, the loss is especially severe. It covers not only the great centuries of vital orthodoxy when the mind of the believing church was shaped and there were evangelicals without evangelicalism. It even includes the earlier movements of evangelicals better known to evangelicals from other continents—and the story of such giants of the English-speaking world of faith as John Wycliffe, William Tyndale, Richard Baxter, William Wilberforce, and Hudson Taylor.

Today there is a direct link between remembering and the redirection of evangelicalism. The possibility of a vital thrust forward depends on a vital thrust back. Evangelicals are, in part, children of modernity. But if we are not to be made spiritual orphans by modernity, we must nourish faith and deepen gratitude through appreciation of the great centuries of vital or-

19

thodoxy and "what has been believed always by all Christians everywhere." If we are not to be victims of fashionableness, superficiality, and hysteria, we need the antidote of a collective memory. The best of the Catholic and Orthodox traditions is as vital for evangelicalism as the best of evangelicalism is vital for them.

8. Reforging the public philosophy

To evangelicals in America, religious liberty is the crown jewel in the treasury of freedoms, our "first liberty" and our assured birthright both as believers and as citizens. But while evangelicals are quick to recognize today's threats to religious liberty—both in the United States and around the world—many are slow to appreciate how we contribute to those threats and how we are failing to seize a historic opportunity for the gospel around the world.

Evangelicals can be justly proud of their part in the long, painful struggle for the legal guarantee of religious liberty. But we must also acknowledge the blemishes and inconsistencies in our own record. Most of these stem from an ambivalence at the heart of our position: Is religious liberty for "saints" only or is it for "strangers" too? Is it a matter of "justice" or "just us," without freedom for those of other faiths? Is the freedom to disbelieve inherent in the freedom to believe?

This unresolved tension, which divided John Winthrop from Roger Williams in the seventeenth century, still divides evangelical from evangelical today. For over three hundred years it has lain behind such church-state tensions as the attempt to pass a Christian amendment and the persistence of religious tests for public office at the state level. Today it is the troubling question behind both specific debates, such as prayer in public schools, and general evangelical attitudes toward "Christian America" and the place of religious liberty in public life.

Unless this ambivalence is resolved definitively on the basis of Christian principle, every evangelical initiative in public life has the potential to be counterproductive. However legitimate, wise, and successful the specific initiative, others are liable to view it as troubling—even threatening—if it is not accompanied by a clear commitment to religious liberty for people of all faiths and none.

Unlike the first seven themes raised, the place of religious liberty in public life should be secondary for us. We are called to be faithful whether we are free or not, and to forget this is to court the danger of an idolatry of religious liberty for its own sake. But at the same time, the free exercise of religious liberty is vital to sustain just and free societies, to protect the welfare of our neighbor, to practice the daily imperatives of Christ's lordship in our own lives, to have the freedom to address transcendent truth to worldly power, and thus—above all else—to follow the deepest dictates of our consciences and let God be God.

As we said, in these eight areas our deepest need is for what God alone can do—in reformation and revival. But if addressed with humility, expectancy, and urgency, these themes are central to the renewal of evangelicalism. Only through such a recovery can there be integrity and effectiveness in the believing community. Only in this way can we act so that all we do stems from who we are. Only so can we engage constructively with our culture and nation at every level of opportunity and challenge. Only so can we seek to be people after God's own heart, who serve His purposes in this generation.

Introduction
THE IDOLS IN OUR
CHURCHES AND HEARTS

Evangelicals, once known as "the serious people," are now in serious disarray. Nowhere is this more damaging than in our captivity to modern idols in our churches and our hearts. We evangelicals can justly call ourselves heirs of America's first faith. But we who should be guardians of the faith are falling victim to the world's first and worst sin against faith. We are idolizing the products of what the Bible calls the "imagination of our hearts." We have uncritically bought into the insights, tools, and general blessings of modernity. (Modernity is the character and system of the world that the forces of modernization and development have produced.) This has led us to idolize modern approaches to life, such as politics, management, marketing, and psychology; we also have fallen prey to powerful modern myths, such as change, technique, relevance, and need.

Idolatry is the most discussed problem in the Bible and one of the most powerful spiritual and intellectual concepts in the believer's arsenal. Yet for Christians today it is one of the least meaningful notions and is surrounded with ironies. Perhaps this is why many evangelicals are ignorant of the idols in their lives.

First, consider a simple historical irony. The church has been assaulted for nearly two hundred years by her own weapon. Thinker after thinker, including Karl Marx and Sigmund Freud, have used the biblical concept of idolatry in such forms as the notion of ideology to attack biblical belief itself. But just when Christians are seizing back the weapon and preparing to use it themselves, two surprising developments have occurred. On the one hand, many of the long-prominent idols of the day outside the church have collapsed by their own inner hollowness—Marxism being the most prominent. On the other hand, unexpected forms of idolatry have risen up within the church itself.

Idolatry within the church? How can that be? Adultery perhaps, or stealing, killing, giving false witness, or coveting. But worshiping idols—as something more than a metaphor, such as "idolizing" heroes? Evangelicals who deny the possibility of idols within evangelicalism should remember the closing words of the first letter of John, the apostle of love. They were written not to pagans but to believers like ourselves: "Children, keep yourselves from idols."

Here we face a second and subtler theological irony. In the Bible, part of the antidote to idolatry is knowledge—but by itself that very knowledge can also be an alibi for idolatry. In both Old and New Testaments idolatry is clearly the supreme threat to faith because it grows from the deepest desires and motivations of the human heart and thus is a barrier to repentance, lordship, and the first and greatest commandment: to love the Lord our God and tolerate no third party or rival allegiance in our hearts. But the Bible makes it equally clear that we cannot defeat idolatry by knowledge alone. Mere intellectual dismissal of other gods is not enough. It takes a covenant love for God to root out idolatry, because idolatry remains a threat even though we know with certainty that idols are nothings.

> *Idols are nonexistent, mere fictions, false gods. But this knowledge by itself is not a safeguard against idolatry.*

Put differently, it is true that because God alone *is*, idols are *not*. Idols are nonexistent, mere fictions, false gods. But this knowledge by itself is not a safeguard against idolatry because it is not a stand-alone truth. It requires both an accompanying call to love and obedience, as well as the reminder that the imagination of our sinful hearts has such a reality-creating power that the nonexistent is invested with its own dynamic. Thus, regardless of what the mind "knows," the imagination of the heart can change the mind. It can turn lies into truth, fictions into reality, no-gods into gods, and the quite incredible into the utterly credible. This idol-making propensity of the imagination of our hearts is a continuing and deadly threat to faith. Having once turned from idols to the living God, our task of keeping on turning is never done.

Radical opposition to idolatry is also fundamental to the Protestant principle. Confronting idols is the corollary to letting God be God, living by faith alone, and practicing the principle of *ecclesia semper reformanda*—the church always needs reformation. At the heart of the Reformation was an insistence on the utter dependability of God and an unrelenting protest against any absolutizing of the created, the relative, and the purely human. Anyone or anything that lays claim to our hearts' confidence, attention, and loyalty may grow into a point of reliance apart from God and eventually may become a full-blown substitute for God. Thus Protestant and evangelical are two faces of the same truth. Protestant is the critical stance of evangelicalism, just as evangelical is the positive content of Protestantism. Neither is complete without the other.

Dominant myths and images concern such themes as modernity, progress, change, technique, statistics, and relevance and shape our perceptions of reality.

Yet the Protestant principle is weak in American evangelicalism today, which brings us to a third irony. Contemporary evangelicals are little better at recognizing and resisting idols than modern secular people are. Our modern secular world congratulates itself on its criticism of idols when actually it creates them just as prolifically. Again, the reason lies in the nature of the world's knowledge. If even a true and biblical knowledge of idols—that they are nothings—is inadequate to defeat idolatry, modern forms of knowledge are even poorer. Modern knowledge deepens and widens this dismissive critique of idols. Not only are idols nothings, to modern knowledge idolatry itself and even the reality of the living God are nothings. So modern knowledge is too rational to deal with the imaginations of the human heart. But the image-making and idol-making of the heart go on unchanged. The double outcome of such modern knowledge is a profusion of idolatrous modern myths while simultaneously inflicting a blindness toward its own idolatry.

Our hearts' drive to idolatry means that our conscious thinking is inspired and shaped by images from the imagination, of which we are barely aware. This means that what people know, and what they think they know, is less important than the underlying myths and images that spawn and interpret what they know. When these myths and images are left uncriticized, they have a disastrous effect: They distort the gospel, they blind those who believe them, they grow into idols, and they force those who worship them to become what they worship. What we revere, we resemble.

In our case as modern people, these dominant myths and images concern such themes as modernity, progress, change, technique, statistics, and relevance. These myths and images are products of the imagination and are highly imprecise. But they are not imaginary or ineffective. They are potent—made concrete by artists, manipulated by advertisers, translated into concepts by thinkers, and conveyed day-to-day by the moving storehouse of clichés, catchwords, and commonplaces that is our society's stock response to life. In other words, these myths and images shape our perceptions of reality and form the heart of "the spirit of our age" and "the idols of our day."

This idolizing process is taking place within our evangelical churches in our time. It is a major reason for our modern Babylonian captivity. The cultural forms of idol-worship have changed, but their essential seductiveness and menace have remained potent. The idolatrous imagination has not changed, only the points on which we falsely come to rely. We therefore seek to address the major areas where we see the danger. Our purpose in writing is to provoke fellow-followers of Christ to be on the lookout for the idolizing of modern myths and be prepared to give a rigorous account of our use of the best insights and powers of modernity.

On the one hand, in searching for what is best in modernity, we should ask: where are modern insights and powers legitimate and fruitful? Because all truth is God's truth, we are free to plunder truth wherever it is found. On the other hand, in looking out for what is worst, we should ask several questions. First, where are modern insights and powers double-edged? (The double edge exists because modern insights contain negative and positive aspects, intended and unintended consequences.) Second, where are they excessive? (Useful though they may be, it is possible to trust in them inordinately, making them either unbalanced or unbounded.) Third, where are they autonomous? (Their very brilliance and effectiveness encourages us to treat them separately from other moral, human, and theological considerations.) Fourth, where are they idolatrous? We ask this final question not because the insights and tools are inherently evil, but because—through their very usefulness—they can be points of false reliance and even working substitutes for God.

26

The essays in this book address the major areas where evangelicals have uncritically employed the insights and tools of modernity, leading to a false reliance and thus to idolatry. In chapter 1 Richard Keyes defines idolatry itself and describes the idol-making factory of the human heart. Idolatry, he argues, has a dual nature—we all have "nearby"idols to serve our need for security and "faraway idols" to serve our search for significance.

The next three chapters look at different forms of idolatry arising from evangelicals' engagement in public life. In chapter 2 Michael Cromartie examines the danger of political activism that too often leads to a politicization of faith and an idolization of politics—on both the Left and the Right. John Seel explores in chapter 3 the idolatry of majoritarianism, which results from a false reliance on social standing coupled with an idealization of the past. In chapter 4 Os Guinness describes the opposite temptation, minoritarianism, which in contrast to the confidence of majoritarianism resorts to blaming others and playing the victim.

The therapeutic and managerial revolutions are two powerful forces of modernity that have captivated evangelical churches. In chapter 5, Paul Vitz examines the current status of psychology, arguing that we need to go beyond it, not least because its best insights are fulfilled in the gospel. Guinness, in chapter 6, critiques the broader therapeutic revolution and its place in American society. On the managerial theme, Alonzo McDonald in chapter 7 analyzes the idolatry of immortality inherent in all organizations. In chapter 8, Guinness examines the enormous significance of the church-growth movement, highlighting the danger of its uncritical use of two tools of modernity, marketing and management.

The ultimate idol factory is the human heart. We who write are as prone to idolatry as anyone, for there is no defense against idolatry in abstract orthodoxy alone.

The final two chapters explore the dangers of idolatry within the ministry and within evangelical ideas and thinking. David Wells (chapter 9) outlines the recent trend toward professionalization among pastors, as they seek professional status based on academic criteria unrelated to either truth or spirituality. Thomas Oden (chapter 10) examines the danger of accommodation to the world in our thinking, challenging our fascination with the cult of newness and calling us to a recovery of the past that puts us in touch with our classical Christian heritage.

Let it be clear that we write from sorrow rather than anger. The list of idols that we challenge is not intended to be comprehensive, but only a sampling. Few errors that we question are full-blown; most are only in germ. There is no name-calling in these pages and the attacks are never on people, only on trends. We are well aware that the ultimate idol factory is the human heart. We who write are as prone to idolatry and as needing of grace as anyone responsible for what we write against, for there is no defense against idolatry in abstract orthodoxy alone.

At the same time, it is our burning conviction that, because idolatry is the central problem of faith, it must be the central concern of all lovers of God and disciples of Jesus. There can be no believing communities without an unswerving eye to the detection and destruction of idols. This then is the theme of this book and the wider challenge to evangelicals in America: The challenge of our time is the recovery of the living reality of the gospel, including the all-sufficiency of the one, true God over against the self-sufficiency of our modern age. Either we put our full trust in God, or we do not. If we do not, we are left to the folly of trusting in false gods and the grief of becoming what we worship. If we do, there is no room for any other god.

For the people of God, there is no other way because there is no other God. There is one God, there is no god but God, and there is no rest for any who rely on any god but God.

1
THE IDOL FACTORY

by Richard Keyes

Like someone held at gunpoint with his own pistol, Christians have been threatened and attacked for two hundred years on the basis of their own view of idolatry, turned against them. Such celebrated critics of the gospel as Karl Marx and Sigmund Freud based their debunking of religion on the insights that originally came from this biblical notion. They claimed that religion was not true, but merely a projection of the believer. Curiously, however, now that these critics and their philosophies are themselves in bad shape, Christians have been surprisingly slow in reclaiming their own best weapon.

But what exactly is an idol? And why and how has the human heart become such an idol-making factory? We look first at the biblical understanding of idolatry in order to provide a context for the later discussion of the idolizing of modern myths and images.

OUR PROBLEM TOO

As modern people we usually think of an idol as an animal or human figure made of stone or wood. We see it as an object for religious devotion or magical power for premodern people who might prostrate themselves on the ground before it. If we have updated the idea at all, we might use "idolatry"

Richard Keyes is the founder and director of L'Abri Fellowship in Southborough, Massachusetts. He has also served at L'Abri Fellowships in Switzerland and England, and has written *Beyond Identity*.

to describe someone's obsessional preoccupations with money or of an "idol" like Elvis Presley. We have, in effect, distanced ourselves from the whole idea of idolatry by pushing it out to the extreme cultural and psychological margins of life.

This distance has produced two problems: First, we misunderstand the most comprehensive description of the shape of unbelief used by the writers of the Bible. If we as Christians today see idolatry only at life's margins, we will be ill-equipped to use this powerful critical tool as the apostles and prophets did—to understand and challenge the surrounding world. The second problem is similar to the first but even more important. If we do not understand the nature of idolatry, we will not be able to recognize it or guard against it in our own lives and communities. As noted in the introduction, the apostle John was warning Christians when he wrote, "Keep yourselves from idols " (1 John 5:21).

A great deal is at stake in both of these problems. On the one hand, overlooking idolatry puts us at the mercy of hostile criticisms. Our society has equipped itself with a number of filters through which people can pass any part of Christian truth or experience. Out the other end of the filter comes something quite innocuous, unchallenging, domesticated to the comfort of the secular mind.

"I am depending on God for the future," I once said to a friend. "Oh, I see," she responded. "You need the security that comes from believing that."

Idols are not just on pagan altars, but in well-educated human hearts and minds. The apostle Paul associates the dynamics of human greed, lust, craving, and coveting with idolatry.

What is involved in that reply? On the surface, it was only a bit condescending. At a deeper level, it casually eliminated a whole category of human knowledge. The possibility of a true knowledge of God had been emptied and reduced to compensations for psychological insecurity. Today, the theological backbone has been surgically removed from religious discussion. The effect of this process on Christians is too often confusion, alienation, and intimidation as we are made to feel obtuse, ethnocentric, or just uninformed when we mention God. Too often again, we then express these feelings in either accommodation and keeping a low Christian profile, or else in defensiveness and bombast.

On the other hand, overlooking idolatry makes us blind toward our own problems. Naïveté about idolatry in Christian experience is like the price paid by the city of Troy as its people happily opened their city gates to welcome the Trojan horse (filled with enemy soldiers). Idolatry can corrupt and distort any aspect of Christian thought and life, transforming it into something that is ruinous and death-dealing. It is this danger of idolatry —the blinding to our own problem—that is the concern of this book.

A careful reading of the Old and New Testaments shows that idolatry is nothing like the crude, simplistic picture that springs to mind of an idol sculpture in some distant country. As the main category to describe unbelief, the idea is highly sophisticated, drawing together the complexities of motivation in individual psychology, the social environment, and also the unseen world. Idols are not just on pagan altars, but in well-educated human hearts and minds (Ezekiel 14). The apostle Paul associates the dynamics of human greed, lust, craving, and coveting with idolatry (Ephesians 5:5; Colossians 3:5). The Bible does not allow us to marginalize idolatry to the fringes of life. All too often it is found on center stage.

My task in this chapter is to explore the biblical paradigm of idolatry. We must be able to recognize idolatry more readily; then we can confront it in our lives and in the lives of those around us. In our view of the world, such awareness can help us to remove the filter and begin to see unbelief as God-avoidance at a profound level, a means of hiding from God. In our Christian experience it should alert us to the deadly danger of self-deception.

The General Characteristics of Idolatry

I will begin with the general characteristics of idolatry, starting with some of the most basic assumptions. To speak of an idol in the biblical sense assumes that there is a true God of whom the idol is a counterfeit.

The natural human response to the true God after the Fall is rebellion and avoidance. Sin predisposes us to want to be independent of God, to be laws unto ourselves or autonomous, so that we can do what we want without bowing to His authority. At the most basic level, idols are what we make out of the evidence for God within ourselves and in the world—if we do not want to face the face of God Himself in His majesty and holiness. Rather than look to the Creator and have to deal with His lordship, we orient our lives toward the creation, where we can be more free to control and shape our lives in our desired directions.

If we were not created to be in personal relationship with God, human beings could have simply dismissed the whole religious dimension of life and lived happily and rationally in the here-and-now world, untroubled by meanings, limitations, and mortality. However, since we were made to relate to God, but do not want to face Him, we forever inflate things in this world to religious proportions to fill the vacuum left by God's exclusion. Augustine's famous statement, that we will be restless until we find our rest in God, is true only because of our God-relatedness. This train of thought was continued by G.K. Chesterton, who said that when we "cease to worship God, we do not worship nothing, we worship anything." We do not just eliminate God, we erect God-substitutes in His place. The biblical writers call these counterfeits "idols," and they tell us a great deal about why idols make us restless.

An idol is something within creation that is inflated to function as a substitute for God.

Unbelief has two overriding concerns, one positive and one negative. The positive is that a person wants to follow the path of life that will bring life's fullness—however that person defines fullness. The negative concern is that the person wants to receive the fullness of life without ever having to be accountable or face the ultimate moral challenge from the true God. That challenge is not just that God tells us to be good, unselfish, and kind. Many people quite like that sort of challenge and feel good about themselves as they track their progress. The ultimate moral challenge from God is at a deeper level. He does tell us to be good and unselfish and follow the commandments, but He also tells us that because we are so enmeshed in our sin, that we will not do so. We will be found to be without excuse. Our only hope is in the forgiveness of God.

This is the ultimate moral challenge—that hope rests in complete and excuse-free dependence on God and His forgiving grace, plus nothing. This forgiveness is joyfully offered to us through Christ.

An idol is something within creation that is inflated to function as a substitute for God. All sorts of things are potential idols, depending only on our attitudes and actions toward them. If this is so, how do we determine when something is becoming or has become an idol?

Idolatry may not involve explicit denials of God's existence or character. It may well come in the form of an overattachment to something that is, in itself, perfectly good. The crucial warning is this: As soon as our loyalty to anything leads us to disobey God, we are in danger of making it an idol.

As we will see, an idol need not be a full-sized replacement for God, for nothing can be. We become increasingly attached to it until it comes between us and God, making God remote and His commandments irrelevant or unrealistically prohibitive. In this society, our idols tend to be in clusters. They are inflationary, have short shelf lives, and change, adapt, and multiply quickly as if by mitosis, or cell-division. An idol can be a physical object, a property, a person, an activity, a role, an institution, a hope, an image, an idea, a pleasure, a hero—anything that can substitute for God.

By this definition, all the obvious candidates are potentially idolatrous—wealth, fame, pleasure, power, and so on. We can recognize ways in which we disobey God out of loyalty to them. But many nonobvious things can work as idols as well, causing us to ignore or distort God's commands to us. For example, work, a commandment of God, can become an idol if it is pursued so exclusively that responsibilities to one's family are ignored. Family, an institution of God Himself, can become an idol if one is so preoccupied with the family that no one outside of one's own family is cared for. Being well-liked, a perfectly legitimate hope, becomes an idol if the attachment to it means that one never risks disapproval. Even evangelism, carrying out the Great Commission, can become an idol if people are misused—Christian or not Christian—in the zeal to do it.

To summarize, idols will inevitably involve self-centeredness, self-inflation, and self-deception. Idolatry begins with the counterfeiting of God, because only with a counterfeit of God can people remain the center of their lives and loyalties, autonomous architects of their futures. Something within creation will then be idolatrously inflated to fill the God-shaped hole in the individual's world. But a counterfeit is a lie, not the real thing. It must present itself through self-deception, often with images suggesting that the idol will fulfill promises for the good life.

King David asked that the nations abandon their idols when he prayed, "Strike them with terror, O Lord; let the nations know they are but men" (Psalm 9:20). What a strange thing to ask. Surely they knew that they were men and not giraffes. It is actually not at all strange, however, given the problem of sin and idolatry. Their true status as human beings was the very thing in confusion, the very territory of self-deception. Idolatry gave them an inflated picture of their authority, status, and power. David's prayer was a prayer for undeception, that they might see themselves as they truly were—dependent and morally corrupted creatures of God.

The Strange Shape of Unbelief

Two examples will suggest a certain shape or pattern of thought to our idolatry—one old and one relatively new. Let us begin with the Roman author Cicero, writing in the first century B.C.:

> When we behold the heavens, when we contemplate the celestial bodies, can we fail of conviction? Must we not acknowledge that there is a Divinity, a perfect being, a ruling intelligence, which governs, a God who is everywhere and directs all by his power? Anybody who doubts this may as well deny there is a sun that lights us . . . . For this reason, with us as well as with other nations, the worship of the gods and holy exercises of religion increase in purity and extent every day.[1]

Notice that Cicero wrote of a revival of the popularity of the gods and exercises of religion. Within the polytheism of the time, one could gain access to various invisible powers through religious observances and sacrifices that were designed to exert control on the visible world. Many actual physical idols were involved with this worship. Within Cicero's own generation, the emperor himself was proclaimed divine, helping to consolidate the power of the Roman state.

But notice also a different dimension. Cicero began by referring to "a Divinity," a single transcendent being who was a "ruling intelligence," and who had authority over everything. It seems that the piety of the day embraced both levels of belief—a group of lower gods and spirits that were associated with different functions, but also a higher, more exalted divinity who stood above the whole.

Here is a more recent example. Lance Morrow of *Time* magazine reflected on ambitions that were common to Americans:

> What kind of people do Americans want to be? They want to be a great deal better than they are—not only better paid or better clothed, but better. Not merely passive recipients of favors from the governmental All-Daddy, or on the other side, shrewd looters cooking the books and snickering through the loopholes. The potential idealists inhabit the middle between

those two caricatures. They crave material well-being, certainly. But they also want to be, saying it plainly, active participants in the larger enterprise of their nation. They want to do some good, to make changes.[2]

Here we have the predictable twentieth-century cast of idols—money, possessions, an ever-rising standard of living—all that is involved when we crave material well-being. These things are available to us. We can count them, put them on a graph or in a bank. Material upward mobility offers power for a myriad of things as one of its promises, but it also offers itself as the power to achieve greater wealth still, and therefore more power again. It embraces both ends and means in a seductive spiral upward.

But Morrow's main point goes beyond this. Despite the undeniable greed and the craving for material well-being, Americans are not one-dimensional money-grubbers. They are "potential idealists"—they want to accomplish something morally significant with their lives, to be part of a larger project that is good. If we ignore this second side of American character (and this is not only American, but human character), we misread it.

After the Fall, God-given mastery, or dominion, tends to become domination. Trust, on the other hand, tends to become overdependence.

These examples show two levels of loyalties or allegiances in people's minds and hearts—one more accessible, oriented toward power or control, and another more inaccessible, but providing legitimacy, meaning, or coherence. Could having loyalties on these two levels be a universal characteristic of idolatry? If so, this could help us recognize idols and their work. But first I will suggest a biblical model that might help explain this duality.

THE THEOLOGY OF INSECURITY

In the first chapters of Genesis we find men and women living out the image of God in two directions. One direction is downward in dominion over the creation. They are to control or have mastery over some piece of God's world, not as owners but as stewards. The other direction is upward

35

to God. They are to trust God, to look to Him as their Creator and Sustainer. There was no tension between these two directions until the Fall.

The primal rebellion against God and its consequences are described in chapter 3. Here the whole picture changes. Now people still bear the image of God, but we are twisted and bent, living in a twisted and bent world. The world has become an insecure and dangerous place. Our plans to cash in on the fullness of life are frustrated by disease, accident, bankruptcy, and finally death. Every graveyard shows that the earth subdues us. Our trust is often betrayed in this world since we follow illusions and have extravagant expectations that are utterly unfulfillable. We are no longer strangers to anxiety and disappointment.

What has become of the two directions of the human personality? Both become twisted as they are directed away from God, and they then pull against each other. After the Fall, God-given mastery, or dominion, tends to become domination. Sin predisposes people to turn away from God, who offers reconciliation by grace, and toward something that can allow them to pursue life autonomously, as a law unto themselves. Because the world is an insecure and frustrating place, they seek a certain degree of security from controlling and manipulating key variables (often people) in their lives and surroundings. Control becomes something that in itself alleviates anxiety by all sorts of psychologically symbolic activities, but is also a direct means to getting specific, desired results.

Trust, on the other hand, tends to become overdependence after the Fall. It becomes a grasping or clutching onto things, ideas, institutions, and people. Again, the motivation is security, but here it is not through control as much as by finding an umbrella of legitimacy, meaning, coherence, or safety.

The harmony between dominion and trust is gone, replaced by a tension between domination and overdependence. Many theorists in the psychological sciences point to an internal conflict between a force of independence and of dependence, activity and passivity, individual self-interest and the concerns of community. One of the best known is Friedrich Nietzsche's tug of war between the master and the slave within each one of us. One psychiatrist who is a student of the human life cycle pointed out that when we are two years old, we make two mutually exclusive demands of the world— omnipotence and absolute safety. We then spend the rest of our lives trying to untangle ourselves from these oversized internal demands.[3] The Bible, however, places this tension in its widest framework.

I suspect we all feel the tension between these two motivations, although we differ from each other dramatically in where the balance of power is located within us. For example, if you were suddenly offered a new, very challenging job opportunity, there would be two voices within you. The voice of dominion/domination would say, "Great, this is my opportunity, I'll do it!" But the voice of trust/overdependence would counter with, "I could never do it, I would fail for sure. I'd better stick to what I know I can do."

When we do not turn to God, we instead direct our life to God-substitutes, or idols. Idolatry then will be lived out in terms of this basic duality of human motivations. Idolatry will be expressed in terms of a twisted form of dominion, tending toward domination, as well as a twisted form of trust, tending toward overdependence. Our idol-making will follow this duality that is so deeply imprinted on human psychology.

IDOLS IN PAIRS

Idols come in pairs, and these pairs correspond to the two directions of the human personality just mentioned—dominion and trust, when twisted away from God. An idol is a counterfeit of the true God. And an idol may counterfeit not just God's existence but even aspects of God's character or activity. Idolatry, when seen in its dual character, counterfeits God's immanence in one idol and His transcendence in the other. We shall call these the nearby idol and the faraway idol. These words are not spatial designations as much as psychological ones. The nearby idol is more accessible or tangible. The faraway is more inaccessible, overarching all of life. We will explore the nearby idol first.

Jeremiah pictures a tame god, a user-friendly god, who exists by human manufacture, is at human disposal, and is under human control.

A nearby idol results from the human need for dominion, when directed away from service to God. Dominion is a God-given human gift of mastery, of the ability to affect our surroundings in stewardship to God. But when we are alienated from God, we search for enough security—from controlling some part of the world—so that God seems unnecessary. The nearby idol must provide a sense of well-being through control. It is a psychological counterfeit of the immanence of God.

A biblical example of a nearby idol is described in Jeremiah's scornful remark, "Like a scarecrow in a melon patch, their idols cannot speak;

37

they must be carried because they cannot walk. Do not fear them, for they can do no harm nor can they do any good" (Jeremiah 10:5).

Think carefully about Jeremiah's critique of their religious commitment. He says that their god is like a scarecrow. His point is that their god is entirely under their control (it cannot walk or talk but must be carried), and they even made it themselves. Their god does the job he is supposed to do by increasing their control over an important part of their world—scaring birds from their garden. The god is not just for decoration, it has a practical and powerful function.

Jeremiah pictures a tame god, a user-friendly god, who exists by human manufacture, is at human disposal, and is under human control. This god would never rebuke, warn, threaten, or talk back. The context of Jeremiah's prophesy was a warning against the worship of the Canaanite gods, such as Baal. These gods were not just tame but were powerful. Most were oriented toward fertility. Service to them was acquisitive, and acquisition was by means of various technologies of magic. The purpose was to raise good crops, more livestock, and male children. A nearby god enables its servant to experience a certain leverage over the important forces that control life. Nearby idols can be both the ends of and means to the good life. But especially in the context of social, political, and economic insecurity, their role may become increasingly as arbiters of fear as they offer the power to avert evil and disaster.

The faraway idol is the result of the human need to trust the true God—when that trust has turned away from God. It is a counterfeit transcendence as the object of trust. We often do not recognize the faraway idol as an idol simply because we associate idols with the tangible, visual world. While the nearby idol gives the illusion of the control to get what one wants out of life, it can never satisfy the need for some meaning, coherence, purpose, value, hope, or sense of ultimate safety in life. A nearby idol, though small enough to provide a significant measure of personal control, can never be big enough to provide a sense of meaning.

To give two extreme examples, nearby idols can be such things as a stamp collection or a clean house. Either can be centers of nearly complete control where one's mastery enables a small piece of one's little world to be structured in a way that gives a disproportionate sense of security. It is difficult, however, to derive a sense of meaning, coherence of life, or ultimate safety without going beyond stamp collecting or housecleaning.

The faraway idol may not necessarily be spatially distant, but may provide some overarching positive meaning, even if that meaning is only vaguely describable. Consider two idols worshiped today. For some, Love has become the all-powerful force at a cosmic level. Others worship Progress as all glorious and inevitable. But with some faraway idols, very little can be said to describe them. Still others can be largely negative in form, with convictions about what is not true about the world. For many people, the highest level of truth that they admit to believing in is the certainty that there is *not* a God who will hold us accountable. It could be in the form of atheism, but is more often some form of agnosticism rooted in affirmations about the unreliability of all human thoughts about ultimate things. They are certain about very little else at an ultimate level. But this itself provides a sense of safety from any final evaluation and the freedom to pursue whatever kind of life they so desire.

This is not to say that what is desired will be immoral. On the contrary, many idol-systems have powerful moral dynamics at work. It is just that the content of that morality will be determined independently of the Creator God.

An intriguing biblical example of faraway idols is in the words of Isaiah, "But as for you who forsake the Lord and forget my holy mountain, who spread a table for Fortune and fill bowls of mixed wine for Destiny" (Isaiah 65:11). The language is of setting a table and preparing cups of mixed wine for a god. But notice that a physical or visible statue or figure is not being referred to. It is, instead, the abstract ideas of Fortune and Destiny. He rebuked them for paying homage to Fortune and Destiny, mysterious forces beyond their comprehension.

These gods—also known today as Chance, Good Luck, or Fate—can also deliver the illusion of coherence or meaning in the universe. If the idols are amoral in nature, at least people are left to feel safe from transcendent moral scrutiny. There is safety from judgment. The faraway god is user-friendly also. Neither Fortune nor Destiny ever called anyone to repent.

All idols come in pairs. One is always stronger than the other, and each one corresponds to the two directions of the human personality—dominion, now become domination, and trust, now become overdependence. The Baal worship of the Old Testament is a good example of this paradigm.

Baal is the nearby god, representing powers of rain, fullness of life, and fertility. By use of magic, incantations, rituals, and priestcraft, one could have power over the forces that controlled history, to fulfill wants and prevent fears. Their sexually oriented worship seemed to be at the root of what the Hebrew prophets called "abominable practices." It was not so much that Baal worship allowed sexual license; there was a higher logic to it than that. It was only through passionate human sexual activity that the gods supposedly were stimulated to lust after each other. It was their subsequent sexual relationships that would then produce fertility on earth. The seduction of divinity brought fertility.

Child sacrifice was also linked to this, as a means of access to the invisible and mysterious powers that controlled life. Sacrifices were attempts to activate forces that would produce desired results, or prevent feared ones. In the Bible, child sacrifice was often associated with Molech, the god of the Ammonites.

In the Canaanite pantheon, the faraway god was "El the Benign." He made the world and was mildly benevolent, but he was not as powerful in delivering concrete help as Baal. He was an overarching presence in the background.

STREET PHILOSOPHIES

The idols we are challenging in this book are largely from the dominant myths and images of modernity—Progress, Change, Technique, Relevance, Need, and so on. But let me set out wider examples of idolatries of different sorts. Modern idolatries are characterized by impermanence, flexibility, and multiplicity—they might not last long, they can change shape, and they are legion. This makes an analysis of them difficult, and generalizations dangerous. Near and far idols can relate to each other in many different ways. We will look at several examples, which will suggest their diversity.

Relatively few people today take formal academic philosophy seriously, although philosophy may influence most people more than they know. Everyone has some kind of view about what he or she thinks the world is like, how people got here, how one can know truth from falsehood, and what is a good way to live and why. These ideas might not be systematic or particularly well-articulated, but they are "street philosophies," the ideas that make some sense or order out of a great many modern persons' experiences.

Like more ancient peoples, we have also revived child-sacrifice— both in the abortion industry and in child neglect—out of loyalty to these idols.

An obvious place to begin is with the cluster of nearby idols that group around money, possessions, and the lifestyle they feed. We can experience a certain sort of control in our society if we have them. They come with all the secular sacrifices, offerings, totems, and rituals that promise to deliver the blessings of the good life and avert the disasters we dread. The idolater is likely to sacrifice time, health, family, and other people for these promises. Like more ancient peoples, we have also revived child-sacrifice —both in the abortion industry and in child neglect—out of loyalty to these idols.

Whereas the nearby idol will be a rising standard of living, a large nest egg, and the means to achieve them, the faraway idol is likely to be made up of semi-conscious hopes that financial security will wipe away every tear, or that success will provide immunity from aging and death. (Think of how the advertising industry feeds these illusions.) The far idol might involve moral convictions about the reliability of the universe in rewarding good hard work. The faraway idol might be the Invisible Hand of Adam Smith's free market, which transforms all the individual greed in a capitalist system into a virtuous and just society. On the other hand, the faraway idol could be a notion of Fate or Luck, or it could be a mixture of all of the above.

Woody Allen suggested a variation on this theme when he defined what it is to be middle class. He said that middle class people take life very seriously—with equal seriousness, God and Carpet. Carpet, of course, represents the home with its decorations, color combinations, furniture, appliances, and sound systems. The home can provide a place where one feels secure and in control, where there is a level of predictability and order in an otherwise threatening world.

God in this case stands for some higher being or principle—as in the god of one's choice. Any god who will share his throne with carpet has little to do with the God of the Bible—despite sharing the same name. In contrast, he, she, or it will either ignore the sins of materialism or smile with benevolence on them.

Another closely related idol-system in modern America is the nearby idol of expertise or competence. The idol of expertise could come in any field of activity—investments, computers, construction, or the arts. The sacrifices that it demands are similar to those of idolaters of wealth and possessions. Security can be developed through a sense of control by the highly refined development of one's skills. It gives people a sense of power within a small slice of their worlds, which in turn translates into power on a larger scale in terms of professional success, recognition, and admiration.

The faraway idol could be a confidence in Progress as an inevitable force. Someone's efforts have meaning and moral legitimacy because they are part of the overall improvement of the human condition—technologically, morally, aesthetically, medically. A musician friend once described to me the worldview of many of his colleagues. They had a nearby idol in the highly disciplined skill of playing their instruments (to which they would offer almost anything in sacrifice), and had the faraway idol in the belief that the arts were inherently, morally uplifting and ennobling to the human race.

Then there are idolatries of the body. Nearby gods can be health, diet, fitness, or the body-beautiful culture pursued with obsessional zeal.

Then there are idolatries of the body. In a world where many feel powerless to influence major events, let alone control their own lives, they turn to their own bodies to experience a sense of control, predictability, and power. Nearby gods can be health, diet, fitness, or the body-beautiful culture pursued with obsessional zeal. A measure of order can be experienced in life if one's jogging is improved, an extra two pounds is lost, cholesterol is purged from the diet, arms are expanded, or the waist is shrunk. The sacrifices here will be of other people, money, time, and sometimes even health itself.

The faraway idols could be many here. They might be minimal ones, such as Chance or Luck, but might also be in the form of beliefs about the transcendent importance of self-esteem in a world where body-image is central to self-esteem. For many, Fitness is well ahead of godliness.

We do not have the space to explore different street philosophies and their idolatries having to do with sports, sexuality, power itself, political life, the academic world, science, family, and so on. We will, however, look briefly at the idols of religion.

IDOLS OF RELIGION

Seeing other religions as idolatrous is especially offensive to the modern mind, which readily embraces relativism. The Christian must be especially careful not to provide the fuel for the non-Christian's stereotype of the Christian at this point—as one who rejects all that is not familiar out of a combination of arrogance and ignorance. Other religious convictions and the people who hold them must be treated with respect and understanding, not scorned without investigation. To be fair to the biblical tradition, however, the Christian must be willing to say that there is such a thing as the true and the counterfeit in religions. There is idolatry of different sorts and degrees in other religions.

A good place to begin is with the idolatry of the first-century Pharisees as we find them in the New Testament. We may not be used to seeing them in the categories of idolatry, but idolatry in fact describes them well. The nearby idol was keeping the law. That gave them confidence in their own efforts to secure God's blessing on their futures. Law keeping gave them a sense of control to know exactly where they stood before God. The Pharisees' experience showed a quality of all nearby idols—that the idols tend to demand more and more of those who serve them. The demands of the law became increasingly fine-tuned and all-encompassing. Jesus, for example, deliberately tangled with them over their laws prohibiting work on the Sabbath. They had determined that measures could be taken to keep a wound from getting worse on the Sabbath without breaking the law, but nothing could be done to make it better. Putting on a bandage to stop bleeding was permissible (that was not work), but putting ointment on the bandage was prohibited (that was work because it was healing).

The nearby idols in most parts of the New Age movement have directly to do with power . . . power for psychological change, spiritual growth, methods of healing, and changing the course of history by mind-power.

The faraway idol for the Pharisees was their own heavily edited version of the biblical God and His program. This god was so high and great that his name could not be said out loud. He was also so morally blind that he was impressed with their legalism, and assured them that he would send the messiah to put their boys in power and fulfill all their political ambitions. The Pharisees, who would never have dreamed of turning to a god of a foreign religion, in fact transformed the god of their own tradition into something quite foreign to what the true God had revealed of Himself.

Another entirely different example would be the timeless idolatries of the New Age movement. The nearby idols in most parts of the New Age movement have directly to do with power. In all its diverse manifestations, there is a preoccupation with the power for psychological change, spiritual growth, methods of healing, and changing the course of history by mind-power. Technologies are presented to accomplish these changes, including spiritual growth weekends, meditation exercises, exotic diets, astrology, and crystal power. The movement is known for its ever-changing means of access to power.

The faraway idol for the New Age movement is the god of the major religions of the East. This god is the monistic god of the All, the One, the god of Pantheism, or the Universal Mind.

The seductiveness of a nearby idol for the Christian is that it promises to get things done, to be powerful, to make good changes—but by using means that conflict with God's means.

As we think of the idols of religion, we must not assume that the Christian is immune to idolatry. The most common path is for the Christian to follow one or several of the many powerful nearby idols in our society. They demand sacrifices that contradict and displace obedience to God. As this happens, gradually the Christian transforms the true God into a faraway idol, usually without realizing it. Many of the themes confronted in this book will identify nearby idols in our society that promise power and hope of control to the Christian. This comes at a time when Christians are discouraged by their impotence. The seductiveness of a nearby idol for the Christian is that it promises to get things done, to be powerful, to make changes that might well be good changes—but by using means that conflict with God's means.

Our political, economic, psychological, social, and theological goals can be right and good. But all of those goals can be pursued while by-passing the priorities and ways of living that God has given us to live in. In so far as this is true, those means will become idols to us, and will destroy us along with the legitimate goals that we strive for.

In the Old Testament we see the prophetic warning against following a nearby idol and then assuming that God does not see, does not hear,

44

and will never call us to account for our disobedience. God becomes transformed in our minds into someone who is deaf, blind, and mute, in order that He not challenge or invade the self-chosen shape of our lives. He will not see our sexual escapades, will not notice it when we hold back the wages of the poor, or when we walk across the faces of His people. It is likely that the more loyalty we have to a nearby idol, the more distant God Himself will become in our experience.

THE IDOL'S FRUIT

The fruit born by an idol is one of the key factors in a biblical analysis of idolatry. Since an idol is a counterfeit, it is a lie. Deception is its very identity. The idol deceives both about what it is and about what it does. It is a counterfeit of either the immanence or the transcendence of the living God. But idolatry also deceives us about what it will deliver. Its promises dazzle and blind us.

Typically, the nearby idol, which promises to link us to control, power, and order, ends up enslaving us, overpowering us. There is a role-reversal. This is why obsession, compulsion, and addiction are associated with nearby idols. If we try to make something finite fill the place that only God can fill, we will try to extract an unrealistic level of meaning from that idol. When it does not work, it invites us only to try harder. It should not surprise us in a deeply idolatrous society that books on codependency and addiction form a growth industry. People feel enslaved to substances, to unwanted behavior, and to each other. These idols have promised life, but are death-dealing, anti-human, and constricting. It seems to be exactly this role-reversal that the Psalmist has in mind when in discussing idolatry he writes, "Those who make them will be like them and so will all who trust in them" (Psalm 115:8). The idol begins as a means to power, enabling us to control, but then overpowers, controlling us.

Typically also, the faraway idol, which has promised coherence, legitimacy, and safety, evaporates when it is most needed. What happens to the god who cohabits the same throne with Carpet when we get cancer and look to that god for help? What coherence or validation does Chance or Luck give us when our "luck" has given out? What can any idol do for us when we are faced with death?

The message of the Bible is that just as idols deceive us, so also they eventually disappoint and disillusion us. They are silent when we turn to them for insight and impotent when we go to them for help. The social historian Daniel Boorstin wrote in his book *The Image*, "Never have people been more the masters of their environment. Yet never has a people felt more deceived and disappointed. For never has a people expected so much more than the world could offer."[4]

Another variant pattern is also suggested in the Bible. A caterer at a wedding in Cana in Galilee once remarked that "Everyone brings out the choice wine first and then the cheaper wine after the guests have had too much to drink" (John 2:10). This could be a metaphor of idolatry. It all begins with excitement and great promises. As time wears on, commitments are hardened, discernment becomes blurred, and one begins to realize only dimly, if at all, that the promises are not being kept. That is to say, sometimes there is so little discernment left that there is an inability to see that life is not working and that the idol has failed.

GOD'S VERDICT

The verdict of God is that idols misrepresent Him. The nearby idol gives the illusion that people really can have control over their destinies. The faraway idol produces the illusion that people have some sort of meaning or coherence to their lives, some vindication of themselves as they are, or at the very least, a hope of nonaccountability. The great problem with idolatry is deception. It leaves the mirage of autonomy unchallenged. We are deceived about our actual helpless dependence on God for every single breath. We are deceived also about our true moral guilt and ultimate need for forgiveness.

No idol, near or far, will ever bring us the ultimate moral challenge. Our gods may well challenge us morally, sometimes with extraordinary and severe demands for sacrifice. But they will never confront us with the truth that we fall so far short, that we have no hope apart from the grace of God in His forgiveness. They never allow us to see that, having received the gift of forgiveness, we can then throw ourselves into obedience to God, motivated by gratitude and fullness of life.

One of the most sharp-edged rebuttals of idolatry is found in the prophecy of Jeremiah as he recounts God's rhetorical questions, "Am I only a God nearby . . . and not a God far away? Can anyone hide in secret places so that I cannot see him? . . . Do not I fill heaven and earth?" (Jeremiah 23:23-24).

What is God saying here? He is one God, and He fills heaven and earth. God cannot be divided and conquered. He is not reducible to something "at hand" that we can control or that will promise us control. Nor can He be relegated to some remote, safe spot from which He is too near-sighted to see the way we live. The distinctive wonder of the God of the Bible, as compared to all idols, is that He created the universe by a word of His mouth, and yet He knows the number of hairs that you and I have on our heads, and every sparrow that falls. But He not only knows about us, He cares and is sacrificially involved with us. Graham Kendrick puts it well in his hymn, "Hands that flung stars into space, to cruel nails surrendered."

God is immanent, close to us, available to us. But that does not make him a tame God, controllable, at our disposal.

God is immanent. He is with us, close to us, available to us. But that does not make Him a tame God, controllable, at our disposal. God is also transcendent. He is great beyond greatness. He is the Alpha and the Omega, the beginning and the end. But that does not make Him distant, impersonal, impotent, arbitrary, or beyond moral categories.

The God who fills heaven and earth challenges us morally in both His immanence and His transcendence—that our only hope is in His grace. That same God also offers us the gospel of forgiveness through Jesus Christ. Neither economic prosperity, nor expertise, nor fame, nor beauty, nor admiration will wipe away every tear, but God will.

In the apostle Paul's famous address to the philosophers in Athens, he seemed almost to be speaking from this text of Jeremiah 23. He systematically contradicted their idols, near and far, with four alternating strokes, and corrected them each time with a true vision of the immanence and transcendence of God. I will summarize his address, found in Acts 17, separating his negations and affirmations in the terms of our discussion.

First, Paul contradicts their idea that God is unknown. God is not a far idol that is unknowable (verse 23). Then he contradicts their near idols by saying that God does not live in shrines made by human hands, nor does He need our help for anything (24-25). Next he attacks the far idol when he declares that God is not far from each one of us, for, "In him we live and move and have our being" (27-28). Finally, he negates the near idols again by reasoning that if we are *God's* offspring, then it does not make sense to believe that He is *our* offspring. God is not made of gold, silver, or stone and fashioned by human artistry (29). The apostle seems to have keyed his critique explicitly into the dual nature of their idolatry. He saw the specific way that they had counterfeited both God's immanence, miniaturizing Him, and God's transcendence, vaporizing Him.

47

With each of these negations, Paul makes an affirmation about the one true God, in contrast to the counterfeits. God is knowable, Paul says, and he proceeds to tell the listeners about Him (23). He is the Lord of heaven and earth, and gives life to all people (24). God made the nations to live on the earth, and wants them to seek after Him to find Him (26-27). God is our source, not the other way around (29). In all these points, God is both immanent and transcendent. He is never a God "at hand " or "far off." He is never unable to see, hear, speak, or act. He fills heaven and earth. The apostle Paul went on to declare the ultimate moral challenge—the need for repentance for all people, everywhere, and foretold of the man, raised from the dead, who will one day stand in judgment over the world.

The incarnation of Jesus Christ is the final blow to the dual-idolatry pattern. God became a human being, and still remained God.

Jesus, though He was here with us in flesh and blood, never hinted that He was here to show us how to control God, or even how to control our own lives. In fact, He put almost everyone off balance when they met Him. He is Lord of Lords, King of Kings, but is never too distant to care, to notice, to hear the prayers of His people for their daily bread.

Though idols are counterfeit, empty, and vain, in Jesus the fullness of the true God lived (Colossians 1:19). Idols are self-deceiving, self-serving, and yet self-destroying. Jesus is the Truth, and His ministry was one of undeception. He was the Good Shepherd, who laid down His life for the sheep, to give them abundant life (John 10). For those who follow Him, the good wine is at the end.

Remember that we began with the human claim for autonomy and self-sufficiency that leads to idolatry. The true God stands against this pretense and challenges it. He shows us that we are finite, vulnerable, and mortal; also that we are guilty and without excuse before Him. The attempt to not face the face of God or face ourselves as we are begins the process of idolatry. Jesus confronts our self-deception relentlessly, but also offers Himself to us as our savior. Like the returning prodigal, we are called to "come to ourselves." With such a salvation, the apostle John's warning, "Keep yourselves from idols" is a call for our deliverance and welfare.

2
UP TO OUR STEEPLES IN POLITICS

by Michael Cromartie

Heave an egg out a Pullman window," H.L. Mencken wrote in 1924, "and you will hit a Fundamentalist almost anywhere in the United States today."[1] To the bewilderment of many, this is still true. And if Mencken were living today he might put a slightly different spin on it: "Heave an egg out a window anywhere on Capitol Hill today and you will be likely to hit an evangelical political activist."

A friend in Washington recently remarked to me that the political involvement of evangelicals "was history; they're finished." I demurred and wondered aloud whether he knew of another constituency in the country that had literally caused the Senate switchboard to blow a fuse.

This observer assumed that the various scandals that have received so much publicity had made a mockery of the entire movement, wounding the political influence of evangelicals so badly that the movement would never recover. No doubt he would agree with the Princeton history professor who said in an article on evangelicals in the *New Republic:* "Rarely in modern times has a movement of such reputed potential self-destructed so suddenly. Freethinkers may want to reconsider their skepticism about divine intervention."[2]

Michael Cromartie is director of the Evangelical Studies Project at the Ethics and Public Policy Center in Washington, D.C. He has has edited five books, including *No Longer Exiles: The Religious New Right and American Politics*, and is coeditor of *Piety and Politics: Evangelicals and Fundamentalists Confront the World.*

Contrary to widespread misperceptions, the facts tell a different story. Evangelical influence in politics may have declined, but it has not disappeared. This point is arguable, of course, but one thing is indisputable: Over the past generation evangelicals have played an enormous part in politics just as politics has in evangelicalism. And in both cases, the trend is of recent origin.

ENTER THE EVANGELICAL

Edward Dobson, a former special assistant to the Reverend Jerry Falwell, tells how Falwell came to realize the potential influence of evangelicals on the political process. In 1976, after Jimmy Carter's famous interview in *Playboy* magazine, Falwell on his television program criticized the president for appearing in the magazine. Much to his surprise, Falwell received a call from the president's special assistant, Jody Powell, asking that he refrain from making such comments. "Back off," Powell said to him. Falwell (who calls himself both a fundamentalist and an evangelical) was startled that what he said would cause such concern in the White House. He came to perceive this incident as his baptism into the world of politics.

Many evangelicals have had a similar triggering experience that left them obliged to become politically involved—something they had not been inclined to do previously, largely for theological reasons. The first inclination of these evangelicals was not so much to persuade others of their views as it was to sensitize other evangelicals to become involved in specific public issues. Because many in the movement had been taught for decades that such activity was irrelevant, this was not an easy task.

Eventually, however, strong pressures caused evangelicals to take more explicitly Christian and conservative positions. Evangelical leaders increased their participation, believing, as sociologist Steve Bruce has said, that they "were not getting their due and that their due could be got if they organized to claim it."[3] Evangelicals gained confidence through their effective use of television and direct mail, the declining membership of mainline denominations, and the increasing membership of evangelical denominations. Many became involved after concluding that various judicial decisions by the U.S. Supreme Court gave increasing power to the opponents of traditional Christian values. They became engaged in what Harvard professor Nathan Glazer has called a "defensive offensive" against what they saw as an aggressive imposition of secular views on American society, including their own private communities of faith.

What followed is history. In the late seventies and throughout the eighties evangelicals became a prominent part of the times and the conservative revolution of the Reagan era. As an alternative to the passive piety of earlier days, the reaction and plunge into politics was both understandable and legitimate. But are there dangers in this new political activism? I believe there are.

The problem is not politics itself, only its inflation and distortion. Political involvement is right, good, and necessary.

Politization, which is the act of suffusing everything with politics, has had a baneful influence in the modern world. In our politicized world people demand and seek political solutions for everything. I will argue that one of the dangers to be avoided in our newfound political activism—on both the Left and the Right—is the politicizing of our faith and an idolizing of politics.

But once again the problem is not politics itself, only its inflation and distortion. Political involvement is right, good, and necessary. So in order to encourage a wiser balance and help us distinguish the better from the worse, I will set out the danger of political idolatry in the last of five propositions that express the best and worst of recent evangelical involvement in politics. These begin by way of an historical backdrop.

FIVE FUNDAMENTAL PROPOSITIONS

Proposition #1: Religion and politics have always been intermingled in our country's history. This is not new in American history. Alexis de Tocqueville wrote in his classic book *Democracy in America*: "In the Middle Ages the clergy spoke of nothing but a future state. . . . But the American preachers are constantly referring to the earth, and it is only with great difficulty that they can divert their attention from it."[4] The claim that the faith of American Christians should always be an intensely private affair between the individual and God would come as surprising news to such diverse persons as the Pilgrims, from John Winthrop to Jonathan Edwards, the abolitionists of slavery and Abraham Lincoln, to fifteen generations of the black church, civil rights leaders, and antiwar activists. Religious values have always been a part of the American public debate.

51

The question has never been whether Christians should be involved in politics, but rather what issues they should be most concerned with and what are the most prudent ways to express such convictions. We are commanded by our Lord to love our neighbor. One way to do so is to be concerned about the shape of our public policies. It is our duty to be concerned citizens, indeed to strive, as Richard John Neuhaus has said, "to build a world in which the strong are just, and power is tempered by mercy, in which the weak are nurtured and the marginal embraced, and those at the entrance gates and those at the exit gates of life are protected both by law and love."[5]

Proposition #2: Many evangelicals became politically involved because they felt imposed upon by liberal elites. A sign on a cage in the Washington Zoo says: "This animal, when threatened and provoked, will defend itself." And so it could be said of many evangelicals. For a significant number of evangelicals, the ongoing debate about the proper role of religion and politics is of special interest. They have been accused of "imposing their views" and of "forcing their beliefs" on the community. But is this really the case? Nathan Glazer of Harvard University has said:

> Abortion was not a national issue until the Supreme Court, in 1973, set national standards for state laws. It did *not* become an issue because evangelicals and fundamentalists wanted to *strengthen* prohibitions against abortion, but because liberals wanted to abolish them. . . . Pornography in the 1980s did *not* become an issue because evangelicals and fundamentalists wanted to *ban* D.H. Lawrence, James Joyce, or even Henry Miller, but because in the 1960s and 1970s under-the-table pornography moved to the top of the newsstands. Prayer in the schools did *not* become an issue because evangelicals and fundamentalists wanted to introduce new prayers or sectarian prayers—but because the Supreme Court ruled against *all* prayers. Freedom for religious schools became an issue *not* because of any legal effort to expand their scope—but because the IRS and various state authorities tried to impose restrictions on them that private schools had not faced before.[6]

This imposition of a liberal ethos by the "new class elites"—journalists, television commentators and producers, and the "knowledge class" from the universities—is what aroused many evangelicals to action. Although there always has been plenty to complain about in the wider culture, the rapid changes in American society during the past three decades have sent shock waves through our community. Bruce has pointed out that "Conservative Protestants of the 1950s were offended by girls smoking in public.

In the late 1960s girls were to be seen on newsfilm dancing naked at open-air rock concerts."[7] In short, the era of President Eisenhower's America was far different from the America of the sixties and seventies.

Many evangelicals feel that they live in a hostile culture. "Enough is enough," they cry.

As a result, many evangelicals feel that they live in a hostile culture. "Enough is enough," they cry. The root of their protests is the exclusion of religiously based moral judgments from public debate and decision making. Randall Terry, the leader of Operation Rescue, reflected this mood recently: "Our time of withdrawal is over. We've joined the battle, and are prepared to make serious sacrifices before it's too late. This is a winner-take-all battle for the very soul of the country."[8]

Many sympathetic conservatives have seen this ground swell of evangelical activism as an important opportunity for the Republican party to become the nation's majority party. Evangelicals are contributing to a re-alignment process that could make the Republican party the nation's majority party. According to television network exit polls and surveys by the University of Michigan's Center for Political Studies, at least 80 percent of evangelicals backed President Reagan's reelection in 1984, and 79 percent of evangelicals supported President Bush in 1988.

But others have argued that evangelicals could become an ongoing divisive force in the Republican party. Writing in the *New Republic* just two weeks before the 1984 elections, political journalist Sidney Blumenthal predicted that the disputes between the economic libertarians and the social-issue conservatives would produce a major split in the Republican party. Notably, President Reagan's first-term administration adopted a policy of "repressive tolerance" toward social issues because the president's political aides feared that the Republican party would self-destruct to the degree that social issues became prominent. The senior staff did not want a moral crusade, said Blumenthal.

Blumenthal predicted that the Republican party might crack, even while the evangelical new Right would continue to flourish. He said: "The divisions this sort of politics engender are inescapable. The party that enacts sectarian doctrine into law in the attempt to regenerate a lost world will pay a steep political price."[9]

Has this prediction come true? It is too early to know. Lessons have been learned on all sides, yet it remains to be seen how this dispute will pan out in the years ahead.

In our fallen world, public policy disputes have to be hammered out. But some evangelicals are purists who alienate rather than cooperate.

Many evangelicals, being relatively new to politics, do not realize that the art of prudent and principled compromise is necessary in the political arena. In our fallen world, public policy disputes have to be hammered out, and sometimes one has to give a little to achieve anything. But some evangelicals are purists who alienate rather than cooperate. They have been reluctant to join coalitions—the very brick and mortar of electoral victories—because they seek a public policy certainty. Such certainty is next to impossible to achieve among people who, though they agree on a particular policy, have different presuppositions. Some evangelicals have been divisive, using unnecessarily strident language toward their opponents—and even toward some of their natural allies.

Why has it been difficult for some evangelicals to work closely with others on common concerns? Theological reasons play a part, which leads to my third proposition.

Proposition #3: Evangelicals have crucial differences over what kind of culture God intends for us to establish at this time in redemptive history. Some evangelicals insist that God will only be pleased with society if Christians run things. Often their plea is "Christians should take control." They insist that we should work to get only Christians elected, vote only for Christian candidates, and appoint only Christian judges. They believe that a more righteous society will come about only if Christians are in power. No one but Christians can be trusted to use political power appropriately.

Other believers take a different approach. They argue, and I think correctly, that being born again is no guarantee of political wisdom. Some of the most sincere Christian leaders can be found lacking in prudential judgment. Moreover, those who are in rebellion against God (the unregenerate) have the native capacity to do good things. Doing these things will not bring them redemption and salvation, but they can perform honorable deeds; they can be concerned about traditional family values; they can work to see that all people are protected by law and justice, and treated with dignity and respect. Nonbelievers can speak the truth to others, and lead outwardly virtuous lives—they are what St. Augustine called "virtuous pagans."

Many issues in our political life pertain to the created and fallen order—not the redemptive order. These issues address people as sinners—not people as the regenerate children of God. The civil order, specifically the state, is an institution of God's common grace—not His special grace, which concerns His forgiveness, His mercy, and His loving-kindness. In the words of the theologian John Murray:

> Civil government as such is not a redemptive ordinance. But it provides, and is intended to provide, that outward peace and order within which the ordinances of redemption may work to the accomplishment of God's saving purpose. . . . The tranquility and order established and preserved by the ordinances of government are benefits enjoyed by all. This blessing arising from divine institution we must regard therefore as a common blessing and therefore as of the institutions of common grace.[10]

Evangelicals urgently need to develop a public language, philosophy, and posture that shows our loving concern for the common good of all, and not just the common good of fellow believers.

And what is common grace? According to theologian Louis Berkhof, it is the "light of God's revelation that shines in nature and lightens every man coming into the world."[11] The fruits of common grace include the ability to perform what has been called "civic righteousness," whereby God uses both believers and nonbelievers through the power of the state to restrain evil and sin. Berkhof says that common grace is that general work of the Holy Spirit "whereby He, without renewing the heart, exercises such a moral influence on man through His general or special revelation, that sin is restrained, order is maintained in social life, and civil righteousness is promoted."[12]

The doctrine of common grace appears to be virtually unknown to most contemporary evangelical political activists. Yet this doctrine has been understood by the Protestant Reformers and subsequent generations of theologians (and it has parallels with the Catholic view of natural law) as an essential ingredient in the development of a Christian view of culture and politics. By virtue of common grace, believers and nonbelievers can work together on common cultural and political activities.

These theological points are important to assure our nonbelieving political allies that we are committed to freedom, justice, and moral absolutes, which are mandated by God but are not exclusive to those who care about God's mandate. Evangelicals urgently need to develop a public language, philosophy, and posture that shows our loving concern for the common good of all, and not just the common good of fellow believers. A recovery of an understanding of common grace will do much to diffuse polemical and presumptuous rhetoric that projects an "us versus them" approach to politics.

Proposition #4: When weighing political options in our fallen world, evangelicals must learn the importance of making moral distinctions when considering political realities. For Christians involved in politics, we must be reminded again and again that we are strangers and aliens in every temporal order, for we "do not have an enduring city, but we are looking for the city that is to come" (Hebrews 13:14). According to the prophet Jeremiah, we live in exile: "Also, seek the peace and prosperity of the city to which I have carried you into exile. Pray to the Lord for it, because if it prospers, you too will prosper" (Jeremiah 29:7).

We are still in exile—we are far short of the kingdom of God. On this side of the kingdom we are called to be as wise, faithful, loving, caring, just, and prudent as we can by God's grace. We are morally responsible for the choices we make in our fallen world, often choosing between "relative goods" and "lesser evils." Our duties in exile are shaped by the choices we have, not by the choices we wish we had. There are, as political commentator Charles Krauthammer has said, "no moral foxholes."

We must reflect on our normative ideals in the face of real, concrete situations. Our ethical practice in politics must always be applied, adapted, and compared to the existing alternatives because we live in the "already but not yet" of the fulfillment of the kingdom.

This must be stressed to certain evangelicals who want a third way—those who are neither left-wing nor right-wing, conservative nor liberal, but are just "biblical Christians." Nothing is sufficient or satisfactory for them as they critique issues and positions from their "distinctive" perspective. These brothers and sisters in Christ are like helicopter pilots, hovering over the airport but refusing to land.

It is good to use discernment and ask probing questions. But it is a mistake to evade the choices before us in doing so. To insist on nothing less than the best can undermine the good and play into the hands of the worst. As discerning Christians we are not to withhold our commitment from the available possibilities.

Proposition #5: After learning of their duties to be concerned about politics, many Christians on both the Right and Left have overinflated the importance of politics. So as not to be misunderstood here, my concern is with the people who make their political convictions just as important, or more important, than their theological convictions. They think that believers are *not* Christians unless they hold to certain political views and agendas. They would excommunicate people from the church on the basis of political "doctrines."

We suffer, says the eminent sociologist Peter L. Berger, from an outbreak of "inflationary prophecy." Self-appointed prophets assume that every aspect of God's will may be continually specified in terms of every detail of public policy, on almost a daily basis.

Several examples can illustrate my point. In 1989 the *Washington Post* religion page ran this headline: "Right-Wing Christianity Condemned as a Heresy." It was a story about "The Road to Damascus," a document that was written and signed by third-world pastors who argued that anyone who did not agree with them politically was a heretic whose very Christian faith should be called into question. This new form of excommunication on the basis of being "politically correct" comes from people who profess grave uncertainty about firm doctrinal standards. But when it comes to the gray areas of political judgments, they exhibit the certitudes of the most ardent fundamentalists.

Another illustration is sociologist Berger's visit to a friend's church in Boston. His friend was slowly dying of cancer. That Sunday morning the minister preached a sermon on U.S. government policies in Central America, as the conflict was raging there. More disturbing to Professor Berger than the misinformed views on Central America was how lonely his friend felt in his own church. People there were so concerned about politics that no one ministered to him in his fear of dying.

How sad and how tragic. Berger concludes: "This false preaching denies ministry to those who desperately need it. Our congregations are full of individuals with a multitude of afflictions and sorrows, very few of which have anything to do with the allegedly great issues of history. These individuals come to receive the consolation and solace of the Gospel, instead of which they get a lot of politics."[13]

Let me be clear here: this issue cuts both ways politically. Thus the issue I am addressing is not the substitution of one political or cultural agenda for another. Rather, the issue is the placing of political agendas on the same level or even in place of the more important message of the gospel itself. This is the heart of the idolizing of political ideologies.

> ## *Our unity in the church is based on the fact that we are sinners saved by God's amazing grace, not by our politics.*

I once had a discussion outside the Heritage Foundation, the well-known conservative think tank, with a very conservative Christian journalist who insisted that Jimmy Carter could not be a Christian because "no one could be a Christian and have his kind of foreign policy." Apparently he considered having a conservative "politically correct" foreign policy a requirement for being a citizen in the kingdom of God.

Our unity in the church is based on the fact that we are sinners saved by God's amazing grace, not by our politics. People look for the very Bread of Life and instead some Christian leaders, conservative and liberal, only give them a "political stone." These people, says the apostle Paul, preach a "different gospel":

> I am astonished that you are so quickly deserting the one who called you by the grace of Christ and are turning to a different gospel—which is really no gospel at all. Evidently some people are throwing you into confusion and are trying to pervert the gospel of Christ. As we have already said, so now I say again: If anybody is preaching to you a gospel other than what you accepted, let him be eternally condemned! (Galatians 1:6-7, 9)

In C.S. Lewis's classic *The Screwtape Letters*, a senior devil, Screwtape, writes to a junior devil on how to trip up and distract his Christian patient. In letter number twenty-five he writes:

> My dear Wormwood: The real trouble about the set your patient is living in is that it is *merely* Christian. They all have individual interests, of course,

but the bond remains mere Christianity. What we want, if men become Christians at all, is to keep them in the state of mind I call "Christianity and." You know—Christianity and the Crisis, Christianity and the New Psychology, Christianity and the New Order, Christianity and Spelling Reform. If they must be Christians let them at least be Christians with a difference. Substitute for the faith itself some Fashion with a Christian coloring. Work on their horror of the Same Old Thing. The horror of the Same Old Thing is one of the most valuable passions we have produced in the human heart.[14]

The "Same Old Thing" is the core of the gospel message. Lewis, through his fictional protagonist Screwtape, forcefully reminds us that our ultimate identity is to be found in that message. Again, does this mean that Christians' involvement in politics is unimportant? Of course not. Neuhaus presents it clearly when he writes:

Of course Christians should be engaged in the public square. More and more people need to be told that—more and more persuasively, more and more urgently. Christians need to be engaged in the public square relentlessly, audaciously, defiantly, sometimes even confrontationally. . . . The ministry of the church, however, is to equip the saints for their vocations in the world, and political action is not a large part of every Christian's vocation. There are many—children, the aged, the mentally ill, those who believe they have found better ways of loving their neighbors—all of whom are not less a part of the church simply because they are apolitical. The church's vocation is to sustain many different vocations. And it is to keep those who are politically engaged, engaged with one another, especially when they are politically opposed. They are to be engaged with one another not only within the bond of civility but, much more importantly, within the bond of the love of Christ. The truth of the gospel transcends our disagreements about all lesser truths. And it is by that truth that we are knit together in mutual dependence and accountability. By that truth, the church is enabled to be a zone of truth in a world of impassioned mendacities—not the least of all in the world of impassioned political mendacities.[15]

We must love our neighbors. One way to do so is to be concerned with the shaping of our public policies. But though politics is important, we must always remember, as the Dutch theologian H.M. Kuitert has said, "the dead are not raised by politics!"[16] Our personal salvation and the forgiveness of our sins do not and did not come by a political decree. Our very best political efforts will not reconcile us to the Father.

The Christian gospel calls us to be responsible and concerned citizens. But because it resists the idolizing of anything created and human, it therefore limits the importance of all things political. Many in our churches would be surprised to hear that some things are more important than politics. Our church leaders deceive the public and fellow Christians if they lay claim to an expertise (whether political, economic, scientific, or whatever) that in fact they do not have. The very idea that Christian moral sensitivity somehow bestows the competence to make public policy recommendations on every subject imaginable is presumptuous and even arrogant.

Oxford evangelical theologian Oliver O'Donovan reminds us that "Western theology starts from the assertion that the kingdoms of this world are not the kingdom of God and of his Christ, not, at any rate, until God intervenes to make them so at the end . . . this does not mean that the secular state can be independent from God and his claims, or that the pious individual can cultivate a private existence without regard for the claims of his society. It simply means that earthly politics, because they do not *have* to reconcile the world, may get on with their provisional task of bearing witness to God's justice."[17]

An example of what can be lost if the politicization of the *evangel* occurs in the pulpits of evangelical churches comes from a sobering story by Wilfred McClay. The Tulane University professor recently attended a funeral service of a young woman friend from the university. She had died tragically while giving birth to her second child. McClay wrote after hearing the minister's eulogy, which was given to an overflow crowd of mourners:

> Where the rest of us had been stunned into reflective silence, awed and chastened by this reminder of the slender thread by which our lives hang, the minister had other things in mind. . . . He did not try to comfort her family and friends. Nor did he challenge us to remember the hard words of the Lord's Prayer, "Thy Will be done." Instead, he smoothly launched into a well-oiled tirade against the misplaced priorities of our society, in which billions of dollars were being poured into "Star Wars" research while young women such as this one were being allowed to die on the operating table. That was all this minister had to say. His eulogy was, in effect, a pitch for less federal spending on defense and more spending on the development of medical technology. . . . The only thing omitted was an injunction that we write our Congressman, or Ralph Nader, about this outrage.
>
> I could hardly believe my ears. . . . Leave aside the eulogy's unspeakable vulgarity and its unintentional cruelty to the woman's family. Leave aside the the flabby and clichéd quality of language and speech. Leave aside the self satisfied tone of easy moral outrage. . . . Leave aside the fashionable opinions. . . . I am willing to concede, for the sake of argument, that the minister may have been right in everything he said. All of

these considerations are beside the point. Nothing can alter the fact that he failed us, failed her, and failed his calling, by squandering a precious moment for the sake of a second-rate stump speech, and by forcing us to hold our sorrow back in the privacy of our hearts, at the very moment it needed common expression. That moment can never be recovered.

Nothing that religion does is more important than equipping us to endure life's passages, by helping us find meaning in pain and loss. With meaning, many things are bearable; but our eulogist did not know how to give it to us. All he had to offer were his political desiderata. For my own part, I left the funeral more shaken and unsteady than before. Part of my distress arose from frustration, that my deepest thoughts (and those of many around me, as I later discovered) were so completely unechoed in this ceremony and in these words. But another part of my distress must have stemmed from a dark foreboding that I was witnessing another kind of malpractice, and another kind of death.[18]

McClay was speaking about an experience in a mainline Protestant church. But which of us, who has spent time around newly aroused evangelical Christian activists, can deny that the warning given above is not a warning we need to hear?

As an evangelical working in a Washington think tank, I daily urge evangelicals to be more concerned about their political and civic duties as American citizens. I have been in numerous meetings with many of the leading evangelical political activists and scholars in this country. The point is made over and over: we need to be aware and involved in the political process. But we must never lose touch with the power and ultimate truth of what C.S. Lewis called the "Same Old Thing." To do that for even the best of new things would be the same old danger—idolatry.

3
NOSTALGIA FOR
THE LOST EMPIRE

by John Seel

American history in the twentieth century seems to come in prepackaged, bite-size decades. Each decade is shaped by a pivotal event or a distinctive social attitude. We remember the sixties as a period of social unrest surrounding the Vietnam War and the seventies as the "Me Decade," in Tom Wolfe's description. The eighties will be remembered for the conservatism of Ronald Reagan and the rise of the religious Right. It was a decade of religious political activism, when evangelicals emerged from their ghetto.

Few history books will highlight April 29, 1980, as a historical date, yet that spring day symbolizes the eighties well. For on that day a massive rally gathered on the Mall in the nation's capital. At "Washington for Jesus," Christian leaders, celebrities, politicians, pastors, and their followers announced their intentions to take over the political and moral direction of the country. They selected April 29 because it was "the date in 1607 when the Jamestown settlers planted a cross at Cape Henry, in what is now Virginia Beach, and claimed this nation for God, as His vehicle for spreading the Gospel to every nation."[1]

John Seel, a doctoral candidate in American studies at the University of Maryland, is forum director of the Trinity Forum. He was formerly administrative director of the Williamsburg Charter Foundation and cofounder of the First Liberty Institute at George Mason University.

This gathering, in the spring of the new decade, illustrates many of the eighties' themes—the evangelicals' new engagement in politics, the grassroots mobilization, the charges that the liberals had abandoned our nation's heritage, the confidence in political solutions to solve the nation's problems, and the appeal to history as a basis of Christian grounds for authority. For evangelicals, these themes have been the breeding ground for another kind of idolatry, a desire for and reliance on majority status.

FROM ISOLATION TO ACTIVISM

Still staggering from the sixties, Americans faced a quieter crisis of leadership in the seventies. From Richard Nixon's Watergate to President Carter's "malaise," from the oil embargo to the Iranian hostage crisis, the leadership of the nation seemed to be in disarray. Public disillusionment reached epidemic proportions. As one observer noted in 1975, "People are confused and angry about everything from marijuana to Watergate. Feeling helpless and left out, they are looking for a scapegoat, eager to exorcise all that is evil and foul, cleanse or burn all that is strange and foreign."[2]

In the midseventies, Christian leaders began to mobilize this discontent. Many felt that evangelical public leadership was long overdue. When Jimmy Carter professed to be "born-again," the movement received national media attention. Identifying oneself as an "evangelical" actually seemed chic as *Newsweek* proclaimed 1976 the "Year of the Evangelical." But for many evangelicals this engagement in national life represented a monumental shift in attitudes.

Two factors had been roadblocks against evangelicals engaging with the culture previously. First, evangelicals were hampered by a pietism that narrowed their concern to the devotional and evangelistic. Sociologist Robert Wuthnow wrote of this period that "the operational relevance of the supernatural . . . largely collapsed into the interior of the self."[3] Not until the late sixties and early seventies did the deep significance of the lordship of Christ over the whole life and all of culture begin to emerge in the writings of such authors as Francis Schaeffer. For many young evangelicals this opened a new world in which to integrate their faith—the world of art, film, literature, and finally politics.

Second, evangelicals were hindered by a cultural isolation—a fifty-year institutional retreat from mainstream American life. The Scopes Trial in 1925 and the death of William Jennings Bryan—"the General Custer of fundamentalism"—marked the beginning of a cultural retreat by evangelicals. Abandoning mainstream denominations and culture, evangelicals formed their own subculture in the forties and fifties with a wide range of supporting organizations, including associations, educational institutions, publishing companies, and parachurch ministries.

The consequence was an increasing insularity in perspective and outlook. Evangelical leadership rarely emerged from outside a handful of institutions, whether from Wheaton College or Dallas Theological Seminary. This isolation deepened during the sixties and seventies, as exemplified by the move of *Christianity Today* from the nation's capital, Washington, D.C., to suburban Carol Stream, Illinois (near Wheaton).

So when evangelicals emerged into the national spotlight in the late seventies, their ways of thinking had been shaped by three decades of religious privatization and social isolation. Shocked by intrusions into their private world by Supreme Court decisions in the sixties (prayer in schools) and the seventies (abortion rights), evangelicals began to mobilize politically.

GOD'S COUNTRY, GOD'S ARMY

Two distinctive beliefs emerged from their activism. First was the belief that America is a divinely anointed nation with a divinely appointed mission. The leadership of the religious Right frequently appealed to this divine sanction. One advocate wrote, "What was the purpose of this 'miracle nation' that some called 'manifest destiny?' Many things, one of which would be that God would establish one nation that would do more to fulfill His basic objective for this age, to 'preach the gospel to the ends of the earth,' than any other nation in history."

Second was the belief that the moral direction of America could be reversed by exerting political influence. One leader's comments reflect the confidence of the era, "If Christians unite, we can do anything. We can pass any law or any amendment. And that is exactly what we intend to do." Or as another expressed it, "We have enough votes to run the country. And when the people say, 'We've had enough,' we are going to take over."

Many evangelicals, like many Americans, had "had enough." They worried that the moral fiber was loosening in America. They longed for the stability of the fifties. Evangelicals longed for the Protestant consensus that had defined American life for almost a hundred and fifty years. They still resonated with John Winthrop's call for a Christian commonwealth and identified with his warning that "if we shall deal falsely with our God in His work we have undertaken, and so cause Him to withdraw His present help from us, we shall be made a story and a by-word through the world."[4]

Evangelicals were nostalgic for a lost empire. Reasserting moral leadership was a natural response. It seemed both a Christian and American thing to do.

"GOD BLESS US"

For many years our identity as evangelicals has been closely tied to a specific vision of America. Until recently, Protestantism has largely been a taken-for-granted reality in American public life. To many evangelicals, to be truly American is to be Christian. Church attendance has been on the same par as belonging to the Rotary Club or Junior League. Will Herberg noted, "By every realistic criteria, the American Way of Life is the operative religion of the American people."⁵ This civil religion reached its zenith during the Eisenhower presidency and is typified by Ike's often quoted remark, "Our government makes no sense unless it is founded on a deeply felt religious faith—and I don't care what it is."

Many American evangelicals have been more American than Christian, more dependent on historical myths than spiritual realities, more shaped by the flag than the cross.

But the danger for American evangelicals is being shaped more by their attachment to shared historical myths than their commitment to biblical truths. At times it has seemed that if evangelicals were to wake up as citizens of an African or Asian nation, their identity as followers of Christ would be profoundly shaken. Why? Not simply because of the differences in language, food, and culture, but because many American evangelicals have been truly more American than Christian, more dependent on historical myths than spiritual realities, more shaped by the flag than the cross.

These tendencies came to a climax in the eighties with the rise of the religious Right. What began as an appreciation of the contribution faith made in our nation turned into a false reliance on evangelicals' social standing in America. The evangelical identity shifted from being grounded in the source of blessing to being grounded in the blessing itself. Their status as pilgrims in search of the heavenly kingdom was less important than being citizens of a "Christian America." Following the pattern of most idolatry, something to be appreciated became a point of overattachment, a source of reliance, and finally an idol that led to public pride and self-deception.

Jesus confronted this form of idolatry in people whose primary identity was in their Jewishness. They lived with a hope of overcoming Roman occupation and restoring the nation of Israel to its past greatness. The Samaritan woman, for example, asked Jesus where the true place of worship was, Mount Gerizim or Jerusalem (John 4:20). Jesus reminded her that salvation does not lie in a place but a Person; true worship is not tied to national loyalties but to heart attitudes. Such was the disillusionment of the Jews who lined the streets of Jerusalem cheering "Hosanna" on Palm Sunday and jeering "Crucify Him" a week later.

After the climax in the eighties, today the Moral Majority has disbanded and the religious Right is less visible. But many of the issues to which the movement devoted itself remain unresolved. So while fewer headlines are being made on account of religious political activism, the attitudes that emerged still dominate evangelical discourse and action.

This chapter examines one aspect of these attitudes—majoritarianism. In contrast to the democratic principle of majority rule, majoritarianism is the belief that those in a majority (as proponents claim Christians are) can press their will on any sphere of community life by virtue of their numbers. Majoritarianism is essential coercive and insensitive to differences and is blind to such principles as the common good and minority rights, which balance the bare expression of the will of the majority.

What began in the seventies as a reassertion of moral leadership increasingly became a reliance on a sense of entitlement in the eighties—relying on social standing coupled with an appeal to the past. As this replaced a reliance on God, it became an idol—an idolatry affecting many within the church. We will explore five attitudes that are symptoms of such a false reliance.

FIVE ATTITUDES OF THE MAJORITARIAN IDOL

Attitude #1 is "We were here first!" This is priority as entitlement. Evangelical Christians frequently appeal to the fact that Christians came to America first and have dominated the culture longer than any other faith community. This is a powerful argument most simply because it is true. The danger in this attitude, however, is that it generates a threefold reliance: first, a reliance on society rather than God; second, a reliance on cultural realities that no longer exist; and third, an illusion of entitlement that finally undermines freedom for the gospel.

"We came to America first. Such precedent entitles us to priority." Whether Puritans in New England or the mosaic of other Protestants in the Middle Colonies, these spiritual forebears were America's first faith. Christians are correct in asserting that they had a special role in shaping the contours of early American culture. Historian Sidney Ahlstrom describes Puritanism's importance in this way: "No other factor . . . was more significant to the ideals and thoughts of the colonial Americans than the Reformed and Puritan character of their Protestantism; and no institution played a more prominent role in the molding of colonial culture than the church."[6]

So much so that by the late nineteenth century, evangelicalism had become a kind of "national religion."[7] A distinctly Protestant morality was taught in public schools through the McGuffey Readers, and college students attended mandatory classes in moral philosophy that were taught by college presidents trained in the ministry. Alexis de Tocqueville said of America after visiting in 1830, "It must never be forgotten that religion gave birth to Anglo-American society. In the United States, religion is therefore mingled with all the habits of the nation and all the feelings of patriotism, whence it derives a particular force."[8]

But does being in America first give evangelicals a special entitlement to dominate this country? The issue can be seen clearly in the controversies surrounding the emotionally charged term "Christian nation." What is meant by this term? If by "Christian nation" one means either that the republic's roots were primarily—though not exclusively—Christian or that the Christian faith has been the prominent faith in America, few would disagree. But many evangelicals speak as if it entails a great deal more.

Although biblical principles dominated the political sphere during the writing of the Constitution, it was Christians and not secularists who sought to avoid special entitlements or entanglements.

For example, a resolution passed by the Arizona legislature in 1988 asserted that the U.S. Constitution created "a republic based upon the absolute laws of the Bible, not a democracy." An evangelical magazine extolled, "America has a great past, a great present, and a great future, because America has a GREAT GOD." Or a researcher for a prominent evangelical ministry argued that religious freedom was only intended for Christians: "The Puritans, along with Christians of every denomination, believed that America must evangelize pagans and immigrants, not that our political system should accept their faiths as equally valid. . . . At no place do the Founding Fathers say that Satanists, New Agers, pagans, Muslims, etc. should have religious liberty."

Such views cannot be justified historically. More important, they actually weaken the freedom for evangelism.

From the beginning of our country the founders granted full political protection for followers of all faiths or none. America is the first nation in history to disestablish religious institutions from political control. Although biblical principles dominated the political sphere during the writing of the Constitution, it was Christians and not secularists who sought to avoid special entitlements or entanglements. James Madison, the author of the First Amendment, argued that a state-sponsored religion would undermine the integrity of evangelism. "It discourages those who are strangers to the light of revelation from coming into the region of it."[9] In short, he concluded that state-sponsored religion destroys the vitality of faith it seeks to protect. "During almost fifteen centuries the legal establishment of Christianity has been on trial. What have been its fruits? More or less in all places, pride and indolence in the clergy, ignorance and servility in the laity, in both, superstition, bigotry, and persecution."[10]

Moreover, the founders did not want to protect just Protestant denominations, as some claim, but people of all faiths or none—including such minority faiths as that of Islam. Six years after the Bill of Rights was ratified (1791), the Senate passed a treaty with Tripoli that George Washington initiated and President John Adams signed. It acknowledges the founders' views:

> As the government of the United States of America is not in any sense founded on the Christian Religion—as it has in itself no character of enmity against the laws, religion or tranquility of Muslims . . . it is declared by the parties that no pretext arising from religious opinion shall ever produce an interruption of the harmony existing between the two countries.[11]

If America ever was or ever will be a "Christian nation," it is not by conscious design or written law, but by free conviction. Freedom is a gamble. The outcome of the American experiment is always uncertain because the foundational beliefs of its citizens are not legislated. Abraham Lincoln stated the point simply, "If destruction be our lot, we must ourselves be its author and finisher; as a nation of freemen, we must live through all time or die by suicide."

Alongside our God-given freedom of conscience is our responsibility for our choices. Hell, it has been noted, is God's final commitment to freedom of conscience. Just as Moses set before the Israelites the alternatives of life or death, blessings or curses; just as Joshua charged them saying, "Choose you this day whom you will serve," both freedom and responsibility are clearly set forth in Scripture.

Protecting religious liberty for all does not imply agreement with all, but rather a respect for human dignity and freedom of conscience.

Yet in spite of God's example and the teaching of the Bible, Protestants have not consistently protected the rights of others. Throughout our history we have sought to exclude the freedom of Catholics and Jews in order to maintain the political or cultural status quo. Even today many evangelicals confuse a vigorous defense for the inalienable rights of alien faiths as an automatic accommodation—a form of backdoor relativism. Protecting religious liberty for all does not imply agreement with all, but rather a respect for human dignity and freedom of conscience. The lessons of history have shown the folly of enforcing religious belief either at the point of a sword or from the dictates of law.

The semiestablishment of Protestantism in America was not only unfortunate for minority faiths, it was unfortunate for evangelicals also. Because we dominated the culture for so long, we became weak in our convictions and sloppy in our practice. We forgot spiritual first-principles as well as civic first-principles. Like American automakers, we forgot that there is no manifest destiny in market share—in either cars or beliefs. For evangelicals to throw their rhetorical weight around today in such words as "We were here first" is about as effective as telling the Japanese to buy more Chevrolets.

In every age the church must be faithful in the context of the existing culture. Christians cannot claim that dominance in a historical period or place entitles us to legislate our religious beliefs or appeal to special privileges. The church derives her legitimacy solely from her commitment to God and her allegiance to His kingdom.

Evangelism will be effective and Jesus will be winsome on the basis of the reality of our message, the integrity of our lives, and the love we show to our neighbors. Our message will not be compelling because we simply declare "We were here first." By relying on past glories, on a mythic "Christian nation," we have weakened the civic rights that give evangelicals the freedom to spread the gospel. Wanting to strengthen the gospel, instead we weaken its freedom. Such is the attitude of priority as entitlement.

Attitude #2 is "We are right." This is morality as superiority. The term "Moral Majority" was coined for Jerry Falwell in 1979 by Paul Weyrich for natural and politically astute reasons. With the high media visibility and popular dominance of the "drugs, sex, and rock and roll" culture, it was felt that the silent majority needed to have a voice and an organization through which tradition and morality could be reaffirmed. But for all the good accomplished, the reliance on morality in the "Moral" Majority was always open to two charges, the first being the question, 'Whose morality?" and the second being moral hypocrisy.

Evangelicals have long lost their monopoly status in American society, so that moral leadership demands persuasion before legislation.

First, the issue of whose morality concerns the changes in the make-up of the United States over the last decades of the twentieth century. After the sixties, America no longer had the moral consensus of the fifties. And a Judeo-Christian worldview and morality influences the United States less and less today, as all of the world's religions as well as the increasing number of citizens with no religious preference have a growing influence in America. Many evangelicals either have discounted the significance of pluralism or have pretended that it does not exist. They assume that societal pluralism equals philosophical relativism. But they are not the same. Societal pluralism is a description of a social fact—a society with a growing ethnic and religious diversity. Moral relativism, on the other hand, is a philosophical conclusion—a belief that all truth is the same.

71

Pluralism creates competition in the marketplace of ideas—there are more contenders in the cultural war. Evangelicals have long lost their monopoly status in American society, so that moral leadership demands persuasion before legislation. The culture we face is more like that of first-century Rome than that of nineteenth-century America. But unlike the early Christians, many American evangelicals are unwilling to pay the price that persuasion requires in a competitive and often hostile world of ideas and beliefs. Frequently evangelicals have looked like Confederates at the end of the Civil War, longing for a Dixieland of the imagination and trying to exchange a cultural currency that has decreasing value.

The second and more telling problem, especially to followers of Christ, is the charge of hypocrisy. Majoritarianism leads to pride, to contempt for others, and to arrogance about the end justifying the means. And thus to hypocrisy.

The emergence of these attitudes is understandable in light of both the political mood and the patterns of the eighties—the single-issue politics, mass mail fund-raising, and media-driven adversarial coverage. These attitudes were as natural as the culture wars from which they sprang. But how are we perceived by unbelievers? Do they see Jesus, or do they see enormous egos, powerful special-interest groups, vicious public rhetoric, and religious bigotry? Does the "we versus they" language, the Satanizing of nonbelievers in spiritual-warfare novels, or the vilifying of our pro-choice opponents model Jesus?

Jesus said, "You have heard that it was said, 'Love your neighbor and hate your enemy.' But I tell you: Love your enemies and pray for those who persecute you, that you may be sons of your Father in heaven" (Matthew 5:43-44). His harshest words were not directed to unbelievers, but to religious hypocrites and self-righteous saints. We too can often appear very self-righteousness. Like the community of Pharisees: "Confident of their own righteousness," we have "looked down on everybody else" (Luke 18:9).

In response we defensively appeal to the scandal of the cross, when in fact, too often we are the scandal and it is love that is crucified. Peter exhorted believers to "live such good lives among the pagans that, though they accuse you of doing wrong, they may see your good deeds and glorify God on the day he visits us" (1 Peter 2:12). In contrast, one Christian activist advises, "We must be an aggressive, feisty, dig-in-your-heels, kick-and-scream bunch."

In short, by basing our identity on our social standing, we have become concerned only for our own groups, our own convictions, our own ministries, or simply ourselves. "When we worship the holiness of our own convictions instead of our holy Lord," Oswald Chambers warns, "there is an element in human nature that makes us all possible popes and intolerant upholders of our personal views."[12]

When evangelicals emerged from their pietistic ghettoes in the late seventies and asserted their political muscle, most Americans perceived the move to be a power play. Evangelicals were not perceived as being concerned for all Americans, but rather for the interests of "me, mine, and ours." The perceptions often were accurate. The celebrated textbook cases in Alabama and Tennessee, for example, were not about the rights of all Americans, but about "my rights, our rights." The spirit of these cases might best be summarized by the attitude, "If Madeline Murray O'Hair got prayer out of the classroom, we'll get humanism out of the textbooks." The opportunity to defend the rights of conscience for all Americans was forfeited.

The majoritarian idol blinds us to other people; it destroys our love for those with whom we disagree.

Or consider the tactics and language surrounding much of the abortion debate. A pro-choice activist quoted in the *Washington Post* said of pro-life protesters, "They preach love out of one side of their mouth and then stand in front of a clinic screaming and threatening and calling women 'baby killers' . . . Jesus Christ was not about terrorizing people."[13] The language used by pro-life activists is often offensive to even the staunchest of their own supporters, such as when one calls the doctors in abortion clinics "vile, blood-sucking hyenas" in a press conference.[14] Reinhold Niebuhr's warning is applicable here, "The temper and integrity with which the political fight is waged is more important for the health of a society than any particular policy."[15] Too often our attitudes and actions have betrayed not only the issues being advocated, but the simple right to be heard.

"The Pharisee stood up and prayed about himself: 'God, I thank you that I am not like other men.' " (Luke 18:11). Religious idols are the most deceiving—because they make us feel so "religious." Yet nothing is uglier than spiritual pride with a public face. The majoritarian idol blinds us to other people; it destroys our love for those with whom we disagree. We instead become tribal in outlook, judgmental in tone, and coercive in style.

73

If the first attitude undermines freedom for the gospel, this attitude undermines its credibility.

Edward Dobson, a former associate of Jerry Falwell at the Moral Majority, concluded sadly that the religious Right has been an "act of failure" from the beginning. "It was an attempt to change values in the world at large when those values haven't even been significantly changed in the community of faith."[16]

In marked contrast, "the tax collector stood at a distance. He would not even look up to heaven, but beat his breast and said, 'God, have mercy on me, a sinner' " (Luke 18:13). We need to remember that at the foot of the cross is level ground—it is there that we will find Jesus. To be right without humility is to be wrong. Such is the attitude of morality as superiority.

Attitude #3 is "We are stronger!" This is majority as power. Populism is a recurrent feature of evangelicalism. As early as the abolitionist movement, Christians have been part of a grassroots mobilization for the reform of various causes. The recent resurgence of religious populism is partly a reaction to the rise of the new class, who have largely turned their back on traditional values and religion. In this light, the Moral Majority can be seen as a direct challenge to those people who define our world through their writing, speaking, teaching, or entertaining—writers, artists, intellectuals, professors, journalists, and the media. This confrontation pitted the common person against educated elites, Middle-American values against East Coast skepticism. Evangelicals sought to storm the culture through the back door. Confidence soared. Grassroots populism married to the potent technologies of mass mail and television provided an enormous illusion of power in the eighties.

But in hindsight, the movement did not succeed as some had hoped it would for two basic reasons. First, evangelicals had neither a demographic nor a political majority. The basic resort to majority status was never truly accurate. Eighty percent of Americans claim to be Christians. From here, the funnel narrows quickly. Those who consider themselves "born again" include some 60 million Americans, or about 25 percent, many of whom are in mainline Protestant denominations or the Catholic Church. Those who refer to themselves more narrowly as "evangelicals" represent 40 million Americans, or approximately 16 percent of the U.S. population.[17] But those whose faith commitment is a life-defining factor is less than 10 percent of the American population.[18] In addition, evangelicals failed to demonstrate a unified political voting bloc. In the end the religious Right was left with a statistical confidence that did not translate to either spiritual reality or political votes.

> *Evangelicals have relied on grassroots mobilization and majoritarian politics to reform society. But in a pluralistic society, this is no longer effective. Political action alone cannot effect cultural reformation.*

Second, majoritarian politics could not bring about the needed cultural change. Evangelicals failed to engage the people and institutions that shape our society. The populist fallacy is that demographic size translates into comparable social influence. So evangelicals have historically relied on grassroots mobilization and majoritarian politics to reform society. But in a pluralistic and increasingly secular society, this is no longer effective. Political action alone cannot effect cultural reformation. Passing laws, while important, does not ensure morality.

Evangelicals are slowly learning that cultural change is brought about through cultural gatekeepers—those people who have access to and control of the reality-defining institutions of America. As sociologist James Davison Hunter argues, "The power of culture is not measured by the size of a cultural organization or the quantity of its output, but by the extent to which a definition of reality is realized in the social world—taken seriously and acted upon by actions in the social world."[19] Cultural gatekeepers give shape to what we take for granted about our world. Yet few evangelicals hold these positions of influence, and few evangelical ministries seek to reach these people.

But not only have evangelicals made a strategic error, few evangelicals have the cultural capital needed to address these gatekeepers. We are seriously disadvantaged by a crippling anti-intellectualism. Today knowledge is the strategic economic resource in the modern world just as information is the cultural currency. Yet many evangelicals just do not think. When our economy was primarily agricultural, our resistance to thinking was less decisive. But today the consequences are enormous.

This being the case, the prospect for an evangelical cultural influence has been decreasing since the sixties, because a widening education gap has emerged between believers and nonbelievers. For the first time in American history, the more one is educated, the less likely it is that he or she will take faith seriously.[20] Moreover, other studies show that American evangelicals have the lowest levels of education, an academic orientation toward the technical and practical, and tend to be located in southern and rural areas.[21] We seem to be "gatekeeper-proof."

Evangelicals cannot count on their size alone. Numbers may win elections, but minds win cultures. Isolated in our self-contained, evangelical enclaves, such as in Wheaton, Orlando, and Colorado Springs, we have been content to talk to ourselves rather than to engage public discourse meaningfully. We publish books for the Christian market and pride ourselves on our sales figures. Yet there is little leverage in our writing and thinking among the nation's leadership circle. So we continue to picket, boycott, and protest, but for all the numbers, noise, and action, evangelicals are still losing ground. Grassroots mobilization and political coercion that lacks persuasion, or a vigorous cultural strategy, proves futile. "There is little to show after the shouting has subsided," assessed political scientist Robert Fowler of a decade of religious activism.[22]

Thinking ourselves to be politically stronger, we are actually culturally weaker. Such is the fallacy of majority as power.

Attitude #4 is "We've been robbed!" This is history as resentment. As the 1980s progressed, the majoritarian rumblings grew to a crescendo, but the tone shifted from confidence to resentment. The task that had been set out a decade earlier proved to be daunting. Real gains for the religious Right were hard to find. Resentment became a more dominant theme in their rhetoric—it was the halfway house between confidence and retreat.

This attitude finds its way in the idolatry of both majoritarianism and minoritarianism (discussed in chapter 4). In its early stages the appeal to resentment is less a posturing of identity, but instead is the rhetorical equivalent to a "rebel yell"—a call-to-arms. Resentment is used when other tactics prove unsuccessful.

The essence of resentment is blame. Evangelicals blame others for what they perceive to be America's problems. We point fingers at secular humanists, New Age gurus, or media elites, and the conspiracy theories abound. For example, one leader of the religious Right states, "We are being controlled by a small but influential cadre of committed humanists who are determined to turn traditionally moral-minded America into an amoral, humanist country."

The historical fact remains: Christians surrendered their institutions to secular control rather than secularists stealing their institutions away.

But the historical fact remains: Christians surrendered their institutions to secular control rather than secularists stealing their institutions away. Evangelical historian George Marsden notes, "Secularization in America took place not by a developing hostility between religion and the dominant culture, but by a blending of their goals."[23] It was not a conspiracy by others, but our own collapse.

Evangelicals have found that creating scapegoats is far easier than facing our responsibilities. This attitude keeps us from seeing our own worse enemy—ourselves. T. S. Eliot once wrote,

> One reason why the lot of the secular reformer . . . seems to me . . . easier [than that of a Christian reformer] is this: that for the most part [the secularist] conceives of the evils of the world as something external to himself. . . . If there is evil incarnate, it is always incarnate in the other people—a class, a race, the politicians, the bankers, the armament makers, and so forth—never in oneself. . . . For most people, to be able to simplify issues so as to see only the definite external enemy, is exhilarating. . . . This is an exhiliration that the Christian must deny himself. . . . It causes pride, either individual or collective, and pride brings its own doom.[24]

Some evangelical leaders call us to political mobilization or to strategic marketing. But God would have us begin with the church in mourning. Writing to an evangelical publication, a subscriber wrote, "I'd say your magazine does a better job of accurately defining the mess our society is in than it does in suggesting really biblical solutions. I wish I sensed more often that your pages are splattered with tears—and I mean real ones."[25]

To renounce the deception of resentment is to begin a lament: "Hear the word of the Lord; open your ears to the words of his mouth.

Teach your daughters how to wail; teach one another a lament" (Jeremiah 9:20). We blame others, not ourselves. Such is the attitude of history as resentment.

Attitude #5 is "We can do it!" This is momentum as false confidence. Few presidents in this century have come to Washington with a clearer policy agenda and public mandate than Ronald Reagan. The Republican party positioned itself as "America's Party," a party of patriotism, old-fashioned values, and pride. They were the guardians of Americanism. A confident populist president swept the evangelical vote. "It is springtime again in America," the president boasted. From the celebrations surrounding the Statue of Liberty to the Los Angeles Olympic Games, many Americans were in a feel-good mood. Evangelicals simply rode the cultural wave of confidence. Nothing seemed impossible—the revolution had begun.

The consequent majoritarian tone blended well with the tenor of the times—upbeat, confident, and smiling. One leader boasted, "I hope I live to see the day when, as in the early days of our country, we won't have any public schools. The churches will have taken them over again and Christians will be running them. What a happy day that will be."

But because majoritarian confidence is dependent on external circumstances, it is also highly volatile. As to the worst Little League coach, winning becomes everything. Assessing George Gallup's latest measures of success in a national opinion survey becomes a dominant concern. Nothing is wrong with assessing results, except when confidence is based on or limited to results. Then the "messianic rhetoric" reveals a deep insecurity. The bully, deep down, is actually scared.

Followers of Christ are called simply to be faithful in our moment of history. Such are the demands of faithful discipleship.

Frequently the question is asked of evangelical pundits, "Are you optimistic or pessimistic about the state of evangelicalism?" Some leaders suggest that the "evangelical moment" has yet to be realized. Others say it has come and gone, and that night is falling over the church.

But is this the right question? Does not this question reveal our misplaced confidence?

We are not called to win or to lose, for this is for God to decide. Followers of Christ are called simply to be faithful in our moment of history. Nothing more, nothing less. On a friend's desk is this reminder: "No reservations. No retreats. No regrets." Such are the demands of faithful discipleship. Asking about winning or losing, optimism or pessimism makes sense only if we buy into the majoritarian deception of relying on our social standing—on external circumstances.

My father is a cancer surgeon. In his daily struggle against a killer disease he realizes that the cure rate is not the final index of his stewardship. He once wrote, "The person, not the disease, is the ultimate object; and the healing of his soul the only valid cause."[26] The physician "joins with the patient in a battle in which no quarter is given or asked, a battle which he may sometimes win, or sometimes lose, but which he never ceases fighting."[27] The surgeon's credo, and one that expresses our task as faithful disciples, is proclaimed by the Welsh poet, Ethelwyn Wetherald:

> *My orders are to fight;*
> *Then if I bleed, or fail,*
> *Or strongly win what matters it?*
> *God only doth prevail.*
> *The servant craveth naught*
> *Except to serve with might.*
> *I was not told to win or lose,—*
> *My orders are to fight.*[28]

When we are preoccupied with winning, we are really losing. Our focus is off our true task. Our focus is off Jesus. Such is the attitude of momentum as false confidence.

GONE LIKE THE MIST

Majoritarianism—the false reliance on social standing coupled with an idealization of the past—is one of the most common and destructive forms of idolatry within the American evangelical church. It has done more to tarnish the gospel than the most outrageous scandals of the televangelists. It replaces moral responsibility with spiritual pride that finally leads to a contempt of others. Says one respected commentator of these attitudes, "The echoes of the Iranian militants are loud and clear."[29] Says Thomas Atwood, a former member of Pat Robertson's staff, "[The religious right activists] often came across as authoritarian, intolerant, and boastful, even to natural constituents."[30] But the pragmatic political failures of majoritarianism are not nearly as serious as the spiritual idolatry that grows from it.

79

The mark of an idol is in what it finally produces. We have examined five attitudes caused by majoritarianism—priority as entitlement, morality as superiority, majority as power, history as resentment, and momentum as false confidence. Each is a fertile seedbed for pride. Dorothy Sayers warns, "The devilish strategy of pride is that it attacks us, not in our weakest points, but in our strongest. It is preeminently the sin of the noble mind."[31] In contrast we are admonished in Scripture to "Humble yourselves, therefore, under God's mighty hand, that he may lift you up in due time" (1 Peter 5:6).

Richard Keyes suggested in chapter 1 that idols often come in pairs. And so is the case here. The flip side of majoritarian confidence is minoritarian victimization, the subject of the following essay. Majoritarianism is a "faraway idol," which serves our search for a counterfeit transcendence and sense of place. Minoritarianism is a "nearby idol," which serves as an arbiter of fear and our need for control. Both are serious idols within the church.

When challenged, faraway idols evaporate like the mist. And so our confidence in the past, our security in numbers, our optimism for immediate success gives way under cultural pressure. Nostalgia for the lost empire gives way to the whimper of playing the victim. Such is the nature of false reliances.

The idolatry of majoritarianism demands our repentance. For God's "pleasure is not in the strength of the horse, nor his delight in the legs of a man; the Lord delights in those who fear him, who put their hope in his unfailing love" (Psalm 147:10-11). Or again, "Not by might nor by power, but by my Spirit, says the Lord Almighty" (Zechariah 4:6). Or simply, "When we are weak, then we are strong" (2 Corinthians 12:10).

4

MORE VICTIMIZED
THAN THOU

by Os Guinness

Ohn a gray, rainy day in November 1990 a church ground-breaking ceremony took place in the Boston area. It should have been a day of unmixed
joy. Church planting is tough in the rocky spiritual soil of New England, and
the new facility was innovative. Two congregations—of separate Jewish
and Gentile believers in Jesus—were combining under one roof as a living
demonstration of the human dividing walls being broken down by the cross
of Christ.

But the joy was mixed. Plans for the new church had run into stiff
community resistance from the start. Neighbors opposed the project vocally,
local authorities were difficult, regulations were used as obstructions, and
other churches were silent and unsupportive. The property had even been set
on fire and windows shot out. Only legal action had made it possible for the
ground breaking to proceed at all.

At the ceremony itself, groups of hostile neighbors showed up.
Some obstructed cars and then called the police to complain about blocked
traffic. Others tore up paper and then accused the church of littering.

Os Guinness is a writer born in China and raised in England but now living in
McLean, Viginia. Author of several books, including *The Gravedigger File* and
The American Hour, he is former executive director of the Williamsburg Charter
Foundation and has served as a Visiting Fellow at the Brookings Institution in
Washington, D.C.

The pastor was formally cursed. Two church members were spat on in the face. Understandably, the children among the sixty new worshipers were terrified. They huddled together at one side, holding hands.

Such incidents as this—some milder, some more serious—appear to be multiplying in the United States in the early 1990s. Among the stock explanations, two factors are cited most often. One is the deepening privatization of American life, epitomized by the so-called NIMBY ("not in my backyard") mentality that resents any intrusion into suburbia. The other is a form of reverse politicization—a popular recoil from the high-octane religious activism of the 1980s. All believers are tarred with the same brush and all religious activity is branded as troublesome.

For Christians, the rise of such incidents is disturbing and important on several levels. But what matters most is our response. Going to court is a sound decision when constitutional freedoms are at stake, as in zoning restrictions. But what of reactions at the level of motivations and rhetoric? Should our response be that of the pastor of the new church—that legal and personal grievances are different; opposition is to be expected, and it is a privilege to bear the offense of the cross? Or that of other local Christians who were outraged, unwilling to let the personal offense pass by, and eager to sue? "You know," said one church member to a friend of mine, "we no longer have to take it lying down."

The traditional Christian response to injury is clear. The response to personal injury must differ from the response to injury to others; in all instances, the life and teaching of Jesus determines the response. As Gaspard de Coligny, a French admiral assassinated on the eve of St. Bartholomew's Day, 1572, for his Protestant beliefs, declared: "I will freely forget all things, whether evil weal or injury, done unto me alone, provided that the glory of God and the public [welfare] be safe."[1]

Within American evangelicalism today some have abandoned a distinctively Christian response to injury and have resorted to a Christian version of a current popular strategy—redress through blaming, or playing the victim. The minority temptation is the extreme opposite of the majoritarianism addressed in the previous chapter; yet it also has its advocates and its reasons, and it also takes various subtle forms. Like majoritarianism, the minoritarian tendency can also grow unchecked until it becomes idolatrous.

If Christians are to live by faith as they are made just by faith, they can no more rely on the idol of minority status than they can rely on the idol of majority status. The telltale stratagems of the minority mentality—fear, blaming, and playing the victim—are an unfaithful way of establishing identity, seeking security, exercising responsibility, and redressing injury. It used to be an old evangelical maxim that "one person with God is a majority."

But that saying was a corrective to minoritarianism without being an endorsement of majoritarianism. It proclaimed that only God—not majority or minority standing—should count decisively for people of faith. To live on any other basis is to put an idol in the place of God.

THE GOLDEN ERA OF EXONERATION

At first sight, the evangelical appeal to minority status in America is bizarre. Evangelicals can lay claim to being America's "first faith" and were almost "the church of America" as recently as the late nineteenth century. So for evangelicals to claim minority status seems as appropriate as an elephant posing as a mouse.

But seen against the background of wider cultural shifts, it becomes understandable. When Nelson Mandela made his triumphal tour of the United States in 1990, one of the best-selling T-shirts carried a simple message: "It's a black thing. You wouldn't understand." Few slogans better represent the current mood of American society and illustrate how far the culture has shifted since the heyday of the civil rights struggle in the sixties. For Martin Luther King, Jr., justice was never simply a black thing. It was a human thing. After all, it was justice, not "just us."

During the decades since Martin Luther King's rise, the triumph of psychology and the therapeutic revolution has yielded one particular harvest: the golden era of exoneration. Responsibility has been dissolved and American life has become one vast schooling in the arts of blaming and resentment (see also chapter 6). "Depravity" has become "determinism," and this revolutionary shift now produces a culture in which people literally "cannot help themselves" when it comes to doing wrong. Anna Russell satirized the grand national excuse in the conclusion of her "Psychiatric Folksong."

> At three I had a feeling of ambivalence toward my brothers;
> And so it follows naturally, I poisoned all my lovers.
> But now I'm happy, I've learned the lesson this has taught,
> That everything I do that's wrong is someone else's fault![2]

Countless members of countless groups are now walking billboards for their own grievances. One might easily adapt new slogans for the T-shirts. "It's a feminist/gay/native American/disabled/fundamentalist thing. You wouldn't understand." For America is gripped by a new twist on special-interest groups that combines the language of the civil rights movement with the language of the therapeutic revolution.

The new group logic runs like this: Whether a group is ethnic, sexual, racial, or religious, only those in a group can understand and appreciate what it is to be a member of the group. Therefore, no one outside a group has the right to criticize those inside, and to do so is necessarily to be insensitive, oppressive, and guilty of disrespect (or in the vogue campus language, "dissing"). To join a group in America in the eighties and nineties is to become a connoisseur in sensitivity.

Some Christians mistakenly blame this trend on liberals and left-wingers. To be sure, the most brazen versions are the sensitivity crusades led by liberals, especially the PC, or politically correct, movement in universities and public education with its "thought police" and "linguistic martial law." More than 130 campuses, for example, have codes against "hate speech" directed at minorities. My favorite example is the University of Connecticut prohibition of "inappropriately directed laughter."

Within America, the past generation has witnessed a titanic double shift: from the more traditional emphasis on individualism to the more recent emphasis on tribalism, with its accompanying concern with minority rights.

But Christians who wax indignant about sensitivity crusades and the PC movement often fail to see that the trend is not limited to liberals and left-wingers. In doing so we overlook our own Christian versions of the trend and the idols that grow up with them. Above all, we overlook the wider context that makes such things plausible. The same worldwide convulsion that has helped to bring down the Soviet empire and has shifted the focus of danger to democracy from totalitarianism to tribalism has sent tremors through many societies. Old arrangements that balanced unity and diversity have begun to crumble, and new relationships are being created between centers of power and the peripheries. In Europe, for example, one trend is toward the centralization of the European Community while a counterbalancing trend is toward decentralization—as in the breakup of Yugoslavia into independent nations. The nation state of the past is simultaneously too small for the newly globalized world and too big for the newly localized life.

Within America, the past generation has witnessed a titanic double shift: from the more traditional emphasis on individualism, with its accompanying concern with majority rule, to the more recent emphasis on tribalism, with its accompanying concern with minority rights. These shifts have been followed in turn by lesser movements: from individual rights to group rights, from a concern for bread-and-butter policies to a concern for communal well-being, from an appeal to justice to an appeal to sensitivity, from legal redress to linguistic and psychic redress (or "emotional tort law"). Two of the more notable shifts have been a move from pluralism with a relativistic face to pluralism with a particularistic face, and from solutions based on respect for human dignity and civility to solutions based on rules and regulations.

In short, the overall sociological outcome is a new American tribalism and the overall psychological outcome a new American touchiness. In *Time* magazine's memorable phrase, Americans have become overactive and overpassive at once, a nation of "busybodies and crybabies."[3]

FROM SLEEPING GIANT TO POOR LITTLE WHIPPING BOY

Not surprisingly, such a massive shift in the culture at large has affected evangelicals too. The public psychology has changed dramatically, especially following the decline of the Christian Right. In ten short years, our public self-portrait has changed from the sleeping giant of American public life to the poor little whipping boy at the mercy of liberal forces. What Jewish sociologist Will Herberg in the 1950s called a "back to the catacombs" outlook came in fashion again.[4] "In a mere decade," wrote Charles Colson, "the 1980s Moral Majority has become the 1990s persecuted minority. . . . Clearly it is open season for Christian bashing."[5]

> *The direct appeal to victimhood
> is a means of awakening
> Christian consciousness and
> galvanizing Christian action,
> a crybaby "victimology."*

There are two types of evidence of the swing from a Christian majority to a Christian minority positioning. One is more generalized, such as

85

the widespread feeling of fear among evangelicals, the increasing resort to litigation, and the reliance on conspiracy theories. For example, *Publishers Weekly* commented on the themes of books displayed at the annual Christian Booksellers Convention in July 1991: "If you look at the displays as you walk through, the majority of the books being given publicity are books that are driven by fear—fear of what the educational system is doing to your children, fear of what the Antichrist is going to do in a couple of years, fear of what the 12 steps are going to do to the rest of the Church."[6]

The other type of evidence is more focused and deliberate—the direct appeal to victimhood as a means of awakening Christian consciousness and galvanizing Christian action. Crybaby "victimology" is the other side of the coin of the burgeoning "rights" industry. The idea of a Christian anti-defamation league was first floated in 1986, but abandoned because it was likely to backfire in the wake of the televangelist scandals. It caught on fast when reintroduced as central to Pat Robertson's Christian Coalition in February 1990. "Christian Americans are tired of getting stepped on," his brochure announced. The blatant bias of press reporting, U.S. Representative Robert Dornan charged, is just one example of "the anti-Christian bigotry that has run amok in this nation—with the apparent approbation, cooperation, and participation of the dominant media culture."[7] The situation is worse than "bigotry, plain and simple," said Donald Wildmon of the American Family Association. "When the norm of society says, 'You can't participate in the mainstream because you're a Christian,' then there's a serious problem, not just for me but for everybody in society."[8]

Hearing such claims, it is hard not to remember the same people and their friends only a decade earlier. Then, all the talk was of "rousing the slumbering giant," "mobilizing the moral majority" that represented the "largest single minority in America," having "enough votes to run the country," and providing Christians with "the most united front seen in this century." Richard Zone, a leading Christian activist, even boasted on "Sixty Minutes" in 1980 that "Forty million people can amend the Constitution if they had a mind to. They can elect a President. They can throw out a President. We can elect any official. We can change or make any law, and that's exactly what we intend to do."[9]

Such rhetoric was common in the eighties and central to the majoritarian temptation addressed in the previous chapter. But merely ten years later, the evangelical complaint is made up of three main claims—our decreasing status, the increasing bigotry against us, and the hardening of the political process to our influence. These claims decisively mark the end of the eighties' brand of conservative activism. Just as Richard Bach's *Jonathan Livingston Seagull* (1972) was a bellwether book that marked the end of the sixties and the beginning of the seventies, so Frank Perretti's mammoth bestseller *This Present Darkness* and its sequel captured the change in the conservative Christian mood at the end of the eighties.

The aggressive confidence of some Christians in the early eighties collapsed into alarmism and paranoia in the late eighties. For them the root of the problem suddenly deepened from the human to the supernatural. It was not enough simply to trace it to secular humanists and New Agers. The situation was the fault of the devil himself. Without realizing it, many Christian conservatives at the end of the eighties were following the example of the Christian liberals at the end of the sixties. The liberals had ended the sixties with a hollowed-out demonology that owed more to sociology than orthodoxy (the institutional "principalities and powers"), whereas conservatives ended the eighties with a hyped-up demonology as close to popular author Stephen King and medievalism as to the Bible. According to many evangelicals now, our immediate Christian prospects appear to be limited to defamation and persecution.

NEITHER RIGHT NOR WISE

There is unquestionably a good deal of anti-Christian bias and prejudice in parts of American society today, and horror-story examples are not hard to find. This is not surprising in a period that contains both culture wars and hate crimes. As columnist Patrick J. Buchanan wrote upon release of Martin Scorsese's film *The Last Temptation of Christ,* "We live in an age where the ridicule of blacks is forbidden, where anti-Semitism is punishable by political death, but where Christian-bashing is a popular indoor sport; and films mocking Jesus Christ are considered avant-garde."[10] Richard Land, executive director of the Christian Life Commission of the Southern Baptist Convention, says with good reason: "Anti-Christian bigotry is the safest bigotry still exercised in American life. If people made simplistic characterizations of Jews, blacks, or women the way the media routinely do about evangelicals, they'd be ripped apart in the public press."[11]

But when listening to certain aspects of the complaint by fellow evangelicals, it is hard to keep a straight face. Have our numbers and social standing really collapsed so precipitously? How could such innocents as we have called down such unprovoked malevolence out of the blue? As with the confusions over pluralism, many of the current evangelical responses to "victimization" are neither right nor wise. Here are some considerations to help us rethink the issue and root out a false reliance on minority status before it becomes idolatrous.

First, the evangelical complaint about being a small and victimized minority is factually misleading. ("We evangelicals are a tiny minority, you know," a university professor told me solemnly in Kentucky.) Whatever the numbers claimed for evangelicalism at the beginning of the eighties—generally agreed to be between 20 and 40 million Americans—may be taken as roughly the same number at the end. There are simply too many to fit in the catacombs. There is no known empirical evidence of any dramatic decrease over the last decade.

For the oldest and one of the most sizable faith communities to pass itself off as a beleaguered minority is both an insult to real minorities and an extraordinary testimony to its own state of mind.

In other words, the hard numbers are the same; it is the psychology and social status that have changed. Yet at a time when all minorities are accorded a better cultural place in the sun, for the oldest and one of the most sizable faith communities to pass itself off as a beleaguered and defamed minority is both an insult to real minorities and an extraordinary testimony to its own state of mind. The present situation is reminiscent of the 1920s' quip about a fundamentalist being someone who "talks of standing on the rock of ages, but acts as if he were clinging to the last piece of driftwood."

Second, the evangelical complaint is morally hypocritical. At the end of a decade when more of our dirty linen was washed in public than in any comparable ten years in evangelical history, the wonder is not that there is so much stinging criticism from outside the church but that there is so little within. Both the church and the movement have provided a rich stock of targets to keep would-be pundits and satirists in business for years. The eighties, one wag said, was the decade when pillars of the church became columns in the press. What corrupt European state churches did over the centuries by way of accelerating secularization there, corrupt American churches and Christian leaders did with a vengeance in the last decade.

Besides, any liberal prejudice toward Christians has been more than amply repaid. And many of the splinters in the eyes of the defamers are minute compared with the planks in the eyes of the defenders. The fact is, observers of the press say, the old hostility toward the Christian faith in the mainstream press has fallen. (Fred Barnes of the *New Republic* wrote in 1990, "I don't think that's really true now. I don't think hostility is what it is. It is indifference to Christianity, and indifference to spiritual things in general."[12]) Significantly too, analysts at the end of the eighties were more and more impressed by the conservatives' strength in the media. Forthright conservative apologists, such as John McLaughlin, Patrick Buchanan, Robert Novak, and William Buckley, were obvious. But even such programs as the "McNeil/Lehrer News Hour" were criticized for their decided conservative leaning.[13] Rather than a sign of mounting prejudice against Christians, much of the evidence pointed to mounting partisanship on many issues because of the culture wars.

The effect of playing the victim is to reject the ethic of Christ and resort to a politics of resentment. The politics of resentment is the politics of revenge.

Third, the evangelical complaint is politically and psychologically dangerous. Whatever the motivation, the effect of playing the victim is to reject the ethic of Christ and resort to a politics of resentment. The politics of resentment is the politics of revenge—the attempt to get back at what is perceived as degrading persecution. To do this, Friedrich Nietzsche wrote a century ago, is to play at the hole of the tarantula, because it is the black poison of the tarantula that makes the soul whirl with revenge, especially when bitten by "preachers of equality." (As Neitzsche wrote, "'We shall wreak vengeance and abuse on all whose equals we are not'—thus do the tarantula hearts vow."[14])

Expressed from a more Christian basis, the present recourse to resentment is an irony compounded by tragedy. Conservative Christians criticize the concept of tolerance with some justification. But instead of countering tolerance with its Christian corrective—forgiveness—they counter with resentment, its self-righteous and anti-Christian contradiction.

Ironically, this appeal to a politics of resentment is being put forward deliberately by certain evangelical leaders at the very moment when other groups are reexamining or abandoning it. Women, blacks, Jews, and other groups have all traveled the "victims and losers" road. In the short run, there is instant political power in appealing to those who feel victimized —many forms of political tribalism are simply potent "instant brotherhoods of the scapegoated." But over the long run the results are self-defeating. In order to sustain the power, the self-professed victims must celebrate their victimhood so long that they come to see themselves only as victims and end up victimizing themselves. Victim psychology thus becomes the all-purpose excuse for every Christian (or feminist, black, and Jewish) disadvantage and serves only to perpetuate the handicap. Victims become losers for keeps.

Compared with Martin Luther King, "Christian conservatives" are neither Christian nor conservative when it comes to their politics of resentment. For King's moral authority came more from his rejection of resentment than from his nonviolence. In refusing to mobilize black resentment or to claim exemption from common moral standards on the grounds of victimization, he bypassed a politics of raw guilt and retaliation and lifted civil rights to a level of overwhelming moral authority—for blacks and all Americans.

Will we evangelicals do the same with our campaigns? Since King's time, the art of American political organization has generally gone the other way. From black power and the women's movement to gay rights and now Christians and Middle Americans, the tendency has been to corral resentment, celebrate victimhood, and multiply the demands and devices for avoiding all inequalities under the political sun. The upshot is that the old idea of the citizen—the person with the same few clear rights as everybody else in the republic—has been steadily eclipsed.

Now overshadowing the idea of the citizen is a hierarchy of group privileges and sensitivities that are ranked according to their cultural standing in victimhood (a sort of "more victimized than thou"). The result is a triumph of "minoritarianism"—a rights-run-riot hypersensitivity that, in seeing to it that no one loses in any decision, nullifies the vital difference between majority and minority. At the same time, it undercuts enterprise, equal opportunity, and community.

Early in 1990, cable television magnate Ted Turner picked up the criticism of Hegel and Nietzsche and told a group of broadcasters that "Christianity is a religion for losers."[15] All the more extraordinary that American evangelicals and fundamentalists should choose that moment to confirm his Nietzschean thesis by resorting to a loser's politics of resentment even cruder than Nietzsche had attacked.

OUTSIDE THE CAMP

The three previous considerations about the minoritarian idol are all essentially pragmatic, and therefore are eclipsed by the last and principled one: that the resort to fear, blaming, or playing the victim is a denial of Jesus Christ and His call to discipleship. Scour the New Testament from beginning to end and it would be impossible to find a single line to justify the present evangelical politics of anxiety and resentment. Everything points the other way. If, as it is said, faith is paranoia in reverse, paranoia is a contradiction of faith. After all, perfect fear has cast out love.

Think of the underlying dynamics of victimology and the crybaby appeal to minority status. Blaming others, or playing the victim, can be variously a way of establishing identity, a means of seeking security, a form of exercising responsibility, and a method of redressing injury—wittingly or unwittingly. All these motives are deeply human, and to some extent, they are gratified through victimhood. What is more, they are as natural as sun in California during America's golden age of exoneration when Americans have become connoisseurs of grievance. Above all, the approach works, at least in the short run. But is it Christian?

The answer is an emphatic *no*. Followers of Christ will be called many names, but our only identity comes from the One whose call reveals our names and natures. Followers of Christ may no more like shouldering the cost of their commitments than followers of other ways, but no one who knows what our Master bore can bear to shrug off the blame on others. In reality, the brotherhood of the victimized ones is a twisted counterfeit of the fellowship of the crucified one. Followers of Christ flinch at times from the pain of wounds and the smart of slights, but that cost is in the contract of the way of the cross.

Whatever needs we find assuaged through victimhood—whether identity, security, responsibility, or redress to injury—the result for the Christian is a spurious and disloyal comfort, an idol in our hearts and a liability in our movement.

No child of a sovereign God whom we can call Our Father is ever a victim or in a minority. Trust in the utter dependability of God is the antidote to fear, just as forgiveness is to resentment. Vengeance is God's, not ours. But having counted the cost, our commitment is to take up the cross daily and follow Jesus. Such commitment is not only to be His, entirely His and forever His, but at all costs His. When we have to, we follow him outside the camp. As Dietrich Bonhoeffer wrote, "When Christ calls a man he bids him come and die."[16]

"BLESS YOU, PRISON"

A fuller discussion of this issue could enter into deeper levels of distinctions and qualifications—for example, why and when the resort to law is legitimate and prudent for Christians and when it is not. But attitudes of the heart, as touched on here, are the deepest issues of all. That is the level from which either true faith or false gods spring.

Victim-playing is a wrenching, poignant issue to me because I have vivid boyhood memories of Chinese Christians preparing for their baptism of fire—persecution under Mao Tse-tung after the Communist victory in China in 1949. Forty years and countless martyrdoms later, we can see the results of their unfathomable courage—the blood of the martyrs has once again become the seed of the church. But this was no comfort to them at the time. Theirs was a courage that could afford few illusions and no self-indulgence. Without rights, redress, or respite, they were truly victims, but their sole cry as victims was to God. To their captors and persecutors they were like their Master—steadfast and forgiving.

When Allied troops liberated the Ravensbrück concentration camp in 1945, they stumbled onto the indescribable horror of the Nazi Moloch-machine in which 92,000 women and children had died. But they also came across signs of unquenchable faith. The following words were found written on a piece of wrapping paper near the body of a dead child:

> O Lord,
> Remember not only the men and women of goodwill,
> But also those of ill will.
> But do not only remember the suffering they have inflicted on us,
> Remember the fruits we brought thanks to this suffering,
> Our comradeship, our loyalty, our humility,
> The courage, the generosity,
> The greatness of heart which has grown out of all this.
> And when they come to judgment
> Let all the fruits that we have borne
> Be their forgiveness.
> AMEN AMEN AMEN[17]

By contrast, there is a bitter irony in the fact that we evangelicals who have long celebrated the purifying effects of persecution in places like China now complain publicly of victimization in the United States. Perhaps it is time to recognize with Samuel Rutherford, "Oh, what I owe to the file, to the hammer, to the furnace of my Lord Jesus . . . Grace tried is better than grace; it is glory in its infancy."[18] Then we will be qualified to begin learning the costly insight of Aleksandr Solzhenitsyn and look back even on the Gulag moments of our lives and say without hesitation: "*Bless you, prison, for having been in my life!*"[19]

In the end, it is the fact of the cross that makes our present evangelical blaming and victim-playing so utterly blasphemous. Shame on us for our thin skins and our petty sensitivities. And beyond the cross is another fact that makes such grievances insignificant, too. In a short while, our final glory will make every pain inconsequential. As John Donne writes, "But then there is *Pondus Gloriae, an exceeding weight of eternal glory,* and that turns the scale; for as it makes all worldly prosperity as dung, so it makes all worldly adversity as feathers."[20]

5
LEAVING PSYCHOLOGY BEHIND
by Paul C. Vitz

Modern American psychology, like the land of ancient Gaul, is divided into three parts. The largest and most familiar part is the popular psychology of "self-esteem" found throughout our society. Self-esteem—and the obsession that everyone must have it—is familiar to almost all of us these days. And self-esteem programs affect the lives of countless schoolchildren, as this idea—and ideal—have taken firm root in the world of education.

The second part of psychology derives primarily from a specific psychology experience: individual psychotherapy and counseling. By now, millions of Americans have seen a psychologist at some point in their lives. When Philip Rieff and others describe America as a "psychological society" in which there has been a "triumph of the therapeutic," they are speaking mainly of psychotherapy and its effects.

Third comes what might be called "group psychotherapy," although it usually does not use trained psychotherapists. Today the best example of this kind of psychology is the recovery group movement. Beginning with Alcoholics Anonymous in the thirties, groups of people with some particular problem—especially an addiction—have gotten together for mutual support in following a program to facilitate recovery from their prob-

Paul C. Vitz is professor of psychology at New York University and the author of several books, including *Psychology as Religion: A Cult of Self-Worship* and *Censorship: Evidence of Bias in Our Children's Textbooks.*

lem. Here again, especially in recent years, millions of Americans, including large numbers of Christians, have participated in such recovery groups.

This division of psychology into three types is necessary because each type has its own advantages and failures and each has a different relation to the Christian faith. In addition, each displays its own distinctive facets of the contemporary idolatry of psychology.

THE CURSE OF SELF-ESTEEM[1]

Historically, the concept of self-esteem has no clear intellectual origins; no major theorist has made it a central concept. Many psychologists have emphasized the self, in various ways, but the usual focus has been on self-actualization, or fulfillment of one's total potential. As a result, it is difficult to trace the source of this emphasis on self-esteem. Apparently, this widespread preoccupation is a distillation of the general concern with the self found in many psychological theories. Self-esteem seems to be the common denominator pervading the writings of such varied theorists as Carl Rogers, Abraham Maslow, "ego-strength" psychologists, and various recent moral educators. In any case, the concern with self-esteem hovers everywhere in America today. It is, however, most reliably found in the world of education—from professors of education to principals, teachers, school boards, and television programs concerned with preschool children.[2]

Self worth, a feeling of respect and confidence in one's being, has merit, as we shall see. But an ego-centered, "let me feel good" self-esteem can ignore our failures and need for God.

The research shows that measures of self-esteem have no reliable relationship to behavior, either positive or negative. In part, this is simply because life is too complicated for so simple a notion.

What is wrong with the concept of self-esteem? Lots—and it is fundamental in nature. There have been thousands of psychological studies on self-esteem. Often the term *self-esteem* is muddled in confusion as it becomes a label for such various aspects as self-image, self-acceptance, self-worth, self-trust, or self-love. The bottom line is that no agreed-upon definition or agreed-upon measure of self-esteem exists, and whatever it is, no reliable evidence supports self-esteem scores meaning much at all anyway. There is no evidence that high self-esteem reliably causes anything —indeed lots of people with little of it have achieved a great deal in one dimension or another.

For instance, Gloria Steinem, who has written a number of books and been a major leader of the feminist movement, recently revealed in a book-long statement that she suffers from low self-esteem.[3] And many people with high self-esteem are happy just being rich, beautiful, or socially connected. Some other people whose high self-esteem has been noted are inner-city drug dealers, who generally feel quite good about themselves: af ter all, they have succeeded in making a lot of money in a hostile and competitive environment.

A 1989 study of mathematical skills compared students in eight different countries.[4] American students ranked lowest in mathematical competence and Korean students ranked highest. But the researchers also asked students to rate how good they were at mathematics. The Americans ranked highest in self-judged mathematical ability, while the Koreans ranked lowest. Mathematical self-esteem had an inverse relation to mathematical accomplishment! This is certainly an example of a "feel-good" psychology keeping students from an accurate perception of reality. The self-esteem theory predicts that only those who feel good about themselves will do well —which is supposedly why all students need self-esteem—but in fact feeling good about yourself may simply make you over-confident, narcissistic, and unable to work hard.

I am not implying that high self-esteem is always negatively related to accomplishment. Rather, the research mentioned above shows that measures of self-esteem have no reliable relationship to behavior, either positive or negative. In part, this is simply because life is too complicated for so simple a notion to be of much use. But we should expect this failure in advance. We all know, and know of, people who are motivated by insecurities and self-doubts. These are often both the heroes and the villains of history. The prevalence of certain men of small stature in the history of fanatical military leadership is well-documented: Julius Caesar, Napoleon, Hitler, and Stalin were all small men determined to prove they were "big." Many great athletes and others have had to overcome grave physical disabilities—and a lack of self-esteem. Many superior achievements appear to have their origin in what psychologist Alfred Adler called "inferiority completes."

The point is not that feeling bad about ourselves is good, but rather that only two things can truly change how we feel about ourselves: real accomplishment and developing "basic trust." First, real accomplishment in the real world affects our attitudes. A child who learns to read, who can do mathematics, who can play the piano or baseball, will have a genuine sense of accomplishment and an appropriate sense of self-esteem.[5] Schools that fail to teach reading, writing, and arithmetic corrupt the proper understanding of self-esteem. Educators who say, "Don't grade them, don't label them. You have to make them feel good about themselves," cause the problems.[6] It makes no sense for students to be full of self-esteem if they have learned nothing. Reality will soon puncture their illusions, and they will have to face two disturbing facts: that they are ignorant, and that the adults responsible for teaching them have lied to them. In the real world praise has to be the reward for something worthwhile: praise must be connected to reality.

There is an even more fundamental way in which most people come to genuine self-esteem—actually, to feelings of self-worth and what psychologists call "basic trust." Such feelings come through receiving love; first of all, our mother's love. But this foundational experience of love and self-confidence cannot be faked. When teachers attempt to create this deep and motivating emotion by pretending they "love" all their students and by praising them indiscriminately, they misunderstand the nature of this kind of love. Parental love simply cannot be manufactured by a teacher in a few minutes of interaction a day for each of thirty or more students. The child not only knows that such love is "fake," but that real teachers are supposed to teach, and that this involves not just support but discipline, demands, and reprimands. Good teachers show their love by caring enough to use discipline. Thus, the best, most admired teachers in our high schools today often are the athletic coaches. They still teach, but they expect performance, and they rarely worry about self-esteem.

Christians should have a tremendous sense of self-worth: God made us in His image, He loves us, He sent His Son to save each of us; our destiny is to be with Him forever.

Similar problems arise for those who try to build their own flagging self-esteem by speaking lovingly to their "inner child"—or other insecure inner selves. Such attempts are doomed to failure for two reasons: first, if we are insecure about our self-worth, how can we believe our own praise? And second, like the child, we know the need for self-discipline and accomplishment.

Self-esteem should be understood as a response, not a cause. It is primarily an emotional response to what we and what others have done to us. Though it is a desirable feeling or internal state, like happiness it does not cause much. Also, like happiness, and like love, self-esteem is almost impossible to get by trying to get it. Try to get self-esteem and you will fail. But do good to others and accomplish something for yourself, and you will have all you need.

The subject is vital for Christians, partly because so many are so concerned about it and partly because the recovery of self-esteem has been touted as tantamount to a new reformation. We must note, however, that self-esteem is a deeply secular concept—not one with which Christians should be particularly involved. Nor need they be. Christians should have a tremendous sense of *self-worth*: God made us in His image, He loves us, He sent His Son to save each of us; our destiny is to be with Him forever. Each of us is of such value that the angels rejoice over every repentant sinner. But on the other hand, we have nothing on our own to be proud of, we were given life along with all our talents, and we are all poor sinners. There is certainly no theological reason to believe that the rich or the successful or the high in self-esteem are more favored by God and more likely to reach heaven, indeed there is far more evidence to the contrary: "Blessed are the meek."

In addition, self-esteem is based on the very American notion that each of us is responsible for our own happiness. Thus, within a Christian framework, self-esteem has a subtle, pathological aspect: we may take the "pursuit of happiness" as a far more intense personal goal than the pursuit of holiness. Today self-esteem has become very important because it is thought to be essential to happiness: unless you love yourself, you will not be happy. But to assume that we *must* love ourselves, that God will not love us as much as we need to be loved, is a form of practical atheism. We say we believe in God, but we don't trust Him. Instead, many Christians live by the very unbiblical "God loves those who love themselves."

Another problem is that Christians have begun to excuse evil or destructive behavior on the grounds of "low self-esteem." But self-esteem, whether high or low, does not determine our actions. We are accountable for them and we are responsible for trying to do good and avoid evil. Low self-esteem does not make someone an alcoholic, nor does it enable a person finally to admit his or her addiction and do something about it. Both of these decisions are up to each of us regardless of one's level of self-esteem.

Finally, the whole focus on ourselves feeds unrealistic self-love, which psychologists often call "narcissism." One would have thought America had enough trouble with narcissism in the seventies with the "Me

Generation," and in the eighties with the Yuppies. But today's search for self-esteem is just the newest expression of America's old egomania. And giving schoolchildren happy faces on all their homework just because it was handed in or giving them trophies for just being on the team is flattery of the kind found for decades in our commercial slogans: "You deserve a break today"; "You are the boss"; and "Have it your way." Such self-love is an extreme expression of an individualistic psychology long supported by consumerism. Now it is reinforced by educators who gratify the vanity of even our youngest children with repetitive mantras like "You are the most important person in the whole world."

This narcissistic emphasis in our society, and especially in education and religion, is a disguised form of self-worship. If accepted, America would have 250 million "most important persons in the whole world"— 250 million golden selves. If such idolatry were not socially so dangerous, it would be embarrassing, even pathetic.

ESCAPE FROM PSYCHOTHERAPY

Although psychology has been justly criticized by both secular and Christian critics, there is plenty of evidence that it is often beneficial. How does psychology, in fact, help people? The research literature on the effects of psychotherapy and counseling is now reasonably clear. Most people do benefit from going into psychotherapy and counseling. About 60 percent of clients show some measure of improvement in their lives, as judged both by their own reports and by the reports of therapists.[7] Of course, a small percentage of people, especially those who were seriously disturbed before going into therapy or who had an inexperienced or incompetent therapist, are harmed; there are still others for whom psychotherapy seems to be essentially neutral.

Let's look more carefully at what it is that helps people in the psychotherapeutic and counseling process. Research studies suggest positive outcomes in psychotherapy, but those outcomes appear to be unrelated to the psychological theories used by different therapists. That is, the psychological concepts guiding the therapy do not seem to have much causal connection to the positive effects. It does not matter a great deal whether the therapist uses Freudian or Jungian or Adlerian or humanistic or cognitive-behavioral concepts. The client seems to benefit independently of the therapist's arduously mastered training in a particular theoretical framework.

The major beneficial factors of psychotherapy reflect the character, or therapeutic virtues, of the psychotherapist and especially how he or she interacts with the client. Successful therapists are described as "empathic," "supportive," "caring," and "patient." Thus, one major contributor to the benefits of psychotherapy is the extent to which the therapist establishes a strong and positive relationship with the client—a relationship that lets the client know that the therapist is an ally.

The therapist must give clients support—but not let them off the hook. Or, more simply, the therapist must provide both mercy and justice: tough love.

Also important are the therapist's experience and skill at intervening with interpretations of the client's behavior, and his or her ability to challenge clients' distortions and misunderstandings about themselves and others. The therapist must be more than just a sympathetic, supportive friend. He or she must be able to help clients confront destructive patterns from the past and confront reality. In short, the therapist must give clients support—but not let them off the hook. Or, more simply, the therapist must provide both mercy and justice: tough love.

Positive effects are also due to attributes of the clients themselves. For example, clients must be committed to the therapeutic process. The most obvious way such commitment shows is in a willingness to come to the sessions in the first place. Large numbers of people, for various reasons, are so uncommitted to therapy and the therapist—in many cases, so unconvinced of the benefits—that they do not stay past the first few sessions. (It is uncommon for fewer than four or five sessions to have much effect.) But many clients are committed, and this "client-commitment effect" can also be described as the client's *faith* in psychology. These days many Americans seem to have more faith in psychology than in their religion.

This account of the factors behind the benefits of counseling may be a bit oversimplified but it is generally true. Naturally, professional psychologists are disconcerted by this account, for it suggests that most of the specialized training in psychological concepts, theory, and so on, is unrelated to the positive outcomes of therapy.

But we need to add a few qualifications to this general summary. Some evidence suggests that cognitive and behavioral approaches are slight-

101

ly superior to traditional talk therapies in terms of their actual results. Cognitive approaches are those that emphasize the control of thoughts, emotions, and behavior through rational strategies. For example, a cognitive therapist might help clients develop methods by which to substitute certain positive thoughts every time depressing thoughts came to mind. Behavioral approaches emphasize the control of behavior: they rely in large part on the use of reinforcements to strengthen positive behaviors and punishments to discourage negative behaviors. For example, a marriage might be strengthened by the simple requirement that the wife is to stop nagging and the husband is to start showing love through kisses; or a problem child could be improved when there is no TV if homework is not done.

A number of points need to be made about cognitive-behavioral psychology. First, it works best for specific and clearly bounded problems, such as phobias, anxiety attacks, modest depressions caused by particular negative thoughts. Second, this kind of psychology is based on conscious thought and reason—which means that it is consistent with the "psychology" found explicitly in Scripture. Much of the Old Testament wisdom literature, such as Proverbs, clearly embodies this kind of approach to the mind—and to the problems of life.[8] In the past, many pastors have based their advice to troubled parishioners on this sort of "psychology." Today's cognitive and behavioral psychology is more systematic and carefully developed, but the underlying principles are the same. Finally, cognitive-behavioral psychology, for all its benefits, is not the kind of psychology that people so wildly embrace today.

In short, we can say that the benefits of psychotherapy and counseling come primarily from the therapist's empathic support and wise interventions, combined with the commitment and confidence of the client both in the counseling process and in the counselor. And yet, despite the benefits of individual therapy and counseling, many people remain trapped in their past; many cannot stop licking their psychic wounds and continue to believe that psychology is the answer to their basic misery. Despite emotional catharsis and support from therapists, many people remain as unhappy and unproductive as they were before they entered therapy: they remain unchanged. The benefits of the psychological support and knowledge they have received in the therapeutic sessions have been slight.

ON BEING A VICTIM

Many clients are unaware of the negative effects of the process of psychotherapy. The very act of constantly looking at and talking about one's past can generate *new* forms of psychological pathology and exacerbate old problems. For example, although many people have suffered from traumatic events in their childhood, they are unaware that this understanding can have harmful effects. The perception of oneself as a victim creates in many people feelings of self-pity, and an understanding of their life as determined by the past and therefore being unchangeable.

Moreover, seeing oneself as a victim frequently results in an increase in resentment and a deeper hatred toward the people responsible for one's suffering. The status of victimhood often gives rise to a strong sense of moral superiority, not only toward the particular perpetrators of the client's traumas but to similar people in society at large. Thus, those who had bad fathers often reject all parent and authority figures wholesale. This sense of self-righteousness can prevent any real understanding or empathy with those who caused our suffering and can isolate us even further from others—except fellow victims. We conveniently forget that those who hurt us were often, themselves, abused in childhood too.

Here a new problem with psychology must be raised. There has been an explosive increase in the number of people who claim to have been abused physically, sexually, or emotionally in childhood. A common perpetrator is an alcoholic father, or a step-father, or a cold, emotionally abusive mother. Many of these claims are undoubtedly correct, as much adult psychopathology has its origin in childhood abuse. The sins of the fathers are indeed visited unto the third and fourth generation.

Christians in psychotherapy and recovery groups must keep in mind that they have a special responsibility not to condemn a parent, as we are not to condemn anyone.

But there is now evidence that a growing number of these claims are seriously distorted or even false. For example, distorted memories often combine two or more figures. Hence a person may fuse the memory of an uncle or neighbor with memories of the father and then accuse the father of incest when it was actually the other man. Sometimes the memories can eventually be sorted out: "corrected." But when false memories derive from very early years, they are often so convincing that they can never be corrected. And in some cases the memory is completely made up—it is an early fantasy recalled as though it were true. The problem of people who report mistaken memories as true has become serious enough that the phenomenon is called the False Memory Syndrome. A growing nationwide group of parents has formed to support each other and reject charges based on the false memories of their children.[9]

One must always remember that charges of abuse are criminal charges and are extremely destructive to those accused. In actual criminal cases there may be some opportunity to rebut the charges, to hear the other side. But psychotherapy is a one-sided process, and therefore simple fairness requires that both the client and therapist should always be aware that claims of abuse may be false or distorted.

Christians in psychotherapy and recovery groups must keep in mind that they have a special responsibility not to condemn a parent, as we are not to condemn anyone. We can be the jury and convict a parent of sin or destructive behavior, but we can never be the judge who passes the sentence. We must remember that vengeance is the Lord's, not ours.

Another consequence of a fascination with the past is the use of enormous amounts of time and energy, so that little remains for doing something positive with one's life. Major decisions, including marriage and a career, are put on hold for years while the past is worked through and stewed over.

Finally, this preoccupation with the past can lead the client into an attitude of moral irresponsibility. As people become preoccupied, even obsessed, with their personal psychotherapy, they often evade responsibility for their present life, fail to acknowledge their own contribution to their psychological problems, and refuse to accept responsibility for change. We have all met people for whom psychology has had some or many of the distressing effects listed above. Perhaps we may recognize them in ourselves. It is from such effects that many need to escape.

But it does not help simply to exhort people to stop being fascinated with their past or to tell them to forget about their dysfunctional family. Something must happen to help the person release the past and start creating a new life, an attitude of looking forward to the future. How are people to escape from a past-oriented, passive, deterministic, and self-preoccupied victim-status? Let me briefly describe the major processes that make this move possible.

Frequently the first step is *forgiveness*. We must decide—and be willing—to forgive those who have hurt us in the past. This is often difficult because it means letting go of what others owe us. If they have done us wrong, to forgive them is not only to cancel that debt but to renounce our moral superiority. Forgiveness is a complex process that involves many stages, as different aspects of resentment and hatred surface over time. But however difficult, forgiveness is absolutely essential if clients—if any of us—are to be freed from the past.

Next comes *reconciliation*, that is, going to the person (if available) and being reconciled and at peace with him or her. This is not recommended for everyone or for every situation, and reconciliation rarely means saying, "I forgive you." Much more frequently it means asking, "Will you forgive me?" Reconciliation helps reestablish a previous relationship, which some painful estrangement had broken. In some cases, reparation will also occur; if you have clearly harmed someone, you may overtly or discreetly be able to make amends.

> *We do not need to be psychologically sound to know and love Christ—for which we should be profoundly grateful.*

Finally, the psychologically troubled person needs to *repent*. Clients must face their need for repentance. Usually when forgiveness has taken place, they are in a position to see how much they have contributed to their own pathology. They choose to hold on to anger and resentment, they choose to hate. They choose to be morally superior, to wallow in self-pity. And they can see how they have hurt others: sometimes in retaliation, but many times harming innocent people. Most of us remember ten times we have been hurt for every one time that we have hurt others. In our account books, we only keep one side of the ledger carefully: what others have done to us!

Experienced and sober therapists have long been aware that our culture has been endowing psychotherapy with an unrealistic power to transform people's lives. Wise therapists know that they help many to overcome certain problems, but they also know that psychology is not the answer to life. Sigmund Freud once said about psychoanalysis that "the best it can do is to return the patient to the normal level of human misery." Psychology cannot make you happy—and it cannot even make you fully "whole" psychologically. Only those in heaven will have perfectly healthy minds and bodies. In this world, we will *perpetually* be somewhat sick, mentally and physically. We do not need to be psychologically sound to know and love Christ—for which we should be profoundly grateful.

105

RECOVERY FROM RECOVERY

Recently, group forms of psychotherapy have become extremely popular. Alcoholics Anonymous, Adult Children of Alcoholics, Al-Anon, Overeaters Anonymous, and many other kinds of groups have been helpful to millions of Americans. Such groups are generally described as "recovery groups," as their aim is to help people recover from addictions or traumas that often have their origin in childhood experiences and dysfunctional families.

No definitive research demonstrates the benefits of any of these groups—especially the more recent groups, such as those that focus on the psychological problems of relatives of addicts. But there is a fair amount of research on the programs of Alcoholics Anonymous. At present, it is not clear that AA is the only or even the best way of overcoming alcoholism. Behavioral programs, intensive in-patient hospital programs, and other strategies are also successful. This is not to deny that millions of people have benefited from AA, but the almost religious veneration that AA frequently receives may be unjustified.

Most recovery groups are based on "twelve step" programs, originally developed by Alcoholics Anonymous. The underlying concept is that alcoholism—or a different addiction—is a disease. There is now good evidence that the disease theory of alcoholism is mistaken.[10] An addiction is very serious and destructive, but it does not appear to be a disease. That is, recovery from alcoholism requires a moral choice and cognitive commitment to change. No true biological disease can be changed by an act of the will and by commitment. If so, the problems of cancer and AIDS would have been licked long ago.

In twelve-step programs, the first step is for people to admit, to themselves and to others in the group, that they are helpless to do anything on their own about their addiction. Although this step expresses the person's total helplessness, the statement itself is understood to be a first act in overcoming the addiction. Nevertheless, some people have criticized this first step as reinforcing a sense of fatalism and passivity.[11]

Many of the steps have a strong religious or moral component. The second step invites the person to "come to believe that a Power greater than ourselves could restore us to sanity." The fourth step declares: "Make a searching and fearless moral inventory of ourselves." A social dimension is represented in the group meetings themselves and in the help that the members often provide for each other outside of the meetings. In short, these recovery groups have quietly revolutionized psychology by introducing major dimensions almost completely absent in traditional psychotherapy: the religious, the moral, and the social.

The founders of Alcoholics Anonymous, serious Christians, based their first recovery group on these steps. These basic principles represent a qualitatively different approach to personal problems as compared to standard individual psychotherapy. Such factors account for the positive religious or spiritual character of most recovery groups, for these are all profoundly Christian ideas. Other religious elements include confession of one's past failings and (when appropriate) attempts to reconcile with those whom one has harmed. Whatever the ability of AA (in comparison with other approaches) to stop people's drinking, there is good reason to believe that these religious principles have greatly facilitated the reconstruction of many people's lives and produced a wide variety of psychological benefits. No doubt recovery groups offer such benefits as friendship and solace for loneliness; yet the main psychospiritual appeal of such groups is a sense of the power of God and sorrow for sin, placed within a context of social support.

Nonetheless, serious religious criticisms must be made of these recovery groups. Despite the theistic emphasis, all the twelve-step programs omit forgiveness of others (and of oneself) as an explicit step. This is a central problem and a surprising omission. After all, the Christian faith has long focused on the importance of forgiveness, and even the secular world is slowly beginning to take note of this most healing of interpersonal processes. My friends in AA, however, point out that forgiveness often occurs in somewhat indirect or reduced forms because AA emphasizes (and rightly so) getting rid of resentment. In any case, forgiveness, which is enshrined in the Lord's Prayer, is a Christian *requirement*: we must forgive others if we wish to be forgiven ourselves. Only recently have some Christian psychologists and others begun to recommend the introduction of forgiveness into recovery group psychology and family therapy. This is an important new development.[12] Forgiveness will certainly serve to complete many people's recovery process.

Within recovery groups, other problems affect a growing number of people. The problems can be viewed as psychological side effects of the recovery process itself. Just as a drug, though generally positive, may have negative side effects for some users—and for some, the side effects may be worse than the disease—so a psychological process can have negative and profound effects. What side effects have been observed in recovery groups? First, the notion that God is to be understood as each individual defines him (or her or it) is not only fundamentally heretical, but it can also promote psychological harm. For certain people, God becomes little more than a narcissistic projection of their own needs and desires—and of their strange views and eccentricities. Some decades ago the popular ventriloquist Edgar Bergen had a dummy named Charley McCarthy. God is some people's Charley McCarthy: they make Him say and think what they say and think. The notion of a God of justice whose "thoughts are not our thoughts," and the "fear" of whom is "the beginning of wisdom," is seriously at odds with this sort of do-it-yourself deity.

Another problem with recovery groups is that their claims are becoming extreme, even irrational. The wild enthusiasm for recovery groups and especially for the theory that the dysfunctional family is the universal cause of our psychological problems is a sign of a cresting fad—another American psychological enthusiasm. For example, a prominent recovery group psychologist said that "Ninety-four percent of all families are dysfunctional." Perhaps "dysfunctional" is understood so loosely that the statement is meaningless, such as, "Ninety-four percent of all people are not completely physically healthy." On the other hand, without research, statistics, and other good evidence, such claims are so ridiculous that those who make them may be classified as modern snake-oil salesmen selling the newest universal cure for whatever ails a person. Because such statements invite backlash, the very real contribution of recovery groups might be thrown out along with their overblown claims.

Just because a recovery group has driven out a devil of addiction does not mean that seven new and worse devils cannot come to take its place —and one of the worst of these new devils may be spiritual pride.

In recovery groups it is not uncommon to hear critical and condescending remarks about the church in general and individual churches in particular—and about people who are misguided enough to be outside of recovery groups. As one AA friend of mine put it, "There is an often voiced sentiment in the rooms of AA that their spirituality represents an attitude toward God that is superior to that held by organized religion." As a result, attitudes of self-righteousness are far from rare. Such comments as "If you are not in recovery, you're part of the problem," make this clear. The recovery group can become a little church. When it does, it is its own little sect: it is not part of the Body of Christ. It has no theology or tradition that can put brakes on the normal human tendency to develop self-serving biases and error.

In other words, just because a recovery group has driven out a devil of addiction does not mean that seven new and worse devils cannot come to take its place—and one of the worst of these new devils may be spiritual pride. Perhaps one of the most reliable ways to avoid the cult-like effects of recovery groups is for members to attend regular church services, where they truly belong to Christ's church.

Finally, there are people for whom the recovery group process itself becomes an addiction. They replace their dysfunctional family with a dysfunctional recovery group; they become, once again, an "enabler" and defend and cling to the recovery group as they once defended and clung to their family.

BEYOND PSYCHOLOGY

Forgiveness and repentance are not part of any standard psychological theory. From Sigmund Freud to Carl Jung to Carl Rogers to cognitive and behavioral therapy, these concepts receive no emphasis. And yet, the healing power of forgiveness—of being reconciled with those who have hurt you and of repenting and being reconciled with God—has been known for thousands of years. Another way of putting this is to say that psychological problems, however real, often do not have psychological answers; they have moral, spiritual, and theological answers.

A little reflection should make the truth of this important point clear. Our major psychological problems are set up by the absence of love and the presence of hatred and cruelty in our earliest years. From physical, sexual, and psychological abuse to the accidents of abandonment, separation, and death to permissive, negligent parents who failed to set limits and discipline, we are wounded as children. Psychotherapy can help us discover how and when and where all of this took place. We may overcome our repressions and our denials and discover, buried in our past, the traumatic events that hurt us and leave us still aching. But this discovery cannot make up for the hurts or take away the pain. Indeed, as noted, too much preoccupation with the past can exacerbate the suffering or bring new pathologies with it. We may even invent our memories of past abuses.

In any case, it is a simple fact that if your parents failed to love you, and even hurt you, there is nothing that psychology can do to make up for it.

No psychotherapist can make up for the lost love of childhood. A fifty-minute hour once a week, years after the events, is ridiculous as an answer. Likewise, group sessions when you are thirty years old cannot make up for family failures when you were seven. If your mother did not love you, the best—the only—resolution to this problem is to forgive her, with all that entails, and repent of your own sins, with all that entails. If we can do this, we can let go of the past, close those painful chapters of our lives, and turn and face the future. We can begin to think about a new life, about new goals, about the next and much more positive and exciting chapter to life's story.

Psychology cannot heal our deepest hurts or answer our strongest yearnings, and it is certainly not a pool in which to gaze perpetually at our own reflection.

Looking back over the three parts of psychology, we are in a better position to see modern psychology for what it is and avoid any idolatrous reliance on it. We can see the search for self-esteem as a well-meaning but misguided fad. We can recognize that psychotherapy has a definite but limited usefulness; we can acknowledge that people with addictions and other problems can often benefit from recovery groups. But psychology cannot heal our deepest hurts or answer our strongest yearnings, and it is certainly not a pool in which to gaze perpetually at our own reflection. At its best, psychology is a stepping stone—we should use it to move on.

If we can understand psychology in this way, then we can finally respond to the truth in the saying: "Life is not a problem to be solved, it is a story to be lived." And in finding our new story we need look no further than to the greatest story ever told.

6

AMERICA'S LAST MEN AND THEIR MAGNIFICENT TALKING CURE

by Os Guinness

In 1909, at the height of one of the busiest periods of immigration in American history, two arrivals from Europe stood at the rail of their ship as it passed the Statue of Liberty and entered New York harbor. The older one, a fifty-three-year-old Jew born in Moravia, poked the younger man from Switzerland in the ribs and said with excitement, "Won't they get a surprise when they hear what we have to say to them?"[1]

But the two men were not on their way to Ellis Island. Nor were they immigrants. The speaker was Sigmund Freud. His companion was his friend and disciple Carl Gustav Jung. And in the form of psychoanalysis and its legacy, "What we have to say to them" has had as much impact on the United States in the twentieth century as any one set of human ideas and words. Their accomplishments represent one of the great developments in the understanding of human nature. Within six years of their arrival their ideas had "set up a reverberation in human thought and conduct of which few as yet dare to predict the consequences,"[2] wrote Walter Lippmann in the *New Republic*.

The result has been hailed as "the triumph of the therapeutic" and the arrival of "psychological man." What were once the esoteric ideas of a small and controversial European elite have mushroomed in America into a dominant academic discipline and a vast, lucrative industry. More than five hundred brand-name therapies now jostle to compete for millions of clients in an expanding market of McFreud franchises and independent outlets that pulls in more than $4 billion a year. In America today it is more hazardous to believe you are not sick that to believe you are. The couch has become as American as the baseball diamond and the golden arches. As Peter L. Berger quipped, "If Freud had not existed, he would have had to be invented."[3]

In the 1990s, the roving spotlight of national attention is on the recovery movement. The twentieth century is closing with the same national nervousness and psychic epidemic as did the nineteenth century. But the recovery movement is only the latest, fastest growing, most popular, most accessible, and most religious of the many therapies that make up the broader therapeutic movement. So dominant have these therapies become— so self-evident in their claims and so seemingly effectual in their cures—that they have been well described as "the therapeutic revolution." And when Christians handle them thoughtlessly and uncritically, they easily become "another gospel."

At its worst, the therapeutic movement grows into what Harvard psychiatrist Robert Coles calls "the secular idolatry which it has been the fate of psychology and psychiatry to become for so many of us."[4] Indeed, together with the managerial revolution (see chapters 7 and 8), the therapeutic revolution is the leading source of contemporary Christian idolatry. At the very least, we must employ critical discernment that is far removed from breathless naïveté as we engage with the therapeutic movement today.

No Other God Has Wounds

Any criticism of the therapeutic revolution is bound to appear heartless. People, after all, are in pain and until that pain is remedied, all words can seem cold and even cruel. Our purpose here, as throughout the book, is to develop discernment, not to dismiss the movement outright. But it is particularly important to stress the difference in the challenge to the therapeutic idol.

In one of their periodic efforts to eradicate religious belief in the Soviet Union, the Communist party sent KGB agents to the nation's churches on a Sunday morning. One agent was struck by the deep devotion of an elderly woman who was kissing the feet of a life-size carving of Christ on the cross.

"Babushka [Grandmother]," he said. "Are you also prepared to kiss the feet of the beloved general secretary of our great Communist party?"

"Why, of course," came the immediate reply. "But only if you crucify him first."

It is an unrivaled wonder of the gospel of Jesus Christ that no other god has wounds. That reminder must precede and follow any critique of the therapeutic movement. We recognize that people today are hurting greatly. With the fatal combination of modern dislocations, such as the breakdown in family stability, and modern expectations, such as the impossible promise of individual freedom and fulfillment, people are hurting perhaps more than ever before.

More important, our God is the great healer. He is Jehovah Rapha, the Lord our healer. As the prophet Isaiah says of the suffering servant who will come, "by his wounds we are healed" (Isaiah 53:5). Even orthodoxy, which is usually reckoned to be "dry" and "cerebral," is viewed biblically as "sound doctrine," which, in Greek, is literally "hygienic" and health-giving.

Healing is therefore as central as ever to the mission of the church of Christ. Wherever the theories of psychology and psychiatry are true and their practitioners wise, the church should only give thanks and learn to work with them well. Many of us have benefited personally from the best of what Richard Baxter, a leading Puritan theologian, called "counsellors of the soul." The church of Christ has been in the business of pastoral care for two thousand years, and the therapeutic revolution marks an important milestone in this story.

But at the same time, competition over the cure of souls is not new. Freud and many of his disciples are simply the modern equivalents of the first-century Jewish and pagan exorcists who rivaled the Christian "mission doctors." The triumph of the therapeutic is therefore partly a spur to the church and partly a judgment—a further example of the "unpaid bills of the church." It is also partly a trumpet call to a new round of the conflict of the gods. So we must never lose sight of the issue at stake: People are hurting, and God is the true healer. Errors in the therapeutic movement must be exposed and the idols challenged, but only so that more and truer healing may be effected.

THE ODD COUPLE

The recovery movement has taken not only America but evangelicalism by storm. In the form of Christian (and not so Christian) books, programs, small groups, and counseling centers, it represents the highest floodwater mark of the therapeutic on the church so far. Twelve-step this and that have been given the authority of the apostolic twelve themselves, and the result has been hailed as renewal.

Christianity Today cites psychiatrist Scott Peck's assessment that the founding of Alcoholics Anonymous in Akron, Ohio, on June 10, 1935, was "the greatest event of the twentieth century."[5] But some glowing appraisals of its stepchild, the recovery movement, put this comment in the shade. One Christian author writes, "I believe the recovery movement is like revival." A prominent evangelical publisher says similarly: "Through our recovery books, we're giving people the truth. It's as close to hard-core evangelism as you can get."[6]

But what is overlooked in this enthusiasm is the oddness of the liaison between the gospel and the therapeutic movement. Freud offered the benefits of psychology as a human "talking cure." Surely this is a curious remedy for those committed to the objective and supernatural work of divine healing. But this is only the beginning of the strangeness.

To a people of faith, the therapeutic is one of the two self-consciously substitute theologies designed to replace faith in God.

To a people who view themselves as conservative, the therapeutic is one of the genuinely revolutionary movements in the modern world (another being the managerial). To a people often suspicious of the academic world, the therapeutic is one of the leading disciplines of the social sciences and one of the two great avenues of "collective introspection." (Psychology is an inquiry into the self just as sociology is an inquiry into society.) To a people dependent on tradition, the therapeutic is a leading carrier of "progressive ideas" that claim to liberate people from the inhibitions of truth, morality, and community. And to a people of faith, the therapeutic is one of the two self-consciously substitute theologies designed to replace faith in God.

It is well known that Freud dismissed religion as an "illusion" and saw himself as a "new Moses" with Jung as his "Joshua." He advocated psychotherapy as "a reeducation" for a new human civilization through a complete reversal of Mosaic morality and God-grounded objective guilt. Psychological liberty to Freud was a matter of messianic liberation.

In short, the therapeutic revolution spawned by Sigmund Freud and the political revolution spawned by Karl Marx form the twentieth century's two grand endeavors to order human life and society without God. One works from the private world outward, while the other works from the public world inward. One, more characteristic of Western democracy, now dominates, whereas the other, more characteristic of totalitarian socialism, now recedes. But both are an open challenge to historic Christian orthodoxy. And to most observers, the therapeutic has triumphed over the faith of the Christian church just as it has triumphed over the faith of the Communist party. Sociologist Philip Rieff concludes that the therapeutic is "the most revolutionary of all modern movements—toward a new world of nothing sacred. . . . In the world of my new readers, there is therapy where theology once was. There are hospital theaters where churches once were."[7]

In sum, where the American church at large and the evangelical community in particular have been unguarded about the therapeutic, they have been caught in the toils of a new Babylonian captivity. But this captivity is enforced on couches instead of brick-kilns and experienced in affinity groups instead of chain-gangs.

Triumphant Beyond Notice

The previous chapter unmasks the idolizing of psychology through a specific critique of our evangelical surrender to the therapeutic revolution in the last generation. This chapter is a more general overview of the social and historical setting in which the therapeutic revolution has occurred. It does not dismiss psychology nor does it critique any specific theories or therapies. Its aim is to show the danger of psychology exceeding its proper bounds and growing into an alternative worldview and an alternative gospel.

We must understand the social and historical setting in interpreting the therapeutic revolution. Knowing the particular setting is also necessary for understanding why we evangelicals have capitulated to the therapeutic with so few qualms or struggles. The setting is the spawning ground for idolatry. The triumph of the therapeutic is most complete because it has become our natural ambience, beyond notice or question.

If most evangelicals were immune to the therapeutic revolution prior to the last generation, we were also ignorant of its explosive growth as a social phenomenon. Following Freud's visit in 1909, the next half century was one of startling growth for psychology. It grew from being a concern of a few to a concern of many, from being centered in an elite to centered in the middle class, and from being the province of the sick to the province of the unhappy too.

In the process, the United States became "the world capital of psychological-mindedness and therapeutic endeavor,"[8] in Bernie Zilbergeld's famous description. Although America had only 6 percent of the world's population, it boasted over a third of the world's psychiatrists and over half the world's clinical psychologists. Not surprisingly to its inhabitants or to fans of Woody Allen films, New York City claimed to have more psychiatrists than any single European country. In 1968, the United States had twelve thousand clinical psychologists while no other nation had more than four hundred (the number today is more than forty thousand clinical psychologists). In 1986, there were 133 more Ph.D.s in psychology alone than in all the other American social sciences combined. Eighty million Americans, it is said, have now sought help from therapists. An estimated ten million are doing so every year.[9]

The full force of this social phenomenon was appreciated in the 1950s and 1960s. Philip Rieff wrote of "psychological man" in 1961 and psychologist Thomas Szasz of the "therapeutic state" in 1963. In 1965, Peter Berger wrote of "the psychological society" and of "institutionalized psychologism." But the watershed analysis was Philip Rieff's *Triumph of the Therapeutic* in 1966, followed later by Richard Sennett's *The Fall of Public Man* (1978) and Bernie Zilbergeld's *The Shrinking of America* (1983).

Two considerations lay behind the recent recognition that psychology has moved beyond a discipline to become a social movement. First, the theoretical and institutional core of the therapeutic movement is very different from the wider constellation of theories and therapies that form its fringe applications. Seen this way, Freudian psychoanalysis is only the oldest, most theoretical, most formalized, and most professionalized of the twentieth-century schools of psychology. Freud's psychodynamic school joins the behavioral, humanistic, and transpersonal schools to form the four main schools of the therapeutic revolution. Beyond these lie a loose and sprawling mass of therapeutic theories, organizations, and techniques, also including less rigorous motivation seminars and explicit New Age philosophies.

Benjamin Spock's Baby and Child Care *became the best-selling bible of American child-rearing, but a bible with Freudian underpinnings.*

Second, the roots of the therapeutic revolution are far older and its consequences far wider than could be guessed by tracing it to Freud alone. Friedrich Nietzsche had prophesied earlier of the link between "the last man" and "the convalescent society." Having lost God and any point of transcendence from which to judge themselves, the Last Men are those with only two bogus beatitudes left—health and happiness. The therapeutic movement and its sensibility are the consequence.

Even earlier still, the German poet and dramatist Johann Wolfgang von Goethe wrote in 1782, "Speaking for myself, I do believe humanity will win in the long run; I am only afraid that at the same time the world will have turned into one huge hospital where everyone is everyone else's humane nurse."[10]

The wider social consequences are not hard to see. Psychology has not only become an important new discipline, it has put its stamp on other disciplines and fields including law, politics, literature, religion, and advertising. Advertising, for example, is virtually psychology in reverse. At the same time, psychology has woven itself into the warp and woof of everyday life and speech. From such early terms as "unconscious" to such recent ones as "codependency," the jargon of psychology has become the coin of everyday life. And its themes and insights are now fundamental to such arenas as marriage, sex, and child-rearing. Benjamin Spock's *Baby and Child Care,* for example, became the best-selling bible of American child-rearing, but a bible with Freudian underpinnings. We have become saturated with psychology, Robert Coles writes, "to the point that a Woody Allen movie strikes one not as exaggeration, or satire, but as documentary realism."[11]

The triumph of the therapeutic has finally transformed psychology from a mere discipline to a worldview and a way of life. Triumphing as a social revolution, the therapeutic has gained a self-evident status and a taken-for-granted cultural authority that is rarely questioned. "Diagnosis" and "therapy" are as obvious to twentieth-century Americans as "demons" and "witches" were to seventeenth-century Americans. In law they replaced crime and punishment. In religion they have replaced sin and redemption. We have progressed, Rieff argues, from Political Man of classical times through Religious Man of the medieval world and Economic Man of the Enlightenment to Psychological Man of the modern world.

FAVORITE CHILD OF MODERNITY

The sheer Americanness of the therapeutic revolution creates a common reaction elsewhere in the world. "Ah, well, of course," they say with eyebrows raised. "How very American," "Only in America," and so forth. And, to a degree, this response is justified.

Thus it is not enough to explain "the shrinking of America" as the result of self-fulfilling circularity—as if America has more shrinks because the more shrinks America had, the more problems Americans discovered and the more shrinks appeared to solve them. We need to appreciate the strong affinities, or definite points of magnetic attraction, between the therapeutic movement and the American character. Such traits as the primacy of the individual, the right to happiness, the duty of self-improvement, the openness to and optimism about change, the belief in fix-it solutions, and the omnipresence of consumerism all fit hand-in-glove with the therapeutic movement. Together they smooth the way for an easy and unquestioned acceptance of the therapeutic. Thus therapeutic movements begun elsewhere have come into their own in the United States—Freudianism above all. And other movements "made in America" from beginning to end have flourished here as nowhere else.

But while important, the Americanness of the therapeutic is not the most significant factor. That place must be given to modernity. For Christians need to see that the therapeutic is a natural consequence of a crisis at the heart of our modern world. Even more, we need to see that psychology appears to triumph precisely at the point where religion appears to fail.

> *The therapeutic movement is an apt response to three particular developments in the modern world: modern individualism, separation of the private and the public worlds and the recent collapse of the family.*

As followers of Christ who read the Bible, we should not be surprised that self and society engage in a two-way conversation. Life means an interplay of the individual and his or her community. At a deeper level, the Bible also teaches that life is a two-way conversation between our human capacity to create and the constraints imposed on us by what we have created. This latter process is most pronounced in the act of idolatry. Worshiping what we ourselves have created, we become what we worship. As Psalm 115:8 puts it, "Those who make them will be like them, and so will all who trust in them."

The therapeutic movement pivots on two important extensions of these principles. First, there is a two-way conversation between social reality (the character of society at a particular time) and psychological reality (the way a person experiences himself or herself in the society at the same time). Second, there is an equally important two-way conversation between psychological reality (the way people are experiencing themselves inwardly in a society) and the psychological models available in a society. Such models are the frameworks or lenses through which life is interpreted and its problems solved.

In short, a psychology presupposes not only a theology, but a sociology. What social setting, we must then ask, helps throw light on the emergence and triumph of the therapeutic?

The therapeutic movement is an apt and even a brilliant response to three particular developments in the modern world. First, the origin of the therapeutic movement fits well with the emergence of modern individualism and subjectivism. What would have been superfluous when people were more community-conscious and socially constrained becomes highly relevant in the context of what has been called America's "national trek inward."

Second, the flowering of the therapeutic fits well with the modern separation of the private and the public worlds. Importantly, this separation is the social context of both the modern "identity crisis" and the modern "crisis of faith." In terms of the identity crisis, the separation strikes at the stability of personhood. The individual identity, as it is deprived of its traditional confirmations, becomes uncertain and unstable. In terms of the crisis of faith, the separation of the two worlds strikes at the integration of faith. Faith becomes privately engaging but publicly irrelevant.

Modernity heavily favors psychology rather than religion as the best response to these crises of identity and faith. In the modern world religion is perceived as a part of the crisis while psychology is seen as a part of the solution. In addition, religion is discounted as traditional, whereas psychology is prized as modern and scientific. But to cap it all, religion is virtually restricted to the private world, whereas psychology passes freely across the public/private divide. Industrial psychology, for example, has no counterpart in "industrial religion."

Third, the full harvest of the therapeutic—in the last generation—fits well with the more recent collapse of the family as a possible "haven in a heartless world." It is no accident that evangelicals did and could afford to ignore the therapeutic revolution until the last generation. We may not have answered its intellectual challenge earlier, but our family life was still strong enough to keep out the encroachments of modernity. Today, all that has changed. Television, fast food, and VCRs are only the technological edge of a social revolution that has destroyed our evangelical family life as much as anyone's. With no haven left and "dysfunctionalism" rampant, resort to the therapeutic is as desperate as it is natural.

One further feature of the therapeutic response to modernity is worth noting: psychology's shift from a remedial to a revolutionary role. Psychology's role is remedial when the focus of the problem is the individual. Since the problem is the individual, the solution calls for the individual to readjust to the family or society. Psychology's role is therefore remedial—and humble. But psychology's role inevitably becomes revolutionary when the focus of the problem is not the individual, but the family, the group, or society. Since the problem is society, the solution becomes freedom for the individual to be independent of the family or society. Psychology's role therefore changes—from remedial to revolutionary, from humble to proud, and from midwife to liberator. Talk of the therapeutic "revolution" is no hyperbole. At its most challenging, the therapeutic is a more formidable "alternative gospel" than humanism or the New Age movement can ever aspire to be.

DIGGING OUR OWN GRAVES

There is a perverse feature of Christian cultural surrender: When Christians freely capitulate to some trend or another, our commitment is often as fierce as it is late. Often, it can only be pried loose when the secular world leads Christians to abandon what it earlier led them to adopt. This cycle is already evident in the recovery movement. The euphoria of latter-day evangelical converts is rising just as secular enthusiasm is waning. *Christianity Today* has many advertisements ("Christian Public Service Announcements") for recovery hotlines just as books like *The Freudian Fraud* are being published and *Newsweek* has a cover story on "the curse of self-esteem." The lesson seems to be: Buy late and always be out of date.

Before long, American evangelicals will slowly awaken to this exercise in foolishness in relation to the therapeutic revolution as a whole. The disillusionment will likely come at one of two points—psychology's inability to answer psychological problems from within its own humanistic framework, or psychology's contribution to America's broader crisis. The latter is particularly relevant today.

We evangelicals have a strong heritage of pietism, but have been slow to appreciate its attendant dangers, such as subjectivism and privatism. Yet these are the very weaknesses that the therapeutic revolution magnifies exponentially—to the point where concern for truth, responsibility, objectivity, doctrine, history, and transcendence is nearing the vanishing point in parts of evangelicalism. In our privatism, we are lulled even as the wider culture is.

We evangelicals need to realize that the cultural decline we rightly deplore is definitely linked to the triumph of the therapeutic so many of us celebrate. The therapeutic movement is quite simply one of the prime solvents of American reality and responsibility. As Goethe warned earlier, "Ages which are regressive and in process of dissolution are always subjective, whereas the trend in all progressive epochs is objective."[12]

Goethe's warning is very close to Nietzsche's prediction of—and contempt for—the mediocrity of the Last Men in a day when the myth of "from rags to riches" has been eclipsed by "from addictions to recovery." Today, this warning is picked up in the analyses of such cultural critics as Christopher Lasch and Philip Rieff. For Lasch, the therapeutic is a key part of the permissiveness of capitalist consumerism. In servicing the Last Men ethic of health and hedonism, the therapeutic ethos undermines such values as thrift and denial. The result is a vicious cycle in which new expectations generate new discontents, which in turn generate new therapists. Thus citizens degenerate into consumers (of things) and clients (of therapy). Their reward—and fate—is to be preoccupied with a never-ending supply of new toys, new drugs, and new liberations.

We have come a long way from Calvin to Freud and from Puritanism to psychology. The result has been an unraveling of American ideals.

For Rieff, the therapeutic's significance represents a titanic shift in American character and history. We have come a long way from Calvin to Freud and from Puritanism to psychology. The result has been both a softening and an unraveling of American ideals. The outcome is genuinely dangerous: a "culture of the never satisfied" and, thus, "the most revolutionary of all modern movements."[13] Not surprisingly, the feel-good era of the 1980s was also the golden age of exoneration ("Don't blame me, blame my parents"), and the heyday of counseling as lifelong school of flattery ("I'm happy to be me"). It was also a period of America's slippage in the world.

THE CONFLICT OF THE GODS

Needless to say, the power of the therapeutic movement cuts both ways. To some, its influence is a sure sign of its relevance and benefits. If ever there was an idea whose time has come, they say, it is the therapeutic. We should pluck and enjoy its fruits and especially their healing power for those in pain. For others, myself included, the very plausibility is also a danger sign. How else could something so antithetical to the gospel so beguile the best minds of a generation that the themes and imperatives of the gospel have grown faint?

In using the insights and tools of modernity we must ask: Are we plundering the Egyptians legitimately or are we setting up a golden calf? Are the therapeutic insights and tools legitimate, or are they double-edged? Have the therapeutic tools grown excessive, or even autonomous? Or, worst of all, have they become a false form of reliance and thus idolatrous? O. Hobart Mowrer raised the question in 1960, "Has evangelical religion sold its birthright for a mess of psychological pottage?"[14] He answered that it had. Paul Vitz powerfully amplified this point in *Psychology as Religion* in 1977 as did William Kirk Kilpatrick in *Psychological Seduction* in 1983. Yet if the recovery movement is any indication, their warnings are still unheeded by most evangelicals. A decade later, Kilpatrick's publishers are in the vanguard of the rage for recovery. New depths of Christian credulity have been plumbed.

How does the essential usefulness of the best of the therapeutic become transformed into "another gospel"? How does a mere psychological theory or therapy become idolatrous? Such distortions happen when psychology grows beyond its proper bounds until the therapeutic revolution offers alernatives to the gospel. The therapeutic now offers eight alternatives— all deceptive and all substitutes for God. These eight, shown below, are temptations that the evangelical church must confront.

AN ALTERNATIVE AUTHORITY

"In the beginning was the Word," and in the beginning of pastoral care was theology—right down to the Puritan era and beyond. But as the church has been pushed back to the margins of the modern world, it has suffered the embarrassment of vanishing social authority. In a word, irrelevance. The two most common responses have been to resort either to traditional modes of authority asserted more aggressively or to new modes of authority altogether.

For those who choose the second and more modern option, the two favorite sources of modern authority are the managerial and the therapeutic. Here, it seems, are two roads to instant status and guaranteed relevance. Hence the cry first directed to liberals in the 1960s and transferred to evangelicals in the 1980s: The traditional pastor has given way to the modern pastor who is "a CEO in his study and a shrink in his pulpit."

The result is what David Powlison describes well as the "defer and refer" syndrome. The relationship of the church to psychology becomes intellectually derivative, socially subordinate, and practically weak. High views of authority, even of inerrancy, make no difference. However orthodox the theology, the therapeutic has the final say in practice. Thus, the therapeutic becomes an alternative authority.

Evangelicals still imagine that such translations serve the cause of relevance. But the crisis of Christian authority has a darker side. Robert Coles tells the story of a medical school classmate dying of cancer in a Boston hospital. Each time he wanted to talk to his minister about God and directly spiritual matters, the minister only responded with psychological words and phrases. The dying man was deeply affronted. "He comes here . . . and offers me psychological banalities as God's word!" Purely psychological insights on the stages and phases of living and dying, Coles writes, are "all dwelt upon (God save us!) as if Stations of the Cross."[15]

AN ALTERNATIVE WORLDVIEW

Hostility to religion has long been a recognized feature of the modern world. Above all, religions and ideologies that strive to integrate the whole of life within the cosmos of their worldview experience special difficulties—Judaism, the Christian faith, Islam, and Marxism, for example. But the old idea that secularization would be progressive and irreversible has proved wrong. Religion has not so much disappeared as it has changed into new forms—and totally new forms of worldviews have risen and flourished.

The therapeutic is a leading example. It has become an influential alternative worldview to Christianity. As Bernie Zilbergeld points out, the "therapeutic sensibility" is a belief system that has "an enormous influence on most of us and in important ways has become our sensibility, our way of viewing the world and ourselves. It is probably not unfair to say that it has become as important as the tenets of Christianity once were."[16] Indeed, Lasch writes, "The contemporary climate is therapeutic, not religious." The cult of personal relations is "the faith of those without faith."[17]

In other words, psychology has become one of the leading ways to interpret both the internal and external world apart from faith. It has superseded other explanatory perspectives, such as the supernatural, the moral, the rational, and the economic. Psychological Man views the world and experiences life in psychological categories. Complexes, repressions, denials, inhibitions, obsessions, traumas, and codependencies are far more "real" than original sin or the image of God. As the devil complains in Jeremy Leven's novel *Satan,* "Psychotherapy worries the hell out of me . . . It keeps turning evil into neuroses and explaining away people's behavior with drives and complexes. . . . Modern psychiatrity is putting me out of business."[18]

"Seeking help" is more likely to mean a seventy-five dollar, fifty-minute hour at the psychologist's than a time of prayer and meditation with God or counseling with a pastor, confessor, or friend.

Sadly, not only the devil has been made redundant. Judging from contemporary evangelical speech and publications, great tracts of Christian truth have too. Recently at a celebrated Christian conference center in Texas, the sermon in the worship service began like this: "Talk to each other in sentences that begin 'I feel.' " The service climaxed with a brief mediation on the thought that Communion is "God's way of hugging you."

The anemic condition of the Christian worldview today is demonstrated by the great difficulty Christians have when asked to "think Christianly." By contrast, the triumph of the therapeutic is exemplified in the ease with which modern people resort instinctively to psychology. "Seeking help" is more likely to mean a seventy-five dollar, fifty-minute hour at the psychologist's than a time of prayer and meditation with God or an unstinted time of counseling with a pastor, confessor, or friend.

AN ALTERNATIVE LANGUAGE OF SKEPTICISM

Marx, Nietzsche, and Freud have been described as the three great "masters of suspicion," or connoisseurs of the "art of mistrust." Ironically, as emphasized earlier, they derived such concepts as rationalizing and ideology from the biblical notion of idolatry. They stole the most powerful weapon in the believer's arsenal and turned it against belief itself. Such general mistrust easily leads to skepticism.

The therapeutic offers the alternative language of skepticism. Nowhere is the art of mistrust stronger at the everyday level than in psychology. With its privileged access to the unconscious, psychology can play its "hidden depths card" to trump any observation. Nothing is what it seems. There is always more than meets the eye. The straightforward is really a scheme, the look is a mask, the deed is a game. Hidden purposes are everywhere. The truth is other than you think.

Although many of these individual explanations are useful, the sum total is an exponential increase in introspection and skepticism. The outcome is not a dogmatic unbelief but a deepening uncertainty about everything—including dogmatism and unbelief. Intellectual psychological dismissals of faith as "projection" or "illusion" may even be rarer than before, but they are hardly needed. Given the epidemic of introspection and the ubiquity of such notions as "denial" and the "toxicity" of faith, what is left of faith today may be as withered as the hand of the palsied man who came to Jesus two thousand years ago. Psychology, with its drive to analyze and excuse, criticizes and seeks to undermine faith.

ALTERNATIVE PRIESTS

The modern trend toward specialization and dependency on experts is covered elsewhere in this book (see chapters 8 and 9). The United States, as modernity's "lead society," is the most specialized and professionalized nation on earth. Americans are therefore reared to be clients of expert services as much as consumers and citizens. A secret of the "good life" in America is having a personal expert to contact for every conceivable need. And it seems that no sphere of need—education, health, finance, law, or entertainment—is more important than one's own inner life.

Advocates of the therapeutic therefore hold a front-rank position in the pantheon of America's experts. Whether researchers, academics, medical doctors, counselors, popular writers, or seminar leaders, they have been accredited socially with a competence that is beyond criticism in most circles. After all, it is said, without the help of psychologists, the dark harvest of crises from confused identities and dysfunctional families would be horrific.

Needless to say, the point is true and important. But it obscures two other points that are the negative face of the drive toward expertise. First, the reliance on experts leads toward dependency and a "tyranny of expertise" that is a form of "paternalism without a father" (Lasch) and the ultimate codependency. Second, it encourages the public's demand for what is psychology's natural supply—counseling as business. With its enlarged circle of therapists, psychology supplies us with alternative priests.

Sincere counselors bridle at this point, but there is no question that psychology itself has become an ideology—a set of ideas that serves the interests of an entire industry. For Christians, however, the problem lies deeper. What have been called "professional disablers" (Ivan Illich), with a truly "authoritarian mystique" (Wendy Kaminer), often become blocks to true freedom and growth in Christ. Christ set us free to be truly free—not free to be free from everything except therapists.

AN ALTERNATIVE PATHOLOGY

No aspect of a religion or a worldview is more important than its capacity to understand and answer life's dilemmas—especially those posed by suffering and evil. The Christian faith has been striking in this regard. Original sin, the cross, grace, final judgment—the different truths that make up the Christian understanding and answer to evil have been a source of personal comfort and philosophical assurance to searchers, doubters, and sufferers alike.

Can the same be said of the therapeutic? Is its view of human evil even more radical, its solution even more complete? Nowhere is the triumph of the therapeutic more surprising and more hollow, for nothing about the therapeutic is more deficient than its pathology of human evil.

> *Without the realism inherent in the biblical diagnosis of sin, the therapeutic condemns itself to explanations that are too shallow and solutions that dazzle only to disappoint.*

Occasionally, psychology's diagnosis is as serious as the Bible's, but lacks the biblical solution. It then becomes a form of determinism or fatalism that, if followed to the end, would lead to resigned pessimism. Certain current proponents of "diseasing," for example, have been described as virtually "addicted to addiction." And their clients are "steps-o-man-iacs," those who know they can never get better, but who gain comfort from the fact that addictions are always expanding so they can always find more addicts like themselves. An addiction-therapist speaking on the Good Christian Woman syndrome said bluntly: "My experience is that everybody in this audience is an addict of some kind or another. Unless you're in recovery, you're part of the problem."[19] The result is not only a broken world but a hopeless one. Americans concerned about the economic deficit should realize that the spiraling cycle of human deficits and infirmities is growing faster still.

More often, however, psychology's diagnosis is too shallow. It suffers from what Wendy Kaminer calls "relentless optimism." As *Newsweek* wrote of "psychotheology" in the recovery movement, "But now you know there are no bad people, only people who think badly of themselves."[20] Therapists used to diagnose problems as the result of complexes and inhibitions. But the new catchall diagnosis for all of life's afflictions, from overeating to masturbation, is the psychologically correct notion of the "hole in the soul"—low self-esteem. California's state commission on self-esteem solemnly declares that "lack of self-esteem is central to most personal and social ills plaguing our state and nation."[21] A seeker-friendly church in Michigan, which calls itself The Church of Today, proclaims that "the great sin is not the things people typically see as sin, it's not living up to their potential."[22]

All such notions eventually fall foul of the question asked by Karl Menninger's famous title: *Whatever Became of Sin?* But ironically, Menninger called into question his own earlier work too, for no one had done more to undermine the responsibility of criminals for their crimes than he had in his 1968 book, *The Crime of Punishment.*

We may take it as certain: Without the realism inherent in the biblical diagnosis of sin, the therapeutic condemns itself to explanations that are too shallow and solutions that dazzle only to disappoint. As Oswald Chambers wrote, "Always beware of an estimate of life which does not recognize the fact that there is sin. . . . You are never safe with an innocent man or woman."[23]

AN ALTERNATIVE SELF

A solid sense of personhood is essential to human life as well as to such lesser things as democracy. Psychology is therefore essential today, so long as it can answer the massive crisis of confidence in the self that modernity triggers. But does it? And where psychology knows that it doesn't, do its proponents admit the deficiency?

The modern "identity crisis" is neither new nor American in origin. But in America it has been taken further because our advanced modern technologies and our extreme postmodern theories of the self have converged. In contrast to traditional life, many Americans experience their lives as self-conscious rather than straightforward, socially constrained rather than giving, fragmented and serialized rather than unified, ceaselessly invented and reinvented rather than ever taken for granted. An American's sense of personhood is self-conscious, artificial, changing, and insubstantial. With "sameness" and "continuity" no longer possible, modern identity is protean and problematic. The "imperial self" of grand individualism has been reduced to the "minimal self" of uncertain narcissism. The rage is for "polymorphous potentiality," for everyone can now be anyone.

Psychology by itself has no answer to the grand crisis of the self—either on the theoretical level or the social level. The therapeutic can offer only a problematic alternative self. The social deficiency has been plain for a long time, because most versions of the therapeutic pivot on a self-defeating individualism. Ever since Freud, most practitioners of psychology have lacked a constructive vision of the social order—whether rooted in community, tradition, or faith. They have therefore been deficient in showing how a healthy life can be achieved and maintained.

Today, as postmodern thinking has brought us, evangelicals as well as Americans in general, to a crisis in the very meaning of meaning, the theoretical foundations of the self have been destroyed too. Personhood, truth, and even the notion of a knowable reality have become fictions. Many psychologists have not acknowledged this crisis, or perhaps are unaware of it. Their therapy, then, can never be more than an "adjustment"—the equivalent of rearranging the deck chairs on the S.S. Titanic.

For those who know the depths of the crisis, the issues raised are ultimate. Human nature was once considered to have dignity and weight because humanity was the glory of God and made in His image (*dignitas* being Latin for glory). As Rieff writes, "The true self derived from the one self, self-disclosed in Exodus 3:14: 'I am that I am.' Each self is commanded to be according to this creator-self and not to become a cast no longer in search of their author. The 'self' to which we insistently refer in out therapeutic languages can only be an old sacred world courtesy title."[24]

"Sacred world courtesy title"? "Pastiche personality"? "Mass of relatedness"? Such modern descriptions of the self are woefully inadequate. Those who assess the crisis of personhood and self today confront a challenge: All psychology assumes an anthropology and thus a theology. Those who ignore this challenge choose the path toward ineffectiveness. Those who face it choose a path that leads beyond psychology.

AN ALTERNATIVE FAITH

In many European countries with an established-church background, modernity has conferred a legacy of milder or stronger hostility to religion in general. This is epitomized, for example, in the revolutionary Jacobin cry "Strangle the last king with the guts of the last priest!" The United States, by contrast, has traditionally enjoyed a positive relationship between religion and society because of the genius of the First Amendment. But this has created its own problems in the form of two characteristically American heresies—faith in religion in general (rather than faith in God) and faith in faith as a process (rather than in God).

The therapeutic revolution has long been a leading carrier of the second heresy and the church has long accommodated it. The therapeutic has always proffered an alternative faith. In the nineteenth century, the heresy flowered into the New Thought movement. This was an adaptation of theology to the new vocabulary of science, technology, and popular culture on the one hand, and to the new psychology on the other. Originally a feature of liberal theology and a sibling of the era of "muscular Christianity," the New Thought positioned the gospel as a source of power. Popular treatises flourished with such titles as *The Secret of Power* and *How to Obtain Power Through Prayer.* Thus advocates of New Thought claimed that it was possible to tap the vitalizing reservoirs of "infinite power" through faith.

Later in the nineteenth century, new notions of the subconscious, relaxation, and self-surrender gave rise to new views of faith that could turn transcendent power into immanent power. The result was the gospel of faith as therapy, a catechism of mental hygiene built on "the practical use of faith." From Ralph Waldo Emerson to William James and Harry Emerson Fosdick and down to Norman Vincent Peale and Robert Schuller, the line can be traced from New Thought to the Power of Positive Thinking and today's Possibility Thinking. Every morning, before you get out of bed, a celebrated best-seller advises, the secret of faith is to say to yourself, "I believe!" three times. Or as *Publishers Weekly* remarked of an Orlando megachurch pastor and televangelist, it is no coincidence that he "set up shop in Orlando, home of Disney World. Both promise a magical journey—if you believe."[25]

In the face of this heresy, followers of Christ should be zealous to distinguish faith in God from faith in faith, or justification by faith alone from justification by faith that remains alone. As Adlai Stevenson quipped, "Paul I find appealing, but Peale I find appalling."

AN ALTERNATIVE SALVATION

The overall story of pastoral care in the United States has been summed up as the shift from salvation to self-realization, made up of smaller shifts from self-denial to self-love to self-mastery, and finally to self-realization.[26] The victory of the therapeutic over theology is therefore nothing less than the secularization and replacement of salvation. After all, as Rieff comments, "Religious man was born to be saved, psychological man is born to be pleased."[27]

Optimism is a central feature of this new salvation-as-self-realization—at least for American therapists. Unlike Freud, who was gloomier, they believe there are few limits to human potential and thus to what therapy can do. Their hopefulness is catching. Change, complete and immediate change, is bandied about as a possibility by therapists and believed in enthusiastically by their clients. Even after years of living in the United States as a European, I still am jolted when an American evangelical blithely claims that a conference or seminar "totally changed my life."

Where the experiences are genuinely grounded in Christian truth, they are Pelagian at best—a heresy of the possibility of innocence and perfectibility that is truly unattainable in this life. Where the experiences are purely therapeutic, they are distinctive at times but deceptive always. Arthur Janov promises "a new kind of human being" through his primal scream therapy.[28] His is a typical therapeutic offer, made by a therapeutic evangelist. And therapeutic conversions and testimonies are not far behind. Come from depression to freedom, they say, from impotence to controlling your own destinies. Therapy is the answer. Therapy can change your life.

> *The record of therapeutic success is highly mixed—long-couched patients usually end up financially poorer rather than psychologically better.*

Ironically, the fast-paced parade of therapeutic fashions is the strongest witness to the inadequacy of all the failed therapies that have gone before. But the very speed of the changes spins such an illusion of the latest-greatest and the newest-truest that few have the wit or will to see it. Thus the problem is not that so many are looking for answers, but that so many are claiming to find them.

But people are not so easily changed. There are limits to human malleability. And some changes are for the worse. The record of therapeutic success is highly mixed—long-couched patients usually end up financially poorer rather than psychologically better. Adults in touch with "their own inner children" are often happier rather than healthier. One psychologist admits, "People can get stuck in a victim role with their 'child within.' They come into my office hugging teddy bears, telling me they're recovered."

As Rieff writes, many therapeutic successes are little more than "rubber nipple therapies" designed to be sucked to escape the authority of anxiety.[29] Others are such palpable failures that one is prompted to say, "Physician, heal yourself!" Indeed, there is mounting evidence that psychology is yet another "sick physician" that has failed to cure itself. The eminent British psychologist Hans Eysenck made the point bluntly, "The success of the Freudian revolution seemed complete. Only one thing went wrong: *The patients did not get any better.*"[30]

LONGING FOR HOME

Part Three of Nietzsche's *Thus Spoke Zarathustra* has a section on "The Convalescent." Nietzsche was an expert in words and their roots. "To convalesce" in Greek (*genesen*) is linked to the word "return home." *Nóstos* is the root for our word *nostalgia,* the aching longing for home that we call homesickness. Thus for Nietzsche in the late nineteenth century, the convalescent is the person who collects himself or herself to return home. He (or she) is on the road to himself, so that he can say, "I know who I am." A century later, the recovery movement promises the same. John Bradshaw, its own televangelist, appeals movingly to the "inner child" in all of us and to the universal desire of going home. Through recovery, he promises, "We can go home again."[31]

Here is the final challenge of the therapeutic. Other dimensions of the critique could be added, but one thing is plain: For the followers of Christ, the question of psychology and psychiatry is never simply academic, theoretical, or a limited matter of certain useful insights and tools. All these may be granted gladly, but the main discussion is yet to begin. Far more has been born in the therapeutic and far more is at stake.

For one thing, where the widely advertised healings of the therapeutic movement have been false, superficial, or incomplete, many are still wounded and still need healing. For another, our crying need today as Christians is for a healing that leads beyond healing—to growth and deep maturity in knowing God. But most importantly of all, our understanding of the character and existence of God is at stake. In today's convalescent society, aching with spiritual and cultural homesickness, the ultimate issues are: Which self do we reach when we come to ourselves? Which guide home from the far country do we trust? Which home are we going to? And which father will be waiting for us?

Philip Rieff has spent a lifetime as a student of the therapeutic revolution. He has blunt counsel for a generation born during the revolution's triumph, which recognizes its dangers and desires to see the restoration of faith. He simply quotes Franz Kafka, "For the last time psychology!"[32] Or, as we must say as followers of Christ, "For God's sake, an end to all idolizing of psychology!"

7

THE GRAND INQUISITOR LIVES— IDOLATRY IN ORGANIZATIONS AND MANAGEMENT

by Alonzo L. McDonald

It was a glorious, crisp morning with sunlight radiating all around us as we tripped down the steps of the historic inn near the town center. Our spirits were soaring as we joked about enjoying an overly sumptuous breakfast from the hands of our Pennsylvania Dutch host. He had personally prepared and served the meal with an abundant dose of local folklore, including endless tales about the massive old mill down the street and what it had meant to the town. After the leisurely meal, our mood turned somber as we drove the car alongside the three-story brick facade of the mill; it extended a full two blocks broken only by a narrow lane.

The great doors to the old mill facing the two main streets were firmly locked, probably rusted closed after the workers began arriving several decades ago by automobile instead of by foot. Finally, adjacent to the vacant and dilapidated shipping dock in the rear, we found a small door open, which the caretaker apparently used for his periodic rounds.

As we slowly passed the vast, empty wings and bays of the old factory, the two of us talked more softly and stepped lightly as if walking in a tomb. The echoes off distant walls were eerie and seemed to multiply even

Alonzo L. McDonald is chairman of Avenir Group, Inc., a private development bank. He has four decades of management experience in professional firms, government, the media, and in large and small businesses. He is a former U.S. ambassador, White House staff director, president of Bendix Corporation, managing director of McKinsey & Company, Inc., and a faculty member of the Harvard Business School.

as they faded away. There was little left of value in the stillness where for almost a century a thousand workers, spread across three daily shifts, had made their living, fed their families, and nourished the town's cash registers. The scavengers who purvey used machinery had done their work well. It was now only for the scrap metal crew to collect and cart away anything else that would melt. The only bright spots were a few lonesome rays of sunlight that occasionally shimmered through the rough patches in the roof or around the jagged edges of a broken glass pane, contrasting sharply with the opaque adjacent windows that were thickly coated with dark grime slowly accumulated over three score or more years.

In a deserted office arena we tagged a table whose age in quarterly accounting periods about equaled its weight, and then we marked "to keep" on a handful of classic wooden chairs that had for so long graced the boardroom table. That was all we salvaged from the remains. Refinished and carefully positioned in our modern offices, these quasi-antique fixtures would serve as quaint conversation pieces for a few more years before becoming a bargain dining set in some youngster's post-college housing.

About an hour before noon, I slipped back to the car, heavily depressed and with a tightness in the chest that comes at a certain age when reminded of the transient nature of this world. The depression hung heavy as I realized the scene represented what happens when organizations, once great institutions and fine companies, big and small, succumb to idolatry and blindly follow false gods into oblivion.

As I lay down on the back seat to rest, some basic questions occurred to me. Why did it happen? Why do institutions decline and fall like this? What apparition, what false ideas bound together the minds and actions of the leaders and people of this once respected enterprise to lure them away from their early vision of service and productivity, from their initial useful mission to society, far from the patterns of success that marked their years of spirited actions and prosperity? What if they had evolved, adapted to the changes underway all around them, kept firmly to their mission as a bountifully contributing enterprise? Finally, one more question came to mind, this one concerning Christian organizations: *Why do Christ-centered organizations and ministries so often follow a similar path* (a path that undercuts the organization's spiritual impact and can lead the ministry to spiritual suicide)?

These questions merit our reflection and concern today because the death of an institution—whether a company or a parachurch organization—may in some ways be even sadder than the death of a human being. Sooner or later, of course, the latter is expected. Although an institution does not have the soul of a human being, there are real losses when an institution

134

dies: missed opportunities, a failed mission, and an alarming toll on the community. Hundreds, and even thousands of lives are often changed forever. The grandeur and mortality of human institutions is a worthy part of the human story—though with human institutions, part of the grandeur is actually the illusion of immortality.

THE IDOL OF IMMORTALITY

Like human beings, all organizations, under human control, fantasize about the dream of immortality. Yet unlike human beings, human organizations seem to have genuine reason to hope that the fantasy can become reality. Organizations, after all, are not limited to one human lifetime. They have no fixed life cycles, no known stages of aging, no predetermined deterioration of organs and tissues, and no predictable reduction of capabilities for self-renewal and revitalization.

Faced with no fixed actuarial tables, leaders and management readily embrace the dream of their organization becoming immortal. This assumption is particularly obvious after one or more generations of leadership, a relatively short timeframe as a generation of management usually spans only a third to half the life cycle of a human generation. Therefore, even organizations that are fifty or sixty years young may have survived three or more generations of management leaders. This helps create the illusion of continuity and even permanence. Yet, this is only an illusion. Human organizations are no more immortal than human beings. Only a fraction of the hundred largest corporations in the United States at the beginning of this century still exist today.

Yet the drive for immortality is ever present. If institutions at their best are about the ordering of human freedom, and management at its best is the art of reordering human freedom wisely, the astute manager must seriously consider the dynamic that most undermines human institutions—the overriding drive for immortality, which is the idol at the heart of every human institution.

Religious institutions are especially prone to this temptation. After all, they deal with the eternal, and the soaring comprehensiveness of their belief-systems adds to the illusion of their ultimate importance and, therefore, permanence. In the case of the church universal, the institution has Christ's promise that the very gates of hell will not prevail against it. And as if to prove this divine endorsement, the church has lived in some form for two thousand years, spanning countless cultures as well as generations.

There is therefore a justifiable sense of the continuity of the church. This in turn leads to the assumption of the church's innate right of continued existence. Regardless of what a branch of the universal church or a para-church organization accomplishes or how close or far it is from Christ's purpose, it is easy to think that God Himself will assure its continuity forever—with a little bit of help from His self-appointed servants.

This is a catastrophic presumption. It is at the heart of what Fyodor Dostoyevsky called the church's "correcting the work of Christ." It is best recorded in the "Legend of the Grand Inquisitor," a chapter in Dostoevsky's great novel *The Brothers Karamazov.* In the legend, Jesus Christ comes to the earth again, softly and unobserved. Yet His presence is felt by everyone who crosses His path. The radiance and intensity of His love deeply moves all who see Him or touch His clothing, as in His healing a blind man and raising the tiny daughter of a prominent citizen from her coffin at the portal of the Cathedral of Seville.

As the story proceeds, the Grand Inquisitor, a cardinal of the church nearing ninety years of age, quickly dispatches his guards to capture the intruder. They place Him in "a gloomy vaulted prison in the ancient palace of the Holy Inquisition." The Grand Inquisitor then descends to talk with his prisoner who, never saying a word, listens intently to the Cardinal's tirade. The Inquisitor accuses Christ of unwisely refusing the three temptations recorded in the Scriptures—three fundamental questions that the old Cardinal acknowledges are a miracle of wisdom in themselves. "For in those three questions," he says, "the whole subsequent history of mankind is foretold."

The Inquisitor claims that Jesus made the wrong choice in all three instances for the sake of maintaining full freedom of choice and conscience for every individual. Each has the right to determine his or her own belief or nonbelief. But, the Inquisitor scoffs, "Nothing has ever been more unbearable for a man in a human society than freedom." Yet, he continues, since man will always opt for earthly bread over heavenly bread, the church has decided to cater to human weakness and assume earthly power over its subjects.

"You would not enslave man by a miracle and craved faith given freely, not based on miracle," he grants. Yet he counters, "It's not the free judgment of their hearts, not love that matters, but a mystery that they must follow blindly, even against their conscience. So we have done."

The Grand Inquisitor's tirade climaxes with a terrible claim: "We have corrected your work and have founded it upon *miracle, mystery,* and *authority.* And men rejoiced that they were again led like sheep and that the terrible gift [freedom of choice] that had brought them such suffering was at last lifted from their hearts."[1]

Dostoyevsky had in his sights the corrupt authoritarianism of the medieval papacy, but his parable illuminates the idolatry in all human institutions, religious no less than secular, Protestant and evangelical as well as

Roman Catholic. All human institutions—Campus Crusade for Christ and the Southern Baptist Convention no less than General Motors and the American Republic—are potentially driven by a desire for immortality. This includes the organization led by the editors of this book.

Whenever immortality becomes the central objective of an organization, its demise is inevitable.

In Christ-centered organizations, then, the temptation arises in a thousand forms to pursue immortality by "correcting the work of Christ" and relying instead on varieties of miracle, mystery, and authority. Dostoyevsky wrote a decade before Frederick Taylor took some of the crude early steps toward modern management science, but this evolution makes our warning even more urgent. Legitimate and fruitful though management insights are at their best, they need to be used with care or they can become a new and improved way of perverting the terrible freedom of the gospel. Far from a kiss of life to dying Christ-centered institutions, modern management can also be the kiss of death if its approaches overshadow rather than reinforce the basic mission.

Whenever immortality becomes the central objective of an organization, its demise is inevitable. Concern for the self-perpetuation of the institution and the preservation of the status quo is the greatest idol that any institution will face.

Needless to say, the continuation of a good organization is good and right. There is no virtue in failure. But the legitimate desire for self-perpetuation is similar to the desires for profitability and happiness. These are not achieved through our direct actions. Rather, they are by-products of other endeavors that keep an organization vibrant and forward-looking, contributing more to society than it expects in return. When continuing existence is sought directly as an end rather than as a by-product of serving wider needs, the dynamics of idolatry lead to deception and disaster for the organization.

There are many other dangers in the dynamics of institutions; the ones usually cited include power, money, and prestige. But these are really subsidiary to the desire for immortality, and thus for the preservation of the status quo. In the struggle to sustain organizations, these dangers are less important than they are for individuals, if only because organizations are usually not in the business of nurturing the innate pride or fragile egos of individuals.

False gods that are more devious and difficult to deal with are factors that are basically good most of the time. They become idols only when they are misused or pursued to excess. These can include some or all of the elements of management. The more common examples are systems, organizational formats, patterns of interpersonal relationships, financial controls, planning activities, production methods, sales approaches, advertising themes, customer service concepts, and even quality standards. When these components become the focus instead of simply useful tools, they too can be inflated into false gods whose distortions lead organizations toward the brink of oblivion.

THE ORDERING OF FREEDOM

When it comes to understanding institutions, evangelicals typically make two common mistakes. On the one hand, we are often overcritical of the general idea of institutions—as if those who come to Christ are restored to the simplicity of an Eden-like existence that needs no structures or organizations. It is almost as if institutions are structures of the fallen world, not needed for those who are spiritual. On the other hand, we are often equally uncritical of specific institutions, namely those we like and have come to trust or work for. In both cases there is a lack of realism about institutions, though in the first instance we are unrealistic about their benefits and in the second about their dangers.

Our concern in this chapter is the idolatry of institutions, which is obviously a direct product of the second error. But because the first error is prevalent in Christ-centered organizations, especially the more spiritual ministries, the dangers are worth noting. Here are two positive points to set against super-spiritual pietism that underestimates the proper place and importance of institutions.

First, institutions are vitally linked to freedom. Our human freedom is best ordered and sustained through these structures. Institutions are a matter of form, not freedom. But freedom requires these forms if freedom is to last. As G.K. Chesterton wrote:

> It is the fashion to talk of institutions as cold and cramping things. The truth is that when people are in exceptionally high spirits, really wild with freedom and invention, they always must, and they always do, create institutions. When men are weary they fall into anarchy; but while they are gay and vigorous they invariably make rules. This, which is true of all the churches and republics of history, is also true of the most trivial parlour game or the most unsophisticated meadow romp. We are never free until

some institution frees us, and liberty cannot exist till it is declared by authority.[2]

Second, organizations and institutions are vitally linked to mission. They do not exist by chance, but come into existence by deliberate, and usually thoughtful, actions. There is clearly a need for an organization whenever one person does not have the strength, talents, time, or resources to accomplish a desirable end result by himself or herself. Therefore, coming back to the source of the origins of an organization, we will always find its fundamental raison d'être to be a mission and an accompanying vision to carry out that mission.

A clear sense of mission is essential because institutional infant mortality is particularly high with new organizations. Religious organizations are highly fragile too, as is evident in the multitude of new denominations and parachurch ministries that spring up and wither away. One survey reported that more than three hundred new religious groups and denominations were formed during the last decade in the United States. Following a pattern similar to venture businesses, fewer than one in ten would survive the lifetime of its founder to become an institution of standing that could make a contribution spanning three generations or more.

MAINTAINING THE PRIORITIES

The tension between individualism and collectivism is found in all cultures, though organizations are obviously on the side of the collective rather than the individual. Organizations demand certain collaborative standards and disciplines of their individual members in order to fulfill their reasons for existence. If individuals could freely achieve the same results as organizations, organizations would disappear faster than a morning mist on a sunny day. Under the best of circumstances they are complex and difficult to manage.

Two requirements are essential for an institution to sustain both its freedom and its mission. The first is that leaders must maintain the organization's hierarchy of responsibilities. This natural list of priorities is part of the grand design of how individuals work together in a civilized society. Professional firms sometimes use this ranking to emphasize their own professionalism and distinguish themselves from other organizations. But the same sequence applies whatever the organization. It will come back to haunt those who ignore it or never discover it.

The natural sequence of priorities in an organization is this: first, the customer, client, or target beneficiaries of the organization; second, the organization itself, which provides the benefit; and third, the rights and privileges of the individual members of the organization. In more collectivist societies, such as Japan and parts of Europe, this hierarchy seems normal and reasonable. But in highly individualistic cultures such as the United States, it is often unknown or unacceptable. This helps create a series of dangerous fantasies and transient idols—for example, the belief that institutions are solely for the purpose of the individual, an illusion common to many in the current "me" generation and in parachurch ministries. Consider each priority and its consequences.

Beneficiaries first. As the laws and customs of any civilized society show, the resources needed to establish an institution are justified by the importance of its mission and by the benefits to its beneficiaries. Thus, the mission and its beneficiaries are the final justification for an organization's existence. Any fantasies or false illusions to the contrary only contribute to the fragility of the endeavor, to the detriment of all concerned.

Sample any group of organizations and this fundamental requirement will be evident. For example, nonprofit organizations have been deemed beneficial to society because they contribute to our general welfare. To encourage such benefits, monetary contributions to them have been made tax exempt. Religious organizations are included in this category, as are most educational, cultural, health, and other types of civic-minded organizations. But if these nonprofit organizations lose sight of their accepted missions to indulge in profit-making activities, such as manufacturing or trading, the value of their mission is reduced or lost, and their charters may be revoked. This also occurs if they become self-centered and consume too high a proportion of their revenues to sustain the organization and its employees.

In the United States, these considerations apply generously to religious organizations. They are considered both desirable and necessary to support both the earthly and the heavenly well-being of the people. With our historic commitment to religious liberty and our strong tradition of evaluating religion positively, we have given special privileges to denominations, local churches, spiritual organizations of all sorts, and possibly even cults. They are absolved of income taxes on their revenues and property taxes on their assets.

An organization's mission to its beneficiaries is therefore its first priority, the central focus of its loyalty and direction, and its only real reason for being. If this mission is carried out efficiently and effectively, the organization can prosper, expand, receive public acclaim, and generate an enviable stream of new benefits. But for those who lose sight of the original mission and follow such false gods as self-perpetuation, their decline and ultimate demise is foreordained.

The institution second. After the organization's mission and benefi-ciaries comes the organization itself—which means that the organization outranks those who work for it. The organization, after all, is what is con-sidered essential to provide the beneficiaries with the benefits envisioned. Therefore, its cohesive operation, including a sense of collective teamwork and a spirit of all-for-one, is vital to its success.

In today's world, this point is easily misunderstood. Institutions are believed to be solely for the purpose of the individual, and anything else is considered a "straitjacket" or "alienating." At best, we see declining loyalty between the organization and its people and vice versa. Yet, for those who take part in a successful institution, the rewards can be enormous, whether in terms of earnings, job satisfaction, personal development, or promotions into a variety of responsibilities and activities. Rarely can an in-dividual employee obtain these benefits all at once. Therefore, members of an organization, like the organization itself, must operate within a proper time perspective, and so must society when it judges the success of an organization.

The employees last. It is not popular today to remind individuals that they are subordinate first to the mission and second to their institution. But if an individual is unwilling to accept such a position of service, with reasonable personal constraints and duties, he or she would do well not to join an organization. Such an individual may remain self-employed, unem-ployed, or fend through life in whatever manner fits the individual prefer-ences—such is the gift of freedom of choice. For the opportunities and compensation offered by an organization, however, they come at a price—a price that individuals should recognize and accept upon joining.

Many followers of Christ need to ponder this lesson carefully. Their individualism, to which they are blind because of their spiritual idealism, makes them poor members of teams but wasted as lone-ranger operators.

The great disillusionment comes when the organization's mission is no longer foremost in view and the institution stoops to pursue the idol of immortality or some lesser false god. Employees are then properly frustrated because the mission, which justifies their service, is no longer foremost and evident. Subordination of the employee to the organization becomes highly questionable, which in turn leads to enormous tensions, conflicts, and high costs for all in both emotional and financial terms.

THE INSTITUTION'S IMAGE

Organizations that follow the lure of immortality become obsessed with their image, usually at the expense of contributions to their intended beneficiaries. Occasional polishing of image is appropriate and supports an organization's mission. But here again the idolizing dynamic of excess comes into play, leading to problems over the integrity of public statements, the character of leaders, the handling of finances, and the honesty of its external relationships, products, and services.

As the stakes continue to rise and the mission grows even more distant, the fight for image intensifies to sustain the fantasy of immortality. This often leads to desperate actions at all levels of authority within an institution. Because these efforts are usually not rational or balanced, inherent injustices develop—at first for third-party beneficiaries but later on for subordinate levels of management and finally down to the lowest levels of employees.

As the common idols of immortality and status quo fight side by side for power and position, they reduce the organization's ability to accomplish its basic mission.

At this stage, organizations begin to flounder, their people become dissatisfied and confused, and the decline accelerates. The situation can only be turned around if a revitalized leadership reconfirms a worthy vision and reorients the organization enthusiastically.

One way in which people within an institution speed the organization's decline is by translating the inherent desire for immortality into an advocacy of the status quo. To individuals, the "devil" one knows in the current situation usually seems more attractive than the uncertainty of change and the prospect of a new competitive interplay of talents. Yet this openness for upward movement is the essence of a meritocracy and the primary hope for those at the bottom of the socioeconomic scale who seek a better life. The organization's flexibility to change and adapt to new circumstances and external demands is its only prospect for sustaining itself over several generations. Thus, as the common idols of immortality and status quo fight side by side for power and position, they reduce the organization's ability to accomplish its basic mission. These sweetly singing sirens then entice the organization to its death.

142

Our Utmost for His Highest

The above hierarchy of responsibilities is the first major requirement for organizations to sustain their freedom and their mission. The second major requirement is equally little known to most evangelicals. It is the implicit hierarchy of expectations that the general public uses to judge performance and decide whether to continue supporting institutions and organizations. Because this evaluation system is rarely put into words or publicly acknowledged, it usually can only be discerned by observing the levels of public acceptance, support, and respect for various institutions. Unfortunately, this hierarchy of expectations is often violated. This leads to dissatisfaction in society, and often to litigation in the United States.

What follows is a suggested hierarchy of expectations, from the lower to the higher, that currently operates in the United States. It forms a series of society's quality standards, according to the kind—or mission—of organization. As you will note, Christ-centered organizations are inserted in what should be their proper place in the ranking. Notice, too, how the sequence of levels rises in direct proportion to the degree society expects the organization or individual to be committed to their mission, or—in the case of followers of Christ—to His service. Greater sacrifices or personal limitations naturally coincide with a rise in the fundamental importance to society of the mission in question.

Civic and voluntary organizations. Typically the lowest standards of quality and performance are expected from civic and voluntary organizations. After all, they are recognized to be goodwill activities that are undertaken part-time by nonprofessionals who are motivated largely by their personal interests. Because little or no financial reward is involved, any contribution of time or energy appears to be a plus in the public's mind.

As a result, the contributions of voluntary organizations range from the extremely positive to the somewhat negative. They always reflect far more of the motives and work habits of individuals than do more demanding organizations.

Educational institutions. Contrary to both opinion within the universities and such notions as "academic excellence," American education does not rank high in society's hierarchy of performance expectations. Among the number of academic and educational institutions, one can find exceptional people who have the highest standards. But this is typically not expected of the majority. Within higher education, the principal reason is that so many individual considerations outweigh institutional priorities, at least in potential. These include the principle of academic freedom and the preponderance of individual projects, such as independent research, sabbaticals, and private consulting.

Quality standards are therefore more individual than institutional. This becomes even more pronounced after faculty members receive tenure and feel almost invulnerable to direction, quality control, or even termination.

Government. Government departments, on either a state or a federal level, actually have higher performance standards than most educational institutions. But only marginally so—there is good reason for the Kafkaesque associations of the impenetrable, faceless bureaucracy. With the exception of a few individuals at the top, governments tend to move as bureaucratic snails, producing endless volumes of paper in their preoccupation with means and justifications rather than ends, with processes and procedures rather than services for the general public.

The choice of government as a career usually falls to those students in the middle and lower levels of most graduating classes in the United States. Only the top appointive and elective posts are pursued by the more diligent, resourceful, and ambitious, who may have achieved earlier successes in other fields. As a result, the public expects few constructive results from government and no demanding standards for high productivity, innovations, or personal risk from civil servants.

Public frustration with government is reflected in cynicism about taxes and the negative political campaigns that put people in office. Many of today's successful candidates therefore run "against government," even though they themselves are incumbents.

In contrast to many parts of the world, a striking exception to mediocre standards in government is honesty. For all our slipping standards, the American public still adheres to the Puritan tradition of becoming incensed when it discovers swindling, bribery, or corruption by officials. A person could remain in government at a relatively high position for years while doing little except shuffling correspondence and passing the time, but a hand in the till is still considered a terminal offense.

We might expect the public to be more demanding of local officials than those remote from them, but the reverse is usually true. As a result, there is an internal hierarchy of quality expectations with local government at the bottom, state government in the middle, and federal government at the top of a relatively low average scale.

Commercial operations. Higher than government, educational, or voluntary organizations are commercial operations, such as business corporations. One reason for the high expectations is that money talks loudly in a capitalistic society. It can easily be traded for recognition, upward mobility, and a myriad of material rewards and opportunities. Money opens up a vast array of idols to harden human hearts in a market economy such as ours, idols that are inaccessible to citizens in authoritarian and class-structured societies.

Another reason for the high expectations is that commercial results are readily measurable. The process of making, selling, and exchanging goods and services creates a bid-auction environment in which people can express their appreciation or displeasure toward an entity's commercial performance with their buying decisions. If a product or service is inferior, overpriced, or obsolete, the supplier must replace it promptly and efficiently or the whole organization will be in danger.

Professional practitioners. Higher still on society's ladder of expectations come professional practitioners, such as doctors and lawyers. In fact, this group normally represents the highest standards of performance in modern society—although I will argue that it should really rank second. Dedicated professionals readily understand and accept the three-level priorities outlined earlier—mission, institution, and individual interests. They bring to the job the most intensive training coupled with the clearest view of the human clients and beneficiaries. In addition, they enter a professional environment with a long tradition of high ethical standards and expectations of service. Even their training embraces long years of hard labor as interns and residents in hospitals with exhausting personal work schedules and negligible per-hour compensations.

The professional performs in ways that society recognizes and rewards abundantly. This is why the highest paid professional occupation in the United States is that of the medical doctor, with many individual lawyers and experts of various kinds attaining a similar pattern of material success and recognition—if they have invested the years in education and apprenticeship to excel.

It is easy to illustrate society's expectations in the case of the surgeon. A doctor may be troubled at home, overburdened at work, or personally depressed—or simply be suffering from aches and pains, or fatigue. But none of these things are considered acceptable excuses for botching even a minor surgical task, much less the repair of a vital human organ. Whenever people's high standards are not met, litigation follows. Unfortunately, malpractice suits are often unjustified in today's world, which is a reflection of selfish individuals who seek to extract exorbitant sums just because practitioners are wealthy and are backed by insurance companies. In the jargon and precedent of unjust civil juries, "deep pockets pay regardless of guilt." But even though many may be perverse, malpractice suits lend their own testimony to the standards expected of professionals.

Christ-centered activities. Activities done for Christ, and openly bearing His name, should be the most demanding assignments of all. Since our model is Jesus Christ—the example of human perfection—only the highest standard for use of our talents and capabilities, combined with total commitment to the activity, is acceptable. Those truly Christ-centered activities, whether led by lay people or clergy, require a deep sense of calling, or vocation, and a level of personal dedication beyond that of any professional position. For this reason, among others, too few churches pass the demanding test of being Christ-centered. Even with willing pastors and priests, many are subverted by their internal institutional processes and traditions as well as recalcitrant congregations who do not wish their comfortable church habits and ways of life directly challenged by Christ's example.

What the secular person knows as the pursuit of excellence, dedicated followers of Christ see—in Oswald Chambers's phrase—as "our utmost for His highest."

Christ-centered parachurch activities are frequently transient and rarely are converted into lasting institutions.

The customary life cycle of a Christ-centered parachurch ministry has been simply described in the following four phases: phase one concerns a man or woman who is a leader, and has a vision that is lacking in the wider church; phase two concerns men and women who gather in support of that vision; phase three concerns a movement, as the vision becomes structured and institutionalized; and phase four concerns a monument, as the process described by Max Weber as "routinization" leads to an institutional sclerosis that hastens the death of the original vision. The four phases are often summarized simply as "man, men, movement, monument."

Put differently, Christ-centered parachurch activities are frequently transient and rarely are converted into lasting institutions. The guidance of God and total submission to His will are so fundamental to launch such an effort that the leaders often feel that nothing else is required. The burst of energy from the core group continues to sustain the activity for some time, but other God-given talents of leadership, including basic management processes, are ignored.

146

Over time, as the membership grows and the scope of activities expands, the leaders may begin to devote more and more time and energy to maintaining harmony among their followers. They hereby drift toward another idol—elevating congenial relationships over mission—leading to laxity in organization, planning, execution, and the normal human actions that are essential to sustain a constructive institution.

Followers of Christ often rationalize this lack of discipline, declaring that they are "waiting on God's guidance" for every single decision and action, even those the least gifted among us have been given wisdom enough to perform. In effect, they are too heavenly minded for their own earthly good, and soon they begin to undermine the mission. This in turn sows disillusionment among those who would most enthusiastically support such Christ-centered activities. As a result, a gradual decline sets in that parallels the aging of the leadership and its inability or unwillingness to use God's talents fully in His service.

Instead of adapting in order to capitalize on its initial vision and the God-given impact of its early activities and enthusiasm, the ministry begins to drift. It spends more time in self-deception and rationalization, trusting solely in God for automatic renewal when He has already granted them the ability to initiate the needed changes. Younger people, who were initially attracted to the movement and had dedicated their lives to its vision, become disenchanted with the institutional frailty that distracts from the mission. If they are sufficiently dedicated, they pray for a new vision and eventually adopt an alternate mission that represents a new cause. This leaves the former group to wither away.

People today think of management generically as a purely commercial activity, and one that is therefore secular. But sound management is thoroughly biblical.

This transitory pattern has enormously high human and strategic costs. Yet this is often the frustrating pattern followed by evangelical groups. As the decline sets in, the public's view of the group and its performance also begins to ebb, and fewer new hearts are touched. In the final stages the leadership becomes heavily concerned with fund-raising activities to sustain its membership and their programs, rather than maintaining superb performance of the mission to draw continuing support and new adherents.

In an ideal world, Christ-centered activities would stand head and shoulders above the rest in the realm of performance. They would be followed closely by professional, commercial, governmental, and educational organizations, leaving voluntary organizations a distant but acceptable last.

Yet the saddest assessment for us as followers of Christ is that too many churches and parachurch organizations perform much like voluntary organizations. They reflect a general laxity of performance expectations and an absence of management competence and discipline. This is one reason why our religious institutions are increasingly ignored in a sophisticated, modern society, in which higher and higher standards are demanded for organizations to be considered relevant and productive.

If evangelicals' first major mistake is to be unrealistic about the proper benefits of institutions and management, the second is the reverse: to be equally unrealistic about their dangers. The process of management represents for the institution what the motor and rudder are to a ship—skilled handling. People today think of management generically as a purely commercial activity, and one that is therefore secular. But sound management is thoroughly biblical. Essentially, it is another word for stewardship. Many of the most tried and true management principles are taught or practiced in the Old Testament books of Proverbs and Ecclesiastes and embodied in the example of Jesus Christ Himself.

Precisely because sound and positive management is essential for the success of any organization, it is subject to a great array of the idols of excess. Conscientious but unthinking managers often follow these false gods onto devious side roads, when managers focus more on technique than accomplishment. Managers can easily become immersed in piles of forms and planning data that may be only marginally relevant for orchestrating the talents of human beings and a variety of material resources.

In all kinds of organizations the best management leaders—whether through training or by observation and experience—evolve into a pattern of servant leadership. Although from the viewpoint of others they are perched at the pinnacle of power, these high-performing managers submerge their personal interests into those of the organization and its people. They also require the organization do the same in relation to its clients and customers.

The foremost task for management is to rekindle its vision periodically. This is also its greatest achievement. It encourages greater focus for the organization and more dedication by its people, and thus a greater chance to produce the results demanded by its overriding mission. As such, good management is more of an attitude and an experienced art than a science based on technical know-how. Thus it demands of managers a personal standard of performance appreciably higher than any expected from subordinates.

CHRIST'S WAY OR THE INQUISITOR'S WAY?

The weaknesses, vices, and idolatries of management are no surprise to Christ. He knew all the world's shortcomings or He would not have come. But instead of becoming a king and commanding our rescue, He chose a different course. He beckoned those who would follow Him to come by their own free will—a debatable proposition at best for many leaders of churches and Christ-centered institutions who would truthfully prefer equality for all rather than the inequalities resulting from choice.

In response, Dostoyevsky's Grand Inquisitor underscores the glorious challenge—in his view and that of many, the absurdity—of Christ's commitment to freedom. He argued his own better way that corrects Christ's work through the management of sin. "Oh, we shall allow them even sin— they are weak and helpless—and they will love us like children because we allow them to sin," he declares. "We shall tell them that every sin shall be expiated if it is done with our permission." The Grand Inquisitor foretold the future when he asked Christ a rhetorical question, "Do you know that the ages will pass, and humanity will proclaim by the lips of their sages that there is no crime, and therefore no sin; there is only hunger? 'Feed men, and then ask of them virtue!' That's what they will write on the banner they will raise against You, with which they will destroy Your temple."

A century has passed since Dostoyevsky cried out these words, but they are just as pertinent today. His prediction of religious organizations being seduced by the lure of false gods as they seek to correct Christ's work and manage primarily the worldly needs of human beings is all too common. Many religious leaders today show a greater desire to gain power by organizing the distribution of earthly bread, whether political or psychological, than to open their hearers' hearts to the terrible, individually demanding freedom granted by Jesus Christ.

All too frequently the loyalty this earthly bread buys is just as fleeting as the momentary satisfaction of the food itself. Therefore, instead of acts of charity, these spurious contributions of bread become meaningless exercises because the motivation is not genuine love for fellow human beings or for Christ. Rather they are attempts to expand control and manipulate human need to enhance the appeal of their institutions and justify their continued growth.

Just as with individuals, Christ-centered institutions and their leaders have been endowed with that precious but frightening gift—freedom. They are free to choose between good and evil, giving or receiving, loving or hating, believing or denying. Only the moment by moment choice of faith through continued prayer and personal intimacy with our Creator can overcome our weaknesses, especially our proneness to idolatry. The still quiet voice of God is all about us, but we must remain vigilant if we are to escape the seductive, high-decibel lyres of a chorus of gods and goddesses, who play and dance frantically but appealingly to lure the ship of our lives onto the deadly rocks of idolatry.

After a long period of reflection while lying down in the back seat of the car, I climbed out and took one last walk down the long sidewalk beside the old mill onto Main Street. At the corner stood an enormous brass plaque, embedded in a massive block of concrete, spelling out the name of the now defunct company. Doubtless, years earlier, the placing of that cornerstone had been an occasion of great celebration in the center of this little community. But the organization over time had forgotten its vision, abandoned its mission, and chased futilely after the idols of immortality and status quo. The reward of these false gods was that those who revered them came to resemble them. The old cornerstone with its emblazoned nameplate would serve not as a symbol of life but as a monument to a dead enterprise. Over all that is not born and does not live by faith it can be written, "This too shall pass away."

8
SOUNDING OUT THE
IDOLS OF CHURCH GROWTH

by Os Guinness

The King is dead! Long live the King!" As with royalty earlier, so with popular movements and trends today—the passing of one signals the prevailing of another. Thus in the United States in the 1990s, influence of the Christian Right is clearly on the wane, as noted in chapter 3. Meanwhile the church-growth movement is succeeding it as one of the nationally prominent religious movements.

The church-growth movement is committed to "effective evangelism" through such modern means of "growing churches" as management, marketing, and megachurches. Its goals are laudable and ambitious; as C. Peter Wagner, a leading proponent, states them: "to make more effective the propagation of the gospel and the multiplication of churches *on new ground*" (original emphasis) and thus to "seeing America evangelized in our generation."[1] Can the movement attain these goals? Its proponents argue that its passion for mission and effective evangelism can lead to a harvest of new Christians and reverse the secularization of the West. Some believe such innovations will bring about a reformation in the worldwide church. Others wonder whether the secrets of successful megachurches can be carried over to small local churches. But the greater question is: Will the church-growth movement remain self-critical, or has the reliance on the so-called "new ground" become an insidious new idolatry?

This chapter is an adapted version of *Sounding Out the Idols of Church Growth* (Fairfax, Va.: Hourglass Publishers, 1992). Used by permission.

Any movement that not only hits *Time* and *Christianity Today* simultaneously but is viewed by so many Christian leaders as a remedy for Christian ineffectiveness deserves to be noticed, understood, and assessed. This chapter is such an assessment—a constructive critique of the church-growth movement. My purpose is to raise questions so that we may engage this vital movement with our eyes open and our ears alert to be as self-critical and truly discerning as the gospel requires.

THE MOVEMENT OF THE 1990s

Needless to say, the roots of the church-growth movement are far from the late twentieth-century world of the West—Donald MacGavran's missionary work in India gave rise to the movement in the thirties. But it is no accident that the movement has now passed beyond its missionary phase and its early American phase. In the form of the megachurches, it is coming into its own in a third phase, in a highly popularized form.

Many people identify the church-growth movement narrowly with its specific architects and advocates—most famously, MacGavran, Wagner, and the Charles E. Fuller Institute of Evangelism and Church Growth School—or the most visible examples of its current success—most recently, such best-sellers as George Barna's *The Frog in the Kettle, Marketing the Church,* and *User-Friendly Churches.* Some immediately think of the burgeoning "mega-" or "superchurches" on the "top, ten" list, each with a weekly attendance far above five thousand people.

But as I use the term *church growth*, these individuals and churches are part of a much wider and more important movement that is linked by a series of underlying commitments: to Christian renewal through renewal of the church, as opposed to politics or the culture; to renewal of the church through renewal of the local church, as opposed to the denomination or parachurch ministry; to the renewal of the local church through the renewal of mission, as opposed to other priorities; and, most important, to the renewal of mission along one of two avenues—charismatic renewal or using the behavioral sciences' insights and tools to aid effective evangelism. In this final area, proponents use tools from the fields of management, marketing, psychology, and communications (the "new ground" mentioned earlier). Viewed in this broader way, the church-growth movement is a "back to basics" movement with a special modern twist.

The movement has spiritual, cultural, and historical significance for evangelical churches. First, spiritually the church-growth movement represents a concern for many of the most-needed components of Christian mission, renewal, and reformation. This can be seen by stressing the movement's most obvious emphases—the centrality of the church, the priority of mission, the possibility of growth, the necessity of speaking to outsiders, the acknowledgment of culture and of cultures, the insistence on real results, and the wisdom of using the best insights and technologies proffered by the key disciplines of the human sciences.

Ten years ago the attention was on the Christian Right; today it is on church growth. Then the cry was "Mobilize!"; now it's "Modernize!"

Second, culturally the church-growth movement represents the most influential movement in the American churches in the 1990s, and a significant expression of the search for the lost authority of faith. The church-growth movement and the Christian Right are only two of many movements within the wider Christian community. But the contrast between their respective standings in the early 1980s and the early 1990s tells the story of the cultural shifts that have occurred from one decade to the next. For all the sustained activism of Operation Rescue and the talk of a new conservative political party, the Christian Right is largely a spent force; the shift to the centrality of local churches is both vital and illuminating.

Ten years ago the attention was on the Christian Right; today it is on church growth. Then the cry was "Mobilize!"; now it's "Modernize!" Then the focus was politics and public life; now it is church and mission. Then the reliance was on populism and political strength; now it is on entrepreneurialism and managerial strength. Then the orientation was the past and the restoration of the nineteenth-century consensus; now it is the future and renewal. Then the attention was on special-interest groups, epitomized by the Moral Majority; now it is on the megachurches, epitomized by the recent explosion of churches that have more than three thousand members.

Third, historically the church-growth movement is a significant new initiative in the long story of Christian innovation and adaptation. In essence, it is the most significant attempt by the conservative churches in North America to grope toward a new stance in a society that sidelines faith —because it is increasingly secular in its public life and pluralistic in its private life. This fact is easily overlooked because of the movement's own rhetoric. Church-growth leaders speak and write about Christians and churches who are "hidebound," "stuck-in-the-mud," or "dying for change." "Frankly," one author writes without a sense of historical perspective, "evangelical Christianity has done well on revelation (the Bible) but poorly on relevance (the culture)."[2] This gives the impression of a Neanderthal church incapable of change.

Certainly, stories of diehard resistance to change are easy to find. But the Christian faith is unrivaled among the world religions for its genius in innovation and adaptation. And no branch of the Christian faith has demonstrated this genius more often and more successfully than the evangelical movement.

All innovation is open to question and different assessments. And the darker side of this innovative genius is the church's proneness to compromise with the spirit of its age. But from the adaptations of the early church—for example, Augustine's translations of the language and ideas of Platonism down to the innovations of eighteenth-century Methodism and nineteenth-century revivalism, Christians have been tirelessly determined to innovate and adapt for the sake of the gospel.

Using modernity's insights and technologies could therefore lead to one of the most fruitful periods of innovations in the church's two-thousand-year history. The managerial revolution, for example, could provide the church with a large, varied, and powerful toolbox. To some people, the term "manage" has a sinister ring of manipulation—not least because of the "scientific paternalism" of early management studies. But that is unfair. After all, the core theme of management is essentially that of stewardship, whether of people, resources, or time. John Wesley's nickname in the Holy Club in Oxford was "the manager," and the same brilliance in organization and personal discipline is what gave the Methodists their name.

In sum, innovation is not a problem. If Christians would use the best fruits of the managerial revolution constructively and critically, accompanied by a parallel reformation of truth and theology, the potential for the gospel would be incalculable.

Whatever criticisms need to be raised, this point is beyond dispute: the church-growth movement is extraordinarily influential and significant within American churches today. At its best, it should be applauded. Where it is not at its best, it requires criticism so that it might be. The church of Christ concerned for the glory of Christ needs more—not less—of the best of true church growth.

WEAKNESSES TO WATCH

Like many movements, the church-growth movement is a grand mixture of things good, bad, and in-between. The good is worthy of praise, and we have cited some of the movement's strong contributions. Our present concern, however, is not the good but rather the bad and the in-between, and in particular the range of problems that grow from the movement's uncritical use of such insights and tools of modernity as management and marketing. For if the movement has a threefold positive significance, it also has a fourfold weakness.

First, the very name, "church-growth movement," is confusing because both words are capable of a double meaning. On the one hand, does the term *church* refer to "the people of God," including all the people of God in a local area, or to a particular local church and its facility and programs? The two are not necessarily the same. If the distinction is not kept clear, the admirable growth in the first sense can be used to cover a less admirable growth in the second, which actually hurts the first. One example is when it leads to an essentially consumerist competition between particular local churches that simultaneously thrusts up superchurches and impoverishes other churches and the overall work of God in a local area.

On the other hand, is the term *growth* to be understood quantitatively, in terms of size and numbers, or qualitatively, in terms of depth, character, and spirit? Both sorts of growth are essential to the church, and qualitative growth does not exclude quantifiable growth. Nor does the quantitative growth exhaust qualitative growth. To pretend otherwise through careless use of the terms is a cardinal error of modern times and a fallacy in much church-growth rhetoric. Sometimes the difference is difficult to see. All too often it is easy. As one megachurch pastor boasted about his church to the *Wall Street Journal*, "It is the fastest growing church" in the nation. "I want the biggest church I can think of."

Second, the church-growth movement has two common deficiencies. On the one hand, its theological understanding is often superficial, with almost no element of biblical criticism. As a well-known proponent states, "I don't deal with theology. I'm simply a methodologist"—as if his theology were thereby guaranteed to remain critical and his methodology neutral. But in fact, theology is rarely more than marginal in the church-growth movement and discussion of the traditional marks of the church is virtually nonexistent. Instead, methodology, or technique, is at the center and in control. The result is a methodology only occasionally in search of a theology.

On the other hand, the movement relies on a minimal sense of historical awareness. It is particularly unaware of comparisons with earlier periods that could throw light on the possibilities and pitfalls we face today.

Two periods give fruitful parallels: the late eighteenth century and the story of European liberalism's engagement with the "cultured despisers," and the early nineteenth century and the story of American evangelicalism's fateful sea-change during the era of Jacksonian populism. This earlier nineteenth-century change was not so much from Calvinism to Arminianism as from theology to experience, from truth to technique, from elites to populism, and from an emphasis on "serving God" to an emphasis on "servicing the self" in serving God.

The principle of identification is covered well in such church-growth principles as "niche marketing," "audience-driven," and the "homogeneous unit principle." But without employing critical tension, the principle of identification is a recipe for compromise and capitulation.

Third, the church-growth movement has two common flaws through which the confusions and deficiencies mentioned above become more serious. On the one hand, it employs an unbalanced application of a biblical principle. Known technically as "contextualization," or more simply as "relevance," this principle is indispensable to communication and obviously rooted in Scripture. The supreme pattern of the contextualization and relevance is the incarnation of God in Jesus Christ, and such passages as 1 Corinthians 9:19-22 capture its full dynamic perfectly (climaxing in Paul's summary: "I have become all things to all men so that by all possible means I might save some").

Thus the record of Scripture and Christian history is equally clear: the principle of identification is basic to communication and is covered well today in such notions as contextualization and relevance, as well as in such church-growth principles as "niche marketing," "audience-driven," "seeker-friendly," "full-service churches," and the "homogeneous unit principle."

But Scripture and history are also clear: Without employing critical tension, the principle of identification is a recipe for compromise and capitulation. It is no accident that the charge of being "all things to all people" has become a popular synonym for compromise. If the process of becoming "all things to all people" is to remain faithful to Christ, it has to climax in clear persuasion and genuine conversion. Joining people where they are is only the first step in the process, not the last. Unless it resists this danger, the church-growth movement will prove to be a gigantic exercise in cultural adjustment and surrender.

On the other hand—and here is the main doorway to idolatry—many in the movement employ an uncritical understanding of modernity and its insights and tools. "Truth is truth," as George Macdonald put it, "whether on the lips of Jesus or Balaam."[3] It would therefore be odd for any Christian to deny the illuminating helpfulness of the social sciences. At the same time, however, it is amazing to witness the lemming-like rush of church leaders who forget theology in the charge after the latest insights of sociology—regardless of where the ideas come from or where they lead to. Carelessly handled, innovation and adaptation become a form of corruption, capitulation, and idolatry.

Fourth, the church-growth movement carries two potential dangers. They can be summed up simply in the words "no God" and "no grandchildren." In the first case, the problem results because the insights and tools of modernity can be so brilliant and effective that there no longer appears to be any need for God. In the second case, the problem arises because the tools of modernity are successful in one generation but cannot be sustained to the third generation. The success undermines the succession. Many superchurches are simply artificially inflated local churches that will not be able to survive their supergrowth.

In short, through these weaknesses and above all through its uncritical use of the "new ground" of modernity, the church-growth movement has the potential to unleash a deadly form of idolatry and practical atheism in the churches. The result would be one more contemporary testament to the extraordinary power of religion that has no need for God.

Critical discernment is essential. Two useful pictures of what it means to develop critical discernment should challenge Christians. One comes from the eminent Christian social scientist Peter Berger, who is a renowned analyst of modernity. He warns that whoever sups with the devil of modernity had better have a long spoon. "The devilry of modernity has its own magic." The believer "who sups with it will found his spoon getting shorter and shorter—until the last supper in which he is left alone at the table, with no spoon at all and an empty plate."⁴ Our challenge, then, is to dine at the banquet of modernity—but with long spoons.

The other picture comes from Friederich Nietzsche's *The Twilight of the Idols*. In words that are more biblical than he intended, Nietzsche wrote, "There are more idols in the world than there are realities."⁵ Our task, then, is to "sound out idols," to "pose questions with a hammer," to be iconoclasts, and see whether many of the things taken for granted in our time are in fact hollow, not real—mere "idols of the age."

We now turn to six reminders that will help cultivate critical discernment and help avoid idolatry in the church-growth movement's engagement with modernity. The best of the movement will doubtless pass through unscathed. Much of the rest requires tougher scrutiny.

ONE MAIN QUESTION

When all is said and done, the church-growth movement will stand or fall by one question. In implementing its vision of church growth, is the church of Christ primarily guided and shaped by its own character and calling—or by considerations and circumstances alien to itself? Or, to put the question differently, is the church of Christ a social reality truly shaped by a theological cause, namely the Word and Spirit of God?

> *If the church makes anything other than God's truth and resources the principle of its existence, Christians risk living unauthorized lives of faith, exercising unauthorized ministries, and proclaiming an unauthorized gospel.*

Behind this question lies the fact that the church of God "lets God be God" and is the church only when it lives and thrives finally by God's truths and God's resources. If the church makes anything else the principle of its existence, Christians risk living unauthorized lives of faith, exercising unauthorized ministries, and proclaiming an unauthorized gospel.

Yet, that is precisely the temptation modernity gives to us. The very brilliance and power of its tools and insights mean that eventually there is no need to let God be God. In fact, there is no need for God at all in order to achieve measurable success. Modernity creates the illusion that, when God commanded us not to live by bread alone but by every word that comes from His mouth, He was not aware of the twentieth century. The very success of modernity may undercut the authority and driving power of faith until religion becomes merely religious rhetoric or organizational growth without spiritual reality.

In light of this, it is curious that the church-growth movement's "new ground," its use of modernity, is one of its most prominent but least examined features. This first reminder therefore deals with the first and greatest problem modernity poses for the church-growth movement—because it appears to be no problem at all. It is most dangerous at its best—not its worst—when its benefits and blessings are unarguable. No civilization in history has amplified the temptation of living "by bread alone" with such power and variety and to such effect. In today's convenient, climate-controlled spiritual world created by the managerial and therapeutic revolutions, nothing is easier than living apart from God. Idols are simply the ultimate techniques of human causation and control—without God.

One Florida pastor with a seven-thousand-member megachurch expressed the fallacy well: "I must be doing right or things wouldn't be going so well."[6] One Christian advertising agent, who both represented the Coca-Cola Corporation and engineered the "I Found It" evangelistic campaign, stated the point brazenly: "Back in Jerusalem where the church started, God performed a miracle there on the day of Pentecost. They didn't have the benefits of buttons and media, so God had to do a little supernatural work there. But today, with our technology, we have available to us the opportunity to create the same kind of interest in a secular society." Put simply, another church-growth consultant claims "five to ten million baby boomers would be back in the fold within a month" if churches adopted three simple changes: (1) "advertise"; (2) let people know about "product benefits"; and (3) be "nice to new people."[7]

If Jesus Christ is true, the church is more than just another human institution. He alone is its head. He is its sole source and single goal. His grace uniquely is its effective principle. What moves the church is not finally interchangeable with the dynamics of even the closest of sister institutions. When the best of modern insights and tools are in full swing, there should always be a remainder, an irreducible character that is more than the sum of all the human, the natural, and the organizational.

The church of Christ is more than spiritual and theological, but never less. Only when first things are truly first, over even the best and most attractive of second things, will the church be free of idols, free to let God be God, free to be itself, and free to experience the growth that matters.

Two Main Roots of the Challenge

The second reminder deals with a further problem modernity poses for the church-growth movement—modernity's influence is far deeper and more double-edged than many church-growth proponents realize, because of the nature of modernity's two main roots.

Modernization and modernity remain widely misunderstood today. Some people, for example, turn them into a kind of "rich man's Marxism," a deterministic movement that will inevitably sweep the world with prosperity, progress, and democratic revolutions. Christians, however, tend to fall foul of a simpler misunderstanding. Many use the word *modernity* as if it were a fancy word for "change" or simply a matter of being "up to date." They therefore treat it as something simple and straightforward—as if one can understand it through monitoring the latest trends and statistics—and put it to use simply like a new fax machine or laser printer.

> *Modernity centers above all on the premise that the "top down" causation of God and the supernatural has been decisively replaced by the "bottom up" causation of human designs and products.*

Modernity is much more than that. It refers to the character and system of the world produced by the forces of modernization and development—centered above all on the premise that the "top down" causation of God and the supernatural has been decisively replaced by the "bottom up" causation of human designs and products. Modernity is therefore not a fancy word for "change," and little of it can be understood merely by watching trends and keeping up with the latest technologies. To grasp modernity is a challenge—it requires an understanding of the whole, not merely the parts. Ironically, when we wrestle with a tough-minded overview of modernity, it turns out to be far from modern.

Modernity's replacement of "top down" God-centered living with "bottom up" human-centered living represents a titanic revolution in human history and experience. We can trace its origins in two main ways. One way is to focus on human beings and the impact of their ideas. Thus, the road to modernity proceeds from the revolutionary changes in ideas to the way changes have affected society throughout the centuries. This mode of analysis goes back at least to the seventeenth-century scientific revolution and follows the story through the eighteenth-century Enlightenment and the nineteenth-century romantic movement to the modernist and postmodernist movements in the twentieth century.

The rarer but equally important way to analyze modernity and face the challenge is to focus on society and social change. The path is traced in reverse as we follow the revolutionary changes in society to the way they have affected ideas. This mode of analysis traces back to major structural and institutional developments—supremely those that resulted from the capitalist revolution in the fifteenth century, the technological and industrial revolution in the eighteenth century, and the communications revolution in the twentieth century.

This is not the place for a comprehensive analysis of the twin roots of modernity. What matters for our inquiry is this: The world of modernity that has been produced by such a combination of revolutionary forces must be taken with the utmost seriousness because its impact now pervades religion. Thus when the church-growth movement relies on the insights and tools of modernity for its "new ground," it does not rely on something that is neutral or entirely benevolent. At the very least, there is a gigantic paradox in the relationship between modernity and the Christian faith that church-growth proponents should be aware of.

One way to express the paradox is to say that modernity provides both the single greatest *opportunity* the church has ever faced and its single greatest *challenge*. The opportunity exists because more people in more societies are more open to the gospel in the modern world than in any previous era in history. So modernity is to us what the Greek language and Roman roads were to the first-century disciples, and the printing press and sailing ships were to believers at the time of the Reformation.

And yet, after examining the impact of modernity on a sense of truth, transcendence, and tradition—and on a sense of the totality and integration of faith in every part of life—we can appreciate why modernity is also the single greatest challenge the church has ever faced. Such is the nature and extent of its damage to faith in many parts of the modernized world that it combines the subtlety of the challenge of gnosticism with the open

161

menace of persecutions like those of Nero, Diocletian, and Mao Tse-tung. Some have labeled the lethal impact of modernity on religion as "iron cage," "gigantic steel hammer," "runaway juggernaut," and "acid rain of the spirit." Such descriptions are well merited.

Under the influence of modernity, we modern Christians are literally capable of winning the world while losing our own souls.

Another way to express the paradox is that modernity simultaneously makes evangelism infinitely easier, and discipleship infinitely harder. Ponder the fact that the twentieth century was heralded as "the Christian Century," summed up aptly at the beginning of the century in John R. Mott's slogan—"the evangelization of the world in this generation." Yet the century is ending, as Jacques Ellul says, in a situation closer to the saying of Jesus "When the Son of Man comes, will he find faith on the earth?" The problem is not that Christians have disappeared, but that Christian faith has become so deformed. Under the influence of modernity, we modern Christians are literally capable of winning the world while losing our own souls.

Despite this challenge, evangelicals display a fateful shortsightedness in two directions: toward modernity and toward those parts of Scripture that, by application, are either critical of the premises of modernity or a needed antidote to its seductions. Consider, for example, God's anger at King David for succumbing to the devil's temptation to rely on numbers (1 Chronicles 21, 27). Meanwhile, Asa was condemned because he "resorted to physicians" rather than seeking guidance of the Lord (2 Chronicles 16:12, NEB). Similarly, God judged Israel during the reign of Hezekiah for fortifying their walls, stockpiling their weapons, and harnessing the water resources, "but you did not look to the Maker of it all" (Isaiah 22:11, NEB).

Anyone who ponders such passages can only wonder at the contrast between the enduring realism of Scripture and our dismaying gullibility in the face of modernity.

THREE MAIN DANGERS OF MODERNITY

The third reminder deals with yet another way modernity poses problems for the church-growth movement: through its direct damage to faith. Here at last, one might expect a realistic understanding of modernity. But in fact most Christian believers have not faced up to modernity's fundamental damage to faith, for several reasons. One reason it is easy to overlook modernity's damage to religion is that the overall consequences of modernization are so positive. Which of us, for example, would choose to go back to previous generations if we considered the blessings of health alone, not to speak of the advantages of travel and communication?

Modernity's real damage, however, must be faced. For certain lethal trends are at work in the principles and processes of modernity. Once again, a comprehensive account would take us a long way from our task. But there is broad agreement on the three main trends reckoned to be the culprits.

More and more of what was formerly left to God, or human initiative is now classified, calculated, and controlled by the systematic application of reason and technique. What counts in the rationalized world is efficiency, the substitution of technology for the human, and—from first to last —control over uncertainty.

Stated briefly, the damaging trends are secularization, privatization, and pluralization. Through secularization, modernity removes successive sectors of society from the decisive influence of religious ideas and institutions. Through privatization, modernity produces a cleavage between the private and public sectors of life—the private sector commonly being the only place where religion is free to flourish. Through pluralization, modernity multiplies the number of options people have in the private sphere at all levels—including that of faiths, worldviews, and ideologies. The result of this pluralization is a greater sense of relativism, subjectivism, uncertainty, and anxiety surrounding religion in the modern world.

Unquestionably the component that bears directly on the church-growth movement is what Max Weber called "rationalization." This is the first of the two underlying dynamics of secularization. (The other is differentiation.) Rationalization has meant that religious ideas are less meaningful and religious institutions are more marginal because of modernity's advance. More and more of what was formerly left to God, or human initiative, or the processes of nature, is now classified, calculated, and controlled by the systematic application of reason and technique. What counts in the rationalized world is efficiency, predictability, quantifiability, productivity, the substitution of technology for the human, and—from first to last—control over uncertainty.

For religion, the result of rationalization is what Weber also called "disenchantment" (and C.S. Lewis called "a new enchantment"). All the "magic and mystery" of life is reduced and removed—not so much unwanted as unnecessary. No one in the process is necessarily hostile to religion. Rather, as technique and the "figure it out" rationality spread further and further, the decisiveness of faith is rendered more and more irrelevant. As social scientist Philip Rieff sums it up, "What characterizes modernity, I think, is just this idea that men need not submit to any power—higher or lower—other than their own."[8] Whether said with defiance by the few or left unsaid but practiced by the many, religion that is irrelevant in practice becomes practically irrelevant. There is no need for God, even in His church.

The two most easily recognizable hallmarks of secularization in America are the exaltation of numbers and of technique. Both are prominent in the church-growth movement. In its fascination with statistics and data at the expense of truth, this movement is characteristically modern. Some people argue that the emphasis on quantifiable measures—on counting—is the central characteristic of a rationalized society. Thus the United States has government by polling, television programming by ratings, sports commentary by statistics, education by grade-point averages, and academic tenure by the number of publications. In such a world of number crunchers, bean counters, and computer analysts, the growth of churches as a measurable, "fact-based" business enterprise is utterly natural.

The problem with this mentality is that quantity does not measure quality. Numbers have little to do with truth, excellence, or character. As one sociologist says, "Big Mac," even with billions and billions of hamburgers served, need not mean "Good Mac." But what is misleading at the trivial level of fast food becomes dangerous as one moves through sports prowess, educational attainment, and presidential character to spiritual depth. For church growth viewed in measurable terms, such as numbers, is trivial compared with growth in less measurable but more important terms, such as faith, character, and godliness. Having growth in terms of numbers, of course, does not rule out the more important spiritual growth. But it does not necessarily include this type of growth either.

A telltale preoccupation with technique is also prominent in the church-growth movement and is linked to secularization. Life is viewed as a set of problems, each set having a rational solution, an identifiable expert, and therefore a practical mechanism to effect it. Take the example of the changing profiles of the pastor. Needless to say, distortions of the ministry are not new. In 1886, *Nation* magazine reported: "Indeed, so far has the church caught the spirit of the age, so far has it become a business enterprise, that the chief test of ministerial success is now the ability to 'build up' a church. Executive, managerial abilities are now more in demand than those which used to be considered the highest in a clergyman."[9]

Anyone who doubts this shift has only to look at church-growth literature and check for such chapters as "Portrait of the Effective Pastor." The bulk of such chapters keeps theology and theological references to a minimum—little more than a cursory reference to the pastor's "personal calling" and to "God's vision for the church." In their place are discussions of such themes as delegating, confidence, interaction, decision making, visibility, practicality, accountability, and discernment—the profile of the pastor as CEO.

Unquestionably the discussion is admirable. But unquestionably, too, the discussion is only of "the interchangeable." There is nothing there about the "irreducible," the "remainder," and the otherwise inexplicable. Thus the leadership qualities could apply in a hundred other organizations—after all, they once did, and were simply borrowed. Worse still, the disadvantage of the CEO-Pastor, as increasing numbers of them are discovering, is that those who live like CEOs are fired like CEOs—and spiritual considerations have as little to do with the ending as with the beginning and the middle. Small wonder that one eminent Christian leader returned home from a church-growth conference puzzled. There had been "literally no theology," he said. "In fact, there had been no serious reference to God at all."

FOUR MAIN STEPS IN COMPROMISE

The fourth reminder deals with the dynamics of compromise with the world. Christian history is a two-thousand-year conversation between the church and the world. As Christians we are called to be in the world, but not of it. Throughout the centuries Christians have lived out this tension in many ways. Some, at the one extreme, are neither of the world nor in it, and therefore are isolated. Others, at the other extreme, are both in the world and of it, and therefore are compromised.

NO GOD BUT GOD

Doubtless, few on either side would disagree with the ideals of the other, though cultural conservatives would stress the ideal of resistance to the world and cultural liberals would stress relevance in it. At the same time, almost no one would dispute that the biblical challenge is to be balanced. Everyone, however extreme in reality, would consider his or her own position the perfect model of balance. Beyond question, too, evangelicals have traditionally been toward the conservative pole, stressing cognitive defiance; whereas liberals have been on the progressive side, emphasizing cognitive bargaining with the cultured despisers of the gospel.

But today we are confronted with a staggering change in the dynamism of this age-old dialogue. At the high noon of modernity, the influence of the world has become so powerful, pervasive, and appealing that the traditional stance of cognitive defiance has become rare and almost unthinkable.

Compromise is compromise regardless of when, how, or why it happens—though certainly, there are qualifications to it. Thus Christian compromise with the world is usually unconscious, and not deliberate. It can be a matter of lifestyle as easily as belief. And, mercifully, few people go the whole way. Nonetheless, the Christian must recognize and counter the four distinct steps involved in compromise with the thinking or behavior of the world.

The first and crucial step toward compromise is that of *assumption*. Nothing may be further from a believer's mind than compromise, but like the Chinese journey of a thousand miles, the road to compromise begins in a small way. Some aspect of modern life or thought is entertained not only as significant, and therefore worth acknowledging, but as superior to what Christians now know or do, and therefore worth assuming as true.

Something modern is assumed. As a consequence, something traditional is abandoned, and everything else is adapted. The fourth step toward compromise is assimilation.

The second step toward compromise is that of *abandonment*. Everything that does not fit in with the new assumption (made in step one) is either discounted or cut out. What is involved in this step is not just a matter of altering tactics but of altering truth itself. Something modern is assumed to be true and proper. Therefore everything that is no longer assertable in the face of it must go.

The third step toward compromise is *adaptation*. Something new is assumed, something old is abandoned, and everything else is adapted. In other words, what remains of traditional beliefs and practices is altered to fit in with the new assumption. It is translated into the language and expectations of the new assumption, which becomes the controlling assumption.

The fourth step toward compromise is *assimilation*. This is the logical culmination of the first three. Something modern is assumed (step one). As a consequence, something traditional is abandoned (step two), and everything else is adapted (step three). At the end of the line, Christian assumptions are absorbed by the modern ones. The gospel has been assimilated to the shape of culture, often without a remainder.

Perhaps the most blatant example of this perverse bias toward compromise was the World Council of Churches' dictum in 1966, "The world must set the agenda for the Church." Three decades later, it is hard to believe that such an advance warning of preemptive capitulation could have been trumpeted as a lofty and self-evident principle. But it is also worth checking to see whether there are similar inanities in the church-growth movement today.

Take, for example, the current church-growth infatuation with marketing the church. It echoes Bruce Barton's 1920s' best-seller, *The Man Nobody Knows,* which portrayed Jesus as "the founder of modern business" and His parables as "the most powerful advertisements of all time." Apparently, Jesus' saying "I must be about my Father's business" was taken with a literalistic seriousness worthy of a Muslim fundamentalist.

It still is. Consider the progression in the following sentences, taken from church-growth treatment on the subject of marketing: "The Church is a business." / "Marketing is essential for a business to operate successfully." / "The Bible is one of the world's great marketing texts." / "However, the point is indisputable: The Bible does not warn against the evils of marketing." / "So it behooves us not to spend time bickering about techniques and processes." / "Think of your church not as a religious meeting place, but as a service agency—an entity that exists to satisfy people's needs." / "The marketing plan is the Bible of the marketing game; everything that happens in the life of the product occurs because the plan wills it."

Those statements contain truths, half-truths, quarter-truths, and flat-out errors. "It is also critical," one author adds, "that we keep in mind a fundamental principle of Christian communication: the audience, not the message, is sovereign." That statement is utterly wrong, yet it is almost canonical to much of the church-growth movement.

Is it correct that the "sovereign audience" is "a fundamental principle of Christian communication"? This seems to be a dangerously distorted half-truth and a recycling of the error of classical liberalism. This approach to affluent consumers of the twentieth century may carry the same seeds of compromise as Friedrich Schleiermacher's approach to the cultured despisers of the gospel in the eighteenth century.

Like the Bereans in the New Testament, we have to examine such statements for ourselves and make our own biblical assessment. But while many people still appear moonstruck by the recent discovery of the sovereign audience, it is worth pondering a *New Yorker* lament about what is lost in the brave, new "audience-driven" preaching of the day:

> The preacher, instead of looking out upon the world, looks out upon public opinion, trying to find out what the public would like to hear. Then he tries his best to duplicate that, and bring his finished product into a marketplace in which others are trying to do the same. The public, turning to our culture to find out about the world, discovers there is nothing but its own reflection. The unexamined world, meanwhile, drifts blindly into the future.[10]

FIVE MAIN IRONIES

The fifth reminder deals with the unintended consequences of Christians engaging uncritically with modernity. Irony, ironically, is a profoundly biblical theme that does not figure strongly in the thinking of most Christians. Yet no other religion rivals the Christian faith in providing such a foundation for a strong view of irony. Because human unbelief is essentially a matter of the "truth held in unrighteousness," Christians can always count on the fact that the "truth will come out" regardless of the denials of unbelief, that the consequences of human action will always be other than we intended, and that reality will always have the last laugh. Irony, in short, is not merely a subject for writers or cultural commentators; it is a key part of the Christian understanding of life.

It takes a developed sense of irony to appreciate the present position of Protestant evangelicalism in America. This is significant for our discussion because evangelicalism is the source and chief exponent of the church-growth movement. These ironies are stated briefly, without comment.

First, Protestants today need the most protesting and reforming. Second, evangelicals and fundamentalists have become the most worldly tradition in the church. Third, conservatives are becoming the most progressive. Fourth, Christians in many cases are the prime agents of their own secularization. Fifth, through its uncritical engagement with modernity, the church is becoming its own most effective gravedigger.

For the church-growth movement, what matters are the breeding grounds in which such ironies and unintended consequences multiply. Two are paramount. The first breeding ground is the more traditional one: the uncritical espousal of the ideal of "relevance" and its companion church-growth slogans, "seeker-friendly," "audience-driven," and "full-service churches."

As stated earlier, relevance is a prerequisite for communication. Without it, there is no communication, only a one-sided sending of messages addressed to no one, nowhere. But having said that, it must also be said that relevance is a more complex, troublesome, and seductive matter than its advocates acknowledge. For a start, relevance is a question-begging concept when invoked by itself. And when absolutized, it becomes lethal to truth. Properly speaking, relevance assumes and requires the answer to such questions as: Relevance for what? Relevant to whom?

Truth gives relevance to "relevance," just as "relevance" becomes irrelevance if it is not related to truth. Without truth, relevance is meaningless and dangerous.

If these questions are left unasked, a constant appeal to relevance becomes a way of riding roughshod over truth and coralling opinion coercively. People are thinking or doing something simply "because it is relevant" without knowing why. But it is in fact truth that gives relevance to "relevance," just as "relevance" becomes irrelevance if it is not related to truth. Without truth, relevance is meaningless and dangerous.

In addition, relevance has a false allure that masks both its built-in transience and its catch-22 demand. Dean Inge captured the transience in his celebrated line "He who marries the spirit of the age soon becomes a widower." But it was Simone Weil who highlighted the catch-22: "To be always relevant, you have to say things which are eternal."

For many evangelicals, relevance as the road to irrelevance is still tomorrow's problem rather than today's. But the fate of liberalism should give evangelicals occasion to pause. Evangelicals would do well to ponder the enigma of relevance more deeply. One lesson from the "road to Rome" or the "Canterbury trail" is that there is an advantage to the "irrelevance" of being transcultural and transhistorical. Precisely because the church crosses cultures and generations, G.K. Chesterton could even boast that the church is "the only thing which saves a man from being the degraded child of his own age."[11] There is thus an irrelevance to the pursuit of relevance as well as a relevance to the practice of irrelevance.

The second, and more modern, breeding ground for irony is the church-growth movement's uncritical elevation of modern notions of "need." The mega-churches' entire law, as one proponent puts it, is summed up in their two great commandments: "Find a need and meet it, find a hurt and heal it."

At first sight, a ministry based on meeting needs is surely unobjectionable. After all, its ultimate sanction is the saying of Jesus: "It is not the healthy who need a doctor, but the sick. I have not come to call the righteous, but sinners to repentance" (Luke 5:31-32).

Yet people who use the need-meeting approach overlook certain things. First, this approach has no matching emphasis in truth, and leaves the church carelessly vulnerable to intellectual dismissal. The heirs of Ludwig Feuerbach and Sigmund Freud, for instance, attack the church by charging that "the fundamental dogmas of Christianity are fulfilled wishes of the heart"— which is in fact a fair description of much modern evangelical believing.

> *The modern passion for "felt needs" may turn the church into an echo chamber of fashionable needs that drown out the One voice that addresses real human need below all felt needs.*

Second, meeting needs does not always satisfy needs; it often stokes further ones and raises the pressure of eventual disillusionment. As Immanuel Kant said to a Russian historian Karamzin, "Give a man everything he desires and yet at this very moment he will feel that everything is not everything."

Third, and even more important, modernity has expanded and corrupted the very notion of need by creating a "need on command" society. Needs, consumerism, and professionalism are the three pillars of our modern service society. To be need-less is to be less than human. As Tony

Walters points out, modern consumer society is built on a grand reversal of the Beatles' song: "All you love is need."

Strikingly, the new status of "need" simultaneously elevates a new generation of experts—because of their authority to describe and prescribe— and debases true needs. Thus, need, subject to consumer fashion, becomes shallow, plastic, and manipulable. Needs induced by advertising slogans are often merely wants; as such, they become commodities that are purchased on command through expert prescription. Yet here is the irony: Endlessly engineered and marketed, an obsession with perceived needs results in consumer indifference to *specific, genuine, real* needs. People skilled in learning to need the "needs" that the professional elites identify become deaf to their own true needs—their needs as God, not the world, defines them.

In short, the exaggerated half-truth about the church's "needing to meet needs" once again breeds unintended consequences. Just as church-growth's modern passion for "relevance" will become its road to irrelevance, so its modern passion for "felt needs" may turn the church into an echo chamber of fashionable needs that drown out the One voice that addresses real human need below all felt needs.

Six Main Carriers

The sixth reminder deals with the people who are likely to become the source of the church's problem, because of church growth's uncritical engagement with modernity.

The term "carrier" is often used of modernization, borrowed from the medical field to express the development equivalent of a carrier of disease. Usually the reference is to impersonal, structural forces—such as urbanization, the spread of the market economy, bureaucratization, and so on. But it is useful to remember that modernity is also "carried" by certain character types—in other words, by people whose jobs and skills are the epitome of different parts of the modernization process.

There are six main carriers, or character types, of modernity. One or two others might be added. But not only are they close to the essence of modernity; they are very close to some of us, a recognition that can be disturbing.

First is the pundit, the one for whom "everything can be known, everything can be pronounced upon," centered professionally on the importance of information. Second is the engineer, the one for whom "everything can be designed, everything can be produced," centered professionally on production. (You want to market a perfume, land a man on the moon, plant a new church? The engineer will figure it out.) Third is the marketer, the one for whom "everything can be positioned, everything can be sold," centered professionally on consumer satisfaction. Fourth is the consultant, the one for whom "everything can be better organized, everything can be better delivered," centered professionally on management. Fifth is the therapist, the one for whom "everything can be gotten in touch with, everything can be adjusted or healed," centered professionally on healing. Sixth is the impresario, the one for whom "everything can be conveyed to advantage through the presentation of images regardless of any reality," centered professionally on public relations and "impression management."

Doubtless several of these carriers come close to many of us and all of them merit deeper discussion. I will expand only on the pundit—partly because of the pundit's importance in the proliferation of church-growth gurus and management consultants.

Modernity breeds pundits; indeed it turns modern society into a punditocracy based on the ruling assumption that everything can be known, everything can be pronounced upon. Many factors contribute to the pundit's appeal. The arrival of the knowledge society, the rising status of information and data, the triumph of the New Class, the importance of "ideas brokers" and the "culture wars" (America now has more than a thousand think tanks), the rise of professional, credentialed experts, and the introduction of an entertainment dynamic in thinking (so that we now have gurus-in-residence and intellectual celebrities with a passion to perform). Two other elements that favor the pundit are the rise of short-attention discourse (promoted by television's incredibly shrinking sound bite) and the hunger for meaning and belonging with its attendant growth of prophecy and future-hype.

Put all these factors together and the rise of the pundit becomes natural, and even necessary. Nor does it take much thought to see its influence. Take the example of the role of pundits on such political talk shows as "Crossfire," "The Capital Gang," and "The McLaughlin Group." The features of such shows are well known: the trivializing of issues, the sound-bite reasoning, the contrived aggression, the locker room machoism, the off-camera celebrity pimping for corporations, and the considerable hypocrisy—the same men (yes, men and not women) who expect to be taken seriously when they write in newspapers do not expect to be taken seriously when they josh around on the talk shows. Yet their pundit power to set agendas is enormous. Informed opinion in America has become the replay of yesterday's talk show.

Needless to say, Christian pundits are somewhat different in both subject matter and style. But the differences are less than one should expect and not as important as the less obvious similarities. Two problems commonly develop. First, overreliance on pundits—or on any of the other carriers—leads Christians toward *dependency on professionalism and expertise.*

While Christian ministry is the prototype of the profession, and such traditional professions as law and medicine were openly altruistic as a reflection of their origin, modern professionalism has a different goal and a different outcome.

Professionalism embodies the power to prescribe. Today it is the key to determining need, defining clients, delivering solutions and deepening dependency—whether in healing identity, rebuilding inner cities, or planting churches among baby boomers.

The suggestion is that "The expert knows best." But the "ministry of all believers" recedes once again.

The result, however, is not necessarily greater freedom and responsibility for ordinary people, because the dominance of the expert means the dependency of the client. All that has changed is the type of authority. Traditional authorities, such as the clergy, have been replaced by modern authorities—in this case, denominational leaders by church-growth experts. The outcome is what Christopher Lasch calls "paternalism without a father" and Ivan Illich "the age of disabling professions."[12]

The suggestion is that "the expert knows best," so "we can do better." But the "ministry of *all* believers" recedes once again. Even the dream of the "self-help" movement disguises the gold rush of experts in its wake. In most cases, all that has changed is the type of clergy. "The old priesthood is dead! Long live the new power-pastors and pundit-priests!"

Second, overreliance on pundits leads Christians toward *disregard for the specifically Christian content of the expertise.* In the case of the Christian pundit, for example, a dazzling grasp of modern data and information often obscures a striking blind spot—his or her lack of attention to matters of wisdom, responsibility, and character, which far outweigh the importance of information in Scripture.

More seriously still, uncritical adulation of the Christian pundit runs the risk of opening the doors to modern varieties of false prophets. Jeremiah, you will remember, distinguished the false from the true with his searching question: "But which of them has stood in the council of the LORD to see or to hear his word?" (Jeremiah 23:18). I read Jeremiah's question and can only say, "Have I? Have we?" That divine source alone divides true Christian speaking from false. Without it, all prophecy is false, all punditry shallow—the mere chatter of recycled opinions and retailed personal fancies.

173

CONCLUSION

The challenge of modern church growth is the problem of modern discipleship writ large—how to engage in the world freely but faithfully. Clearly, a tough blend of attributes is required: integrity and effectiveness, enterprise with humility, spiritual devotion along with common sense. To that end, here are two concluding reminders and two cautions to ponder.

The first reminder concerns the paradox surrounding change and relevance. On the one hand, no one and nothing stays the same unless it is willing to change. On the other hand, no one and nothing becomes truly timely unless it is in touch with the eternal. The second reminder concerns the paradox surrounding success. On the one hand, in matters of the spirit, nothing fails like success. On the other hand, in matters of the spirit, nothing succeeds like failure.

The first caution to ponder is historical. In the early 1980s when the Christian Right was the dominant trend, criticism of the movement was often treated as treason. Today, when the trail of its debris-strewn illusions is all too obvious, many former enthusiasts wonder why they did not recognize the movement's shortcomings earlier. Could it be that the church-growth movement in its present expansionist phase is also a movement waiting to be undeceived? It would be wise to raise our questions now.

The second caution to ponder is theological. If modernity is history's greatest reinforcement of the idol-making factory that is our hearts, nothing can resist it short of the truth of radical monotheism: "There is one God, no god but God, and no rest for any people who have any god but God." Only an impossible God, revealing impossible truths and making impossible demands, can call out an impossible people adequate for this challenge.

For all who are committed to church growth and eager to use the best of modernity, it is sobering to realize the lengths of God's iconoclasm. As the Scriptures show, God is not only against the idolizing of alien gods, God is against His own gifts when idolized. The fate of the tabernacle and the temple are both a warning to megachurches built not on rock but sand.

We should therefore remember Peter Berger's contemporary warning: "He who sups with the devil of modernity had better have a long spoon." By all means dine freely at the table of modernity, but in God's name keep your spoons long. We should also remember Origen's ancient principle: Christians are free to plunder the Egyptians, but forbidden to set up a golden calf. By all means plunder freely of the treasures of modernity, but in God's name make sure that what comes out of the fire that will test our life's endeavors is gold fit for the temple of God and not a late-twentieth-century image of a golden calf.

9

THE D-MIN-IZATION
OF THE MINISTRY

by David F. Wells

Ministers are among the homeless of the modern world. They have neither a place in secularized society nor, as it turns out, in the church. Because they are the purveyors of belief, the modern world shunts them to the margins of importance. Because the expectations of what a minister is and does have expanded mightily in the twentieth century, few satisfy their congregations for long and many burn out trying to do so. To find respite they flit from church to church like wandering itinerants, which they are not. They are thus strangely dislodged from both the church and society.

This predicament raises profound personal and social challenges for many pastors. I believe too that it best explains the drive that began in the last century to transform the pastoral calling into a profession. This has created an idol at the very heart of ministry. Insecure ministers who are stripped of importance hope to be elevated through professionalization to the same social standing as other professionals, such as physicians and lawyers. And the Doctor of Ministry degree (D. Min) is the principal tool that seminaries

---

David F. Wells is professor of historical and systematic theology at Gordon-Conwell Theological Seminary in South Hamilton, Massachusetts. He has written and edited several books, including *The Evangelicals: What They Believe, Who They Are, and Where They Are Changing.*

This chapter is adapted from "The New Disablers," in *No Place for Truth* (Grand Rapids: Eerdmans, 1992). Used by permission.

offer to achieve this parity. This degree, then, has become the outward and visible sign of the inward and invisible grace that society bestows on someone who is seen as a professional.

Although obtaining this advanced academic degree may seem quite innocent and understandable, the results are profoundly harmful for the church. As with every idol, the gospel is distorted and something is relied on falsely until it becomes a substitute for God. Professionalization produces a culture—a way of looking at life that is at odds with the view ministers need to have if they serve Christ and His people. Christ and culture collide here— they are both competing for the church's soul. It is no small irony that this worldly culture has loosed its values upon the church through the ministry.

In order to explore these themes I will first show how pastors have become marooned. Second, I will examine the solution being widely adopted—turning pastoral calling into a profession. Third, I will show why this solution works against the church's own nature and best interests.

On the Outskirts of the Modern World

There is no doubt that the growing secularization of the modern world undermines the importance of ministers and ministry. Little in the experience of the secular, modern person suggests that a biblical ministry makes sense. What bankers or lawyers do makes sense; after all, the modern world is about commerce and it generates innumerable disputes. Banks and law courts, therefore, have procedures and offer services the modern public thinks it needs. In contrast, what ministers do is not recognized as necessary in the public square at all—to many, it has no relevance to public life. Ministers and the ministry are therefore pushed to the margins of society more and more. The bonds to what is considered meaningful and important become strained, if not broken. This, however, is not a recent problem.

Beginning about midway through the last century, the attitude toward Christian ministry began a dramatic reversal. The high social standing that ministers once enjoyed has been in decline ever since, and the sure purpose with which they did their work has been fading. During much of the twentieth century, when members of the clergy appeared in novels, increasingly they were strained, unhappy figures, if not outright scoundrels. Such figures as the Reverend Mister Dimmsdale in Nathaniel Hawthorne's *The Scarlet Letter,* or Elmer "Hellcat" Gantry in Sinclair Lewis's story, or the Reverend Andrew Mackerel in Peter De Vries's *The Mackerel Plaza* are all symbols of the public's fallen esteem for clergy, be they Calvinist or Arminian, evangelical, fundamentalist, or Protestant mainline.

The most important change in the clergy's standing, however, is stumbled upon almost incidentally. It is found in novels, when clergy members and physicians are compared unfavorably—as if those proficient in curing the body are as skilled in curing the soul. What the clergy once did, increasingly physicians now are seen to do. Physicians and the clergy appear together in over half of the novels in the modern period in which the clergy have significant roles.[1] In some of these novels they work together, but more commonly the minister comes off looking weak and incompetent next to his or her medical counterpart. The low status of the clergy continues in the eighties and nineties through movie and television portrayals of narrow-minded or foolish ministers.

THE SEARCH FOR CLIENTS

As novelists began to picture ministers as awkward or embarrassing figures, other signs appeared of a coming storm that now engulfs the clergy. Chief among these has been the growing impermanence of pastoral ministry.

Churches in Puritan New England, for example, took time to establish a steady pattern in the relation between pastors and churches. This was, however, largely achieved by 1670. Among Presbyterians and Congregationalists in New Hampshire, the average pastor stayed with a church for twenty years. It was only at the beginning of the nineteenth century that the pastoral duration fell below this level. In fact, it was 1808 when the serious decline set in and spread throughout New England. By 1810, the pastor's time at a church fell to fifteen years; by 1830 to five years; by 1860 to just less than four years. In some regions today, the pastor's tenure at one church averages only about two years, and seldom above three.

Many ministers now wander from church to church, seldom finding secure or lasting lodging.

In the eighteenth century a church and its minister typically entered into a compact that was moral, and sometimes legal, in character to last the duration of the minister's life. The church and minister would become united to one another as in a marriage contract. At the beginning of the nineteenth century, the minister still held a socially important office—he did not simply offer spiritual services for a fee. Permanence was important because the church was at the center of the social order. A premature departure of the minister could very well disrupt a town's life. Many churches actually clung to their ministers—in some cases despite appallingly inept preaching—preferring spiritual deprivation rather than losing their minister. And many churches hired an assistant to prop up an aging or irascible minister to preserve continuity, which was preferable to dismissing the disagreeable or elderly gentleman.

There were exceptions to the permanent pastor, of course; for example, the famous circuit riders of the Methodist church. But today the exception has become the rule. The binding marriage contract between pastor and church no longer exists. The contract has been reduced from life to a matter of only a few brief years. The pastor is linked only tenuously to the church because of an expected short tenure. The final and most exaggerated expression of this fleeting, impermanent link can be seen among the televangelists. They "serve" a flock whom they never see, whose troubles are unknown to them, among whom there are no opportunities for service.

Many ministers now wander from church to church, seldom finding secure or lasting lodging. As a result, they have had to define their ministry in terms of its marketability. Because the market dominates how their ministry is exercised, their internal calling and even their spirituality may be submerged. What were once the central interests of ministers—brokering God's truth, caring for the sick and ailing, building up Christian character and understanding—have been displaced by a whole new line of responsibilities in response to the market. A multiplicity of "felt" needs exist, few of which are central to a biblically ordered ministry. In fact, these new interests may even entirely eclipse the minister's foundational responsibilities.

This change in responsibilities has produced considerable confusion among the clergy. Clearly by the end of the sixties and the early seventies this confusion had taken its toll. Ministers were filled with doubt about themselves and also saw their standing in society plummeting. They began to suffer serious anxieties over their status. The power that inward calling had once exerted on private consciousness—the sense of "standing" before God, of doing His work by making His truth known—apparently was not enough. How, then, would ministers not only gain control over the market, but recover some standing as well? Since the seventies the answer has been to become a profession.

PROFESSIONALIZE!

The word *professional*, in its popular usage today, may mean nothing more than being skilled. For example, a complicated piece of plumbing done "very professionally" might simply mean that the pipes were joined more cleanly than previously thought possible. But clearly, not every exercise of skill qualifies one as a professional.

Definitions of the professional actually vary widely,[2] so for our purposes I take only their most common characteristics. Being a professional today means that one has an ability, usually intellectual in nature, sharpened by training and education and exploited in the interests of both acquisition and aspiration. It therefore carries both the idea of fees charged and a career pursued. And because of the degree of specialization of the professional, he or she has a certain monopoly over the work for which the fees are charged. In order to sustain this monopoly, most professionals are organizationally linked to others pursuing the same vocation in order to control who can do the work and how it should be done.

The most important element in this definition is probably that of specialization. As society has grown more complex, it has become increasingly unwise to depend on trial and error to prepare and fashion workers. Correspondingly, it has become more and more necessary to train people specifically for tasks where, because of the rigor of the training, they alone can perform the function.

This system of training, coupled with the community that results from the organizational bonding among like professionals, produces its culture. By this I mean the ideals, interests, and way of looking at life that are common to those in a profession. This professional culture is now defining how skill and proficiency should be understood in the ministry. And that definition clashes with how the pastors would define pastoral ministry if they defined it theologically, according to its own nature.

Many seminaries were hard pressed financially but now had, in the D.Min., a lucrative product to sell.

After the alarming and disconcerting realization was made that the ministry was culturally adrift, serious consideration was given to finding a solution. The quest for a professional degree for ministers has a long, uneven history, beginning in the forties with the proposals of the American Theological Society. Under the careful direction of the Association of Theological Schools a solution eventually was adopted: upgrade the names of the degrees. What had been the Bachelor of Divinity (B.D.) now became the Master of Divinity (M. Div.) in the early seventies. Shortly thereafter the D.Min. was added to the arsenal of social tools for those seeking upward mobility.[3]

Middle class congregations could now be served by a professional, as many thought they needed to be. Equally, ministers could have their service validated by a doctorate, as many thought they needed. With the doctorate came the comforting assurance that forward progress was being made in their careers. Thus was the D.Min. born. In two decades more than ten thousand have been issued.

It was, of course, the old market mechanism at work. In the seventies many seminaries were hard pressed financially but now had, in the D.Min., a lucrative product to sell. At the same time, many ministers were hard pressed psychologically as they sensed their growing marginalization in society, the decline of their status, and the corresponding loss of power and influence. The shotgun marriage was consummated.

The direction that the D.Min. has taken since its inception has not, however, been reassuring. The quality of the degree undoubtedly varies by institution, but the quality of many of these degrees is downright questionable. What in many other professions are simply summer courses or required refresher courses for continued certification have became the royal route that many ministers travel toward a doctorate. Good students, of course, are able to capitalize on their opportunities even when the instruction is mediocre, and undoubtedly some of our newly minted clerical doctors have done so.[4]

But the question of real interest is what draws ministers to these minimalist degrees and why seminaries offer them. It strains credulity to think that only a love of learning has produced this happy match. After all, among those who have graduated with the degree, 78 percent said that they expected to be more respected in the community and 73 percent expected to be paid more.[5] As a result, some seminaries that might have otherwise suffered a shameful demise survived because of the D.Min degree, and some ministers who might have otherwise floundered in their careers instead advanced. At least, they are seen to have advanced and that, in a world where image matters as much as reality, is what actually counts.

The pastoral ministry is thus being professionalized. The middle class—those who are themselves professionals or who deal with them day-to-day—increasingly defines the minister's work and how it is done. To satisfy the middle class the ministers must present themselves as having a desired level of competence. That competence, as it turns out, is largely managerial—ministers must not only manage the unruly and painful forces within the human psyche but the turbulent and equally unruly forces in the organization of the church as well.

The new model of the minister is nowhere better illustrated than in the pages of *Leadership Journal*. This publication, a spin-off from *Christianity Today* in 1980, is geared specifically to pastors and addresses every conceivable problem the church could encounter in the modern world. But a review of all the essays appearing between 1980 and 1988 shows that less than 1 percent made any obvious attempt to root the answers in anything biblical or doctrinal—despite the fact that many of the problems addressed are addressed directly in Scripture. Instead, the answers were taken heavily from the insights of the managerial and therapeutic revolutions. Furthermore, despite that this magazine attempts to offer wisdom on how to handle the problems of modernity (the clash of the world's values with Christian values), less than 1 percent of the essays attempted to understand the modern world in which the problems arose.[6]

Leadership Journal is not alone in this emphasis on the pastor as professional. Many other magazines and books freely dip their buckets into pop-psychology and pop-management theory in place of a serious reckoning with Scripture. This is no accident. The two cultural characters that capture what is most important in modernity are the psychologist and the manager. These characters now define what the professionalized pastor is becoming: in the pulpit, a psychologist whose business is to spread warm feelings; in the study, a CEO whose business is to have a successful year in terms of numbers.

GOING UP THE GARDEN PATH

Professionalizing the ministry was not, on the face of it, an implausible approach to take. After all, it is how other professionals, such as medical doctors, lawyers, architects, accountants, and engineers, have acquired their standing in society. But professionalization is itself a culture, and one not always friendly to pastoral calling and character. It was grasped as a life jacket, but now those who float by its means must also live by its limitations and dictates. In three main areas its culture may part company with biblical principles. It is critical that we guard against the idolizing of professionalism in the ministry in these areas—careers, professionalized specialization, and biblical truth.

Careers. All professionals have careers where they pursue their work in the interests of both aspiration and acquisition. They seek larger responsibility and visibility and expect to be compensated accordingly. Their work, in other words, is the means for advancing their own private interests. Ministers are peculiarly vulnerable to this way of looking at life because their bonding to the people in their churches is now so tenuous and short-lived. This is the first main area to be aware of in the idolizing of professionalism in the ministry.

Pastors often view the frequent obligatory move from church to church as a hidden opportunity. The moves can be stepping-stones to greater personal visibility or reward. The problem with this, however, is that people who think of careers are inevitably thinking in the language and style of self-interest. Moves are assessed in terms of how they might advance the person toward the next plateau, toward a church one size up, toward a position in the denominational headquarters, or toward a larger salary. Careers serve the self; biblically minded pastors do not. Careers have the potential for distorting and destroying Christian service in exchange for the pastor's self-interest.

Needless to say, most pastors are far from adequately paid. Nonetheless, the way the most adept have been able to ease themselves into salaries of the six-figure kind is disturbing. Furthermore, well-to-do, middle-class congregations are accustomed to the professional world, where they find the specialists they need, whether in law, medicine, or accounting. They are used to paying for these specialist services. They would not use a cut-rate doctor, and they do not want to be served by a cut-rate minister. They preserve their own status by feeding the minister's greed.

Professionalization accustoms us to greed. Indeed, it legitimizes greed. Those who now think so easily about being religious professionals often have no qualms in walking down this same path. Their ability to serve Christ faithfully becomes compromised. If there is still a lesson to be learned about the scandals of the televangelists in the eighties, it is at this point. Their public downfall came about largely because of their sexual misdoings. But what passed almost unnoticed and was at least as serious was their greed. No one, however, seemed to mind their greed, which was documented long before they were publicly disgraced.

Finding the niche. The second main area in which to guard against the idolizing of the professionalization of the ministry lies in the specialization of pastors in nontheological areas. All professionals are specialists who claim a monopoly in their area of expertise. They exercise sovereignty within a narrow domain, and charge high fees accordingly. Control over the work and who performs it is essential for the capitalistic enterprise to survive. Our professions have become cartels.

When professionalization is transferred to the church, the differences between the pastor and the congregation are accentuated, just as the differences between doctors and their patients or lawyers and their clients are apparent. The difference in question is the possession of technical knowledge in the one and its absence in the other.

In what does the minister exercise a monopoly? Certainly not over the meaning of Christian faith—for the whole point of the minister's service is for the laity to become more knowledgeable about its own faith. If ministers are to claim a monopoly over some part of their work, while assuming that the congregation does know something about its faith, they will almost certainly have to become specialists in matters that are peripheral to the life of faith. These might include church administration, denominational politics, or psychological counseling. Ministers come to see their special qualification in the church as providing leadership in matters that are peripheral and nontheological.

What kind of leadership is this? It is the kind that allows unbelief and idolatry to flourish. It reduces the church to nothing more than a helping agency, known for the services it offers and the good feelings it engenders, but with little or no place for God. This kind of nontheological leadership is sowing the seeds of the secularization of evangelical faith. It is a profound symptom of the corruption of evangelical faith today.

The loss of a center. The third main area, the disintegration of the biblical and theological core, has unfortunate consequences. Pastors no longer have any way to judge how their time should be spent. In fact, they are entirely at the mercy of the clientele they serve. But their clientele's expectations have become so bloated that no mere mortal can any longer satisfy many churches.

In a major study[7] done in 1934, the minister was seen to have five roles: teacher, preacher, worship leader, pastor, and administrator. A study done in 1980 found that these roles had almost doubled to nine. In addition to the older functions, the minister was expected to have an open and affirming style, know how to foster friendship in the church, be aware of things denominational, and be able to lead the church's participation in political discussions as well as provide a witness against the world's injustice.

By 1986, another study found that the expectations of the pastor had expanded still further to fourteen roles.[8] And interestingly, these expectations were largely unaffected by whether or not the church was evangelical. Pastoral responsibility was stretched across an ever-widening terrain in the church. In evangelical churches, the top priority was given to planning ability, facility in leading worship, and sensitivity to the congregation. This was followed, in order, by spiritual development of the congregation, pastoral counseling for the needy, visiting the sick, and support of the church's stewardship program. These were followed by three equally ranked activities: providing administrative leadership, the ability to involve the laity in the church's programs, and support for the church's mission in the world. And holding issues of social justice before the congregation was now last as a pastoral priority.

Fortunately, there are ministers who have broken the professional mold. But they have done so against great odds and have had to work on the fringes of evangelical life. Often they have had to turn their seminary training on its head, now seeking in the knowledge of God a unity for what they do in the church, instead of seeking in the life of the church the center that defines what they do. They have had to overcome the distance most congregations sense from things theological. They have had to see through modernity with such clarity to be able to discern where and how its pluralism and secularism work. Thus the ministers have had to preach the truth of God's Word with passion, seeking intersections of that truth in modern life. But not all ministers have successfully negotiated the shoals that lie before them. Take, for example, the matter of preaching.

We have the makings of a kind of faith whose life is only tenuously related to the Word of God, that is not much nurtured by it, that is not much anchored in the character and greatness of God.

Many factors affect the way preaching is done in any given age. It would probably be impossible to establish an indisputable cause and effect relationship between the habits of professionalization and the way in which preaching excellence is judged today. Nevertheless, we can say that the scale of excellence on which preaching is now judged is in accord with what the judges believe the ministry is about.

It is, therefore, a matter of no small interest to discover how two important preaching journals, *Preaching* and *Pulpit Digest*, view this matter. A study of two hundred sermons preached by evangelicals between 1985 and 1990 classified messages into four categories: (1) those in which both the content of the sermon and its organization were determined by the biblical passage under consideration; (2) those in which the content was explicitly biblical but the preacher took the liberty of imposing his own organization upon it; (3) those in which neither the content nor the organization arose from the biblical passage but what was said was identifiable as Christian; and (4) those in which neither the content nor the organization arose from a biblical passage and in which the content was not discernibly or obviously Christian.[9]

The two hundred sermons fell into the following categories: 24.5 percent in the first, 22.5 percent in the second, 39 percent in the third, and 14 percent in the fourth. Of these sermons, less than half were explicitly biblical in content and a significant number were not discernibly Christian at all. They could have been given by a secular psychologist in a setting like the Rotary Club.

Even more significant than these findings are the orientations of the sermons. Only 19.5 percent sought to ground or relate what was said in any way to the nature, character, and will of God. The question was not whether the sermons were about God, for a preacher might wish to discourse upon many other legitimate subjects on a Sunday morning. It was, rather, whether the reality, character, and acts of God were the explicit foundation for what was said about the life of faith, and whether in fact that life of faith made an internal sense without reference to the character, will, and acts of God.

The findings were, then, an attempt to measure the prevailing spirit of the age in today's pulpit. Is it anthropocentric, centered on human beings, or theocentric, centered on God? The overwhelming proportion of the sermons—more than 80 percent—were anthropocentric. It seems that God has become a rather awkward appendage to the practice of evangelical faith, at least as measured by the pulpit. Indeed, from these sermons it seems that God and the supernatural order are related only with difficulty to the life of faith. He appears not to be at its center. The center, in fact, is typically the self. God and His world are made to spin around this surrogate center, for our world increasingly is understood within a therapeutic model of reality.

If, in fact, these figures bear any significant relation to what those in the pews are thinking and hearing, then we have the makings of a kind of faith whose life is only tenuously related to the Word of God, that is not much nurtured by it, that is not much anchored in the character and greatness of God, and that is almost completely unaware of the culture in which it must live—for in virtually none of the sermons analyzed was any attempt made to take account of the modern situation. This is professionalization at both its best and worst. It is at its best because it best reveals the true colors of the culture of professionalization; it is at its worst because it reveals the cost to Christian truth.

Without serious engagement with God's truth and serious reflection upon this world and the Christian's place in it, the church is left empty of meaning and an idol has been erected in its place.

185

And meaning, after all, is what faith is about. If a lesson is to be learned from the demise of liberalism, it is at this point.[10] The continual minimalizing of what faith meant, the reductions and modifications to meet the demands of the age, and the slick shifting and moving to catch the prevailing cultural winds meant that it soon lost the ability to answer the most basic interests in meaning. The path this earlier liberalism followed is now being replicated in evangelicalism, perhaps entirely unconsciously. This is true especially where the culture of professionalization strips faith of a functioning, transcendent reference point in the Word of God.

Two distinct models of ministry are at work in the evangelical church today, with theology in different locations in these models. In the one having roots in the Reformation and in the Puritanism which followed, theology is essential and central; in its modern day evangelical descendants, however, theology is often only instrumental and peripheral. In the one, theology provides the culture in which ministry is understood and practiced; in the other, this culture is provided by professionalization.

The minister, like a small boat cast loose upon the high seas, has become vulnerable to a multitude of perils. Many strong winds blow from the religious consumers within the church.

The difference is not that in one theology is present and in the other it is not. Theology is professed and believed in both. But in the one, theology is the reason and basis for ministry; it provides the criteria by which success is to be measured. In the other, theology does none of these things. Here the ministry provides its own rationale for itself, its own criteria, its own techniques. Theology is not disbelieved, but it does not give the work of ministry its heart and fire.

This shift from the older theological model for ministry in the church to the newer professionalized model produces an entirely different understanding of the relationship of theory and practice. In the older model theology was a synonym for the knowledge of God, for the inward disposition that that knowledge produced, for the wisdom in life that resulted, and for the inclination to serve God and His truth in the world. What was practical was always implied in what was known—it was not another kind of knowledge with a set of separate rules and operating procedures. To know God was to be owned by Him in Christ, to be His servant, to have found the center into which all of life, and not merely that part of it which has to do with ideas, should flow.

But in the new model theology and practice have disengaged from one another. Now the fulcrum around which the ministry turns is no longer God, but the church. Theology, whose habitat is now restricted to the academy by default, only touches the edges of church life. The life of the church actually provides a surrogate "truth" for Christian thought. The skills and techniques requisite for the management of the church determine what theology should be studied, not the importance of the truth itself.

What this means in practice is that the minister, like a small boat cast loose upon the high seas, has become vulnerable to a multitude of perils. Many strong winds blow from the religious consumers within the church. There are those who think in terms of paying the church and the minister to meet their needs. If they are disappointed, they quickly look for alternatives. What the consumers look for most is what the self movement offers, except in evangelical dress. This means that a genuinely biblical and God-centered ministry will almost certainly collide head on with the self-absorption and the anthropocentric focus that are normative in so many evangelical churches.

Idols not only distort the truth, but they deceive and betray those who trust in them. This is clear, too, with the modern ministry. The attempt to steer around these shoals, using professionalization as the rudder, has not only complicated the exercise of a genuinely biblical ministry but has failed in other ways as well. In 1966, according to a Harris poll, 41 percent of the public expressed great confidence in the leadership of the clergy. This figure has dropped steadily and had fallen to only 16 percent in 1989. This was the lowest figure for any of the leaders of the major institutions, such as medicine, the military, government, and the press. The attempt by ministers to reach professional parity with lawyers and physicians has neither impressed the public nor has been successful in its original objectives in the church.

That the strategy has miscarried is a matter of some poignancy. For many of those who seek the refuge of professionalization are also those who display virtue in so many other ways. As ministers they often forfeit the access to affluence that the culture desires. By their own choice, they are relegated to the edges of what the culture considers important. And they are content that their accomplishments be largely unknown and unnoticed—for the moments of pain, bereavement, depression, and confusion that visit their flocks, these deeply perplexing circumstances in which they are called upon to serve as Christ's ministers, are essentially private experiences.

The very willingness of ministers to be countercultural in these ways, however, suggests something more. If such ministers could be persuaded that the translation of their calling into a profession is, in fact, the result of enculturation, then it would not be difficult for them to discover and deepen their own countercultural character. In the process, they would begin to recover the basis for a serious renewal of Christian faith. Let us pray that this may be so.

10

ON NOT WHORING AFTER THE SPIRIT OF THE AGE

by Thomas C. Oden

F rom St. Paul on the road to Damascus to Charles Colson in our own day, conversion is the defining experience of evangelicalism. But dramatic conversions are often controversial, and sometimes are unbelievable or even unacceptable to those close to the one converted. After "Saul" becomes "Paul," many people dismiss Paul because they refuse to lose Saul. And just as many others refuse to accept Paul because they were always suspicious of Saul.

My own pilgrimage of faith has been marked by the conflict, pain, and drama of such a change. For not long ago I could be best described as a "movement person." I embraced one movement after another—and successively learned from them, threw myself into them, and eventually baptized my Christian faith in them if they showed any remote kinship with it at all. But that is exactly why I have come to see the vanity—and idolatry—of chasing after each passing wave of the spirit of the age.

A MODERN DAMASCUS ROAD

I took my first plunge into "movement identity" at sixteen when I joined the United World Federalists to promote world government through

Thomas C. Oden is professor of theology at Drew University in Madison, New Jersey, and an ordained Methodist minister. He has written several books, including *After Modernity . . . What?* and a three-volume systematic theology. His most recent book is *Two Worlds: Notes on the Death of Modernity in America and Russia.*

educational and church groups. I moved from ecumenical debate to a deep involvement in the the antiwar movement in the McCarthy days (as a democratic socialist and theoretical Marxist), the pre-NOW women's rights movement as an advocate for abortion in the mid-1950s, and the civil rights movement. After approximately ten years and several other causes, my movement identity took a new turn. I successively became enamored with the existentialist movement, several therapy movements, and paranormal phenomena and parapsychology, to name a few.

My journey illustrates how one Christian thinker was not immune to those unpleasant viruses that cause an accommodation sickness to modern philosophies and ideologies. In venturing to speak of such accommodation, compromise, and idolatry, I am not thinking of "those other people" or speaking in the abstract, but rather out of my own history. I have lived through the desperate game of attempting to find some modern ideology, psychology, political theory, or sociological understanding that could conveniently substitute for the Christian faith. But that game is over for me—the idols have been dismantled.

The martyrs, saints, and prophets of Christian history can teach us the value of the classical Christian faith. Without their instruction, our faith becomes a bored nodding of the head, the source of an occasional laugh, or in emergency, an item to pawn.

My turnaround from searching for new translations of the Christian faith to being immersed in the study of the classics took place in the early seventies. My irascible, endearing Jewish mentor, the late Will Herberg, straightforwardly told me what Protestant friends must have been too polite to say—that I would remain densely uneducated until I had read deeply in the classical Christian writers. So with long hair, baubles, bangles and beads, and a gleam of communitarian utopianism in my eyes, I found my way into a fourth-century treatise by Nemesius. At length it dawned on me that ancient wisdom could be the basis for a deeper critique of the modern narcissistic individualism than I had yet seen.

After a roller-coaster ride up one movement and down another, I have been drawn back, not suprisingly, to orthodoxy and its companion characteristics—continuity and maintenance. The very thinkers I once condemned scathingly as "conservative" I now find ever increasing in plausibility, depth, and wisdom. Once hesitant to trust anyone over thirty, now I hesitate to trust anyone under "three hundred." Once I thought it my solemn duty to read the *New York Times* almost every day; now seldom. Now it seems more important to know what Chrysostom taught about Galatians 2 or to hear Basil on the Holy Spirit rather than to know all the news that is not quite fit to print.

If we are to understand the original meaning and value of our Christian faith, we must once again see it through the eyes of those who have had to struggle for it and maintain it at the risk of their lives. The martyrs, saints, and prophets of Christian history—more than recent riskless interpreters— can teach us the value of the classical Christian faith. Without their instruction, our faith becomes a mere recollection, a bored nodding of the head, the source of an occasional laugh, or in emergency, an item to pawn.

We as evangelicals need to recover our classical Christian heritage from the early centuries, as Luther sought to recover the Augustinian tradition. Alongside our primary commitment to Scripture, the ancient evangelical tradition can help us turn from compromising our faith with modern movements—in effect, idolizing the modern movements as they replace the true beliefs—and lead to the renewal of evangelical life through the spirit. But we must grasp our contemporary situation accurately if the dialogue on the future of the evangelical faith is to proceed realistically.

THE CRISIS OF MODERNITY

Evangelicals are currently in a prodigal mood to buy into modernity. But there is a simple reason why this is wrong: in market terms, it is the folly of buying high and selling low. Every sophomore economics major knows the simple axiom—buy stocks low, sell them high. The reverse— buying high and selling low—is a recipe for bankruptcy, whether in money or ideas. But those who whore after the spirit of the age can easily lose perspective. Like stock brokers in frenzied panic, many evangelicals are blinded to the difference between a bull and bear market of ideas. Buying into modernity is a risky investment; indeed it may bring us to a Black Monday loss. Many will be left with an empty portfolio. There are two reasons this is no time to buy.

The first reason is that modernity itself is bankrupt. Our first task is to understand modernity. Modernity is multidimensional in character—it is a *period* that began with the French Revolution in 1789, a *mindset* that is reflected by the elite intellectuals, academics, and media manipulators, and, more recently, a deadly *malaise* of this mindset, which has been spiraling downward during the past three decades.

Certain moral attitudes had been considered objectionable, due to classic, persuasive moral arguments against abortion, sexual promiscuity, homosexuality, divorce. By the twentieth century, however, the secular university became the conscience and guide for these moral attitudes.

Modernity is less a time than a conceptual place, an ideological tone. It is less a distinct period than an attitude. Although modernity has had many premodern manifestations, it was not until the nineteenth century that it began to expand from the pockets of the intelligentsia into general circulation in Western society. Certain moral attitudes had been considered objectionable and disreputable, due to classic, persuasive moral arguments against abortion, sexual promiscuity, homosexuality, divorce, moral relativism, and state dependency. By the twentieth century, however, the secular university and the secularizing seminary became the conscience and guide for these moral attitudes. By the last quarter of this century, the modern university became less and less a *universitas* in the classical sense and more and more an exponent and apologist for the particular ideologies and mentality of modernity.

The definition of modernity used elsewhere in this book includes the sociological aspects as well as the philosophical. My focus is the latter. As I will use the term, "modernity" has three distinct interrelated meanings in this discussion, comparable to a target of three concentric circles with a bull's-eye.

The outer, more general circle of modernity refers to the overarching intellectual ideology of a historical period whose influence has lasted from 1789 to 1989—the fall of the Bastille to the fall of the Berlin Wall. The second, intermediate circle of our target defines modernity more tightly as a mentality that is found especially among certain intellectual elites. They assume that chronologically recent ways of knowing the truth are self-evidently superior to all premodern alternatives. This is what I mean by modern chauvinism where the knowledge elites—teachers, clergy, social services bureaucracy—have vested interests in the political control of market exchanges. The inner circle, or bull's-eye of our target, is modernity in the sense of a later-stage deterioration of both of the preceding viewpoints. This deterioration has accelerated generally over the last half century but has reached a dramatic moment of precipitous moral decline in the last three decades.

It is only since the mid-sixties that the bitter fruits of modernity, which have been two centuries in gestation, have been widely grasped, eaten, gorged, disgorged, and found socially undigestible. This vomiting, on a fairly large social scale, has been an event spanning three decades.

My revulsion against the ideology of modernity comes as a late allergic reaction to modern history's own optimistic axioms, which have caused such suffering. I need only mention Auschwitz, My-Lai, the killing fields of Cambodia, Solzhenitsyn's Gulag Archipelago, *Hustler* magazine, the assault statistics in public schools, the juvenile suicide rate, or the heroin epidemic. All point to the depth of the failure of modern consciousness. While modernity continues blandly to teach us that we are moving ever upward and onward, the actual history of late modernity is increasingly brutal, barbarian, and malignant.

In this later stage of deteriorating modernity, four key motifs are in a process of collapse. Each motif is now hammering out the final paragraphs of its own epitaph.

The first is *autonomous individualism,* which focuses on the detached individual as a self-sufficient, sovereign self. This individualism is in crisis today. Western societies are now having to learn to live with the consequences of the social destruction brought about by the excessive individualism of the me-first-now generation.

The second is *narcissistic hedonism,* best symbolized in the waning sexual revolution. The party is over for the sexual revolution, for the party-crasher and terminator has come onto the scene—the unwelcome advent of AIDS. We are now having to live with the consequences of the sexual and familial devastation brought about by egocentric hedonism. It is visible in living color whenever one turns on the television for what is called entertainment, which turns out to be fixated on sex and violence. The social fruits of unconstrained hedonism are loneliness, divorce, and the substitution of sexual experimentation for intimacy, to name a few.

The third is *reductive naturalism,* which is the view that would reduce all forms of knowing to laboratory experimentation, empirical observation, or quantitative analysis. This narrow doctrine is in crisis today. We are now being forced to learn to live with the consequences of reducing sex to orgasm, persons to bodies, psychology to stimuli, economics to planning mechanisms, and politics to machinery. Modernity reduces creation to nature, all causality to natural causality, and replete experience to gaunt empirical explanation.

The fourth modern motif is *absolute moral relativism,* which views all moral values as merely relative to the changing, processing determinants of human cultures. Absolute moral relativism is in crisis everywhere today, as seen comically in the condom dispute in American education and tragically in the hospital wards filled with crack-cocaine babies.

The condom is the best symbol for this declining stage of modern consciousness. No technological artifice better tells the story of autonomous individualism, narcissistic hedonism, and reductive naturalism than this flimsy rubber sheath. There are some runner-up candidate symbols of the joint ironic success and failure of modern technology—maybe the hypodermic needle, Valium, smart bombs, chlorofluorocarbons, or DDT. But none says more about what modernity promises and delivers than the supposedly leak-prone condom (with its unreassuring, 80 percent "success" recorded with educated use).

We have blithely assumed that in theology—just as in corn poppers, electric toothbrushes, and automobile exhaust systems—new is good, newer is better, and newest is best.

It is no time to buy into the ideas of modernity, for they have been tried and found wanting. Modernity is fully corrupted by its own premises. It is now having to face up to its own interpersonal bankruptcy, social neuroses, and moral vacuity. Like Marxism in the former Soviet Union, the assumptions of modernity are no longer credible, apart from a tiny group of introverted intellectuals and tenured radicals.

THE SUICIDE OF ACCOMMODATION

The second reason that evangelicals should not buy into modernity now is the failure of the two-hundred-year-old project that has tried to do so—Protestant liberalism. In the past two hundred years, many liberals have sold out under the influence of modernity. What unites such diverse thinkers as Rudolf Bultmann, Paul Tillich, Charles Hartshorne, Mary Daly, and Karl Rahner? Accommodation to modernity. This underlying motif unites the seemingly vast differences between many forms of existential theology, process theology, liberation theology, and demythologization—all are searching for some more compatible adjustment to modernity.

With ministers and professors of religion casting their lot with modernity, theology stands in a comic relation to its subject matter because it has worked so hard to disavow its distinctive task. No other discipline has devoted so much energy to doing away with its own subject matter (which is God, for theology remains a study of *theos,* whose *logos* [word] is revealed in history).

The faddism of theology has not been accidental. It is necessary if theology is understood as a constant catch-up process, which tries to keep pace with each new ripple of the ideological river. What else could theology become but faddist, under such a definition?

We have blithely assumed that in theology—just as in corn poppers, electric toothbrushes, and automobile exhaust systems—new is good, newer is better, and newest is best. To correct this modern chauvinism will have a shocking effect on seminary campuses long accustomed to a Sweet'n Low® theology. The irony is that these "most innovative" seminaries are regarded in certain circles as better only to the degree they follow this debilitating assumption. So the "best" ones have systematically cut themselves off from sustained discourse with the classical Christian faith.

This is exactly what has happened in religious studies. New theologies appear every spring season with a wide assortment of "new moralities," "new hermeneutics," and (note how the adjectives suddenly have to be pumped up) "revolutionary breakthroughs." On closer inspection, however, we will discover that all these views may be found in the writings of decades ago, except then with mercifully fewer pretensions and less hysteria.

Much of the recent energy of Christian teaching has been poured into attaining an expertise about what might seem to be the "next new cultural wave" (politically, psychologically, artistically, or philosophically). After the emergent movement is spotted on the crest of a distant wave, we try to find some small foothold for the Christian faith on the rolling curl of the wave. As the torrent flows by, we then look for another emerging swell. Thus we have been washed and dumped by several swirling currents, including form criticism, philosophical idealism, nihilism, existentialism, psychoanalysis, process thought, rational-emotive therapy, and management training.

Does this describe recent theology? I have asked varied audiences of Christian clergy and laity that question. Each time I have been reassured that my description is not unfair. It seems accurate to me, as I myself have fairly often experienced working unconsciously just in this way. Hell for the modern theologian, according to this view, is the prospect of being detached from the intellectual momentum of our times.

THREE DEBILITATING LIMITATIONS

What do we do if we do not buy into modernity? While this growing crisis of modernity is a tremendous opportunity for evangelical Christians, it is hardly a time for overconfidence or triumphalism. The lethal virus of modernity is highly contagious and has widely infected orthodox belief. Any response to modernity must begin with a careful examination of our own situation, with a combination of humility and realism. Three debilitating limitations are evident in the current ecclesiastical swamp: (1) intellectual immune deficiency syndrome; (2) an underlying acceptance of many deteriorating premises of modernity; and (3) ignorance of evangelicalism's roots in classic orthodoxy.

First, the evangelical Christian faith began its confrontation with modernity crippled intellectually. Ever since the theological meltdown of the outbreak of revivals in the early nineteenth century, anti-intellectualism has been a dominant feature of evangelicalism. Such powerful ideas as "no creed but the Bible" took hold in popular religious movements. Continuity with a theological tradition was abandoned in the optimistic experiential individualism of frontier populism.

But cutting off the heart from the mind created an intellectual immune deficiency syndrome in evangelical faith. Once faced with the challenges of German historicism, British imperialism, and Western nihilism, most Christians had few intellectual defenses left. Modernity quickly infected the whole of religious belief. Their immunity system lost strength until there was no longer any way of distinguishing orthodoxy from heresy.

Second, in spite of its anti-modern public face and protests, fundamentalism unknowingly accepted many of the foundational premises of modernity, as demonstrated in fundamentalism's way of identifying its doctrinal distinctives. The five "fundamentals" that served as the rallying cry against the encroachments of modernity were themselves a reflection of the nineteenth-century mindset. These fundamentals offer a telling selection of doctrines as the nucleus for Christian thought: the verbal inspiration of inerrant Scriptures, the virgin birth, the substitutionary atonement, the bodily resurrection of Jesus, and the imminent second coming of Christ. Yet the nineteenth-century belief that faith is based on historical facts was much more determinative in the selection of these points than either patristic or Protestant orthodoxy.

Why are these five concerns more "fundamental" than others, such as divine providence, justification by faith through grace, or the triune God? What is the ordering principle of selection? Where is the church? The Holy Spirit? Sanctification? Sin? The principle of selection of these five fundamentals makes good sense only if we see it in the context of the nineteenth-century reliance on historical and scientific objectivity, which was influential at that time but is now waning amid the collapse of modernity.

Why did the high estimation of objective historical evidence take on such importance, when it had caused relatively little debate previously? Because the nineteenth century had witnessed the powerful emergence of historical consciousness (G.W.F. Hegel, Charles Darwin, Karl Marx, Friedrich Nietzsche, Oswald Spengler, and so on) that expressed a consuming interest in historical origins and evidence. Consequently, despite its protests against modernity, fundamentalism was inadvertently swept away by this modern consciousness and unwittingly became an instrument of it.

Fundamentalism could not have happened in any century prior to the nineteenth. All this supports an ironic correlation: modern fundamentalism is more akin to liberalism than either would be willing to admit. Both tacitly assumed that faith was based on objective historical evidence and both were overconfident of their forms of evidence. Carefully note the chief presupposition of the turn-of-the-century fundamentalist program: that the Christian faith is best defended by historically establishing its objective factual origin. So it is not surprising that fundamentalism was far less interested in the doctrinal significance of the resurrection than the objective fact of the resurrection. It did not defend the doctrinal meaning or confessional import of the virgin birth nearly so vigorously as the fact of the virgin birth. This is consistent with the belief that faith is based on factual, historical evidence. In affirming this belief, liberalism and fundamentalism remain very much alike to this day.

Another debilitating limitation is that evangelicals have amnesia about their roots in classical orthodoxy, thereby cutting themselves off from a powerful antidote to modernity.

Many modern evangelicals assume that old ways are predictably oppressive and new ways are intrinsically morally superior. Recently I received an eye-opening letter from a graduate of a leading conservative evangelical seminary, who felt that his professors there considered these writers

> . . . such as Aquinas, Augustine, Calvin, and Luther to be interesting, but not as important as modern theologians. In fact, it appears that contemporary evangelicals are "embarrassed" at the notion of espousing and teaching classical theology. One . . . professor told me that men such as Aquinas and Calvin were great for their day, but their writings are no longer that substantial. The overall feeling . . . is that students need to spend more time in modern theology. This is a tragic shift that seems to be taking place throughout the evangelical community. Over and over again I have encountered evangelicals who are so enamored by the "newness" of modern theological ideas that they abandon the real giants whose writings have stood for centuries.

Some evangelicals tend compulsively to quote only the recent "historically informed" methods of interpretation to the neglect of the classic methods of interpretation of the first five centuries. This step leads backward toward the deteriorating modernity, not forward toward an inquiry into classical orthodoxy.

Our modern individualism too easily tempts us to take our Bible and remove ourselves from the wider believing community. We end up with a Bible and a radio, but no church.

Each succeeding generation must come to grips with the original apostolic witness. Easy substitutes and glossy reinterpretations will not do. When one generation of Christian discipline fails, it is much more difficult for the next generation. But the church must understand itself to be an intergenerational process, because it exists in time. There is no nonhistorical shortcut to fulfilling the church's mission, no easy all-at-once way to accomplish the task of the church on behalf of every generation.

"For no one can lay any foundation," wrote Paul to the disputatious Corinthians, "other than the one already laid, which is Jesus Christ"

(1 Corinthians 3:11). The foundation, strictly speaking, is not just Scripture or tradition but Jesus Christ Himself, who is the heart of Scripture and tradition, who lives out the apostolic testimony as read by the consenting laity worldwide.

Christ promised the early church the Spirit, who came to dwell on the first Pentecost and continues to abide in the lives of the faithful. He promised that the Spirit would remain with this community, and lead it to all truth. This has been happening for the twenty centuries since the ascension. We are moving in the wrong direction when, as individuals, we say, "I've got my Bible; that's all I need," so as to imply "No church, no history, no mission." Protestants now need to recover a sense of the active work of the Spirit in history, and through living communities. Our modern individualism too easily tempts us to take our Bible and remove ourselves from the wider believing community. We end up with a Bible and a radio, but no church.

REDISCOVERING THE TREASURE

The agenda for evangelicalism at the end of the twentieth century, following the steady deterioration of a hundred years and the disaster of the past few decades, is to begin to prepare the Christian community for the recovery of faith in justifying grace in its third millennium. To do this we must return again to the careful study and respectful following of the central tradition of classical Christian interpretation of Scripture texts. This will plant us once again in our foundation so we will not sway with the stiff winds of modernity. There are three ways forward to rediscover this lost treasure.

Our first task is to *listen to the Scripture text itself*. "Obedience to the text" means listening to the text itself instead of modern interpreters of it. This was the most improbable, difficult, and surprising thing that has ever happened to me intellectually. It has revolutionized my understanding of the truth.

The Bible is crucial to the Christian life because these texts alone incomparably convey the history of God's saving action. It is the textual center of orthodoxy. But biblical canon did not drop out of the sky. The canon emerged out of a history. The process of canonization itself evolved out of a specific history (supervised by the Holy Spirit) in which these writings were being challenged by false teachings.

What is the history of orthodox theology other than the history of a widely shared mode of reading the written word? Christian teaching has always been an attempt at cohesive, internally consistent explanation and interpretation of the text. It is an attempt to answer the question of what we mean when we say we believe in God the Father Almighty in a way that is integrated with what we mean when we say we believe in God the Son and God the Spirit.

When we approach the method of classic orthodox interpretation, we can see our sources in terms of a pyramid. Scripture is the foundational base, then the early Christian writers—first pre-Nicene then post-Nicene—as the supporting mass or trunk, then the best of medieval followed by centrist Reformation writers at the narrowing center, and more recent interpreters at the smaller, tapering apex. As we move up the pyramid, each new level must grasp and express the preceding mind of the believing, historic church.

I am pledged not to try to turn that pyramid upside-down, as have those guild theologians who most value only what is most recent or most outrageous. Earlier rather than later sources are cited where possible, not because older is sentimentally prized, but because they have had longer to shape the historic consensus. Sources that express consent with the historic church are more trustworthy than sources characterized by individual creativity, controversial brilliance, stunning rhetoric, or speculative genius.

> *We should be doggedly pledged to irrelevance when relevance implies a corrupt indebtedness to modernity. What is deemed most relevant in theology is often moldy in a few days.*

We do well in recovering our lost treasury is to *commit ourselves to make no new contribution to theology*. We should be passionately dedicated to unoriginality, taking Paul's admonition to heart: "But even if we or an angel from heaven should preach a gospel *other than* the one we preached to you, let him be eternally condemned! As we [of the earliest apostolic proclamation of salvation through Jesus Christ] had already said, so now I say again: If anybody is preaching to you a gospel other than what you accepted [other than what you received from the apostles], let him be eternally condemned!" (Galatians 1:8-9, italics added).

The purpose of Christian teaching is to set forth the classical understanding of God the Father, Son, and Spirit, on which there has been substantial intergenerational agreement between traditions of East and West, Catholic, Eastern Orthodox, classic Protestantism, and evangelical theology of the last two centuries. We do well to listen to the historic consensus received by believers of widely varied languages, social locations, and cultures, whether of East or West, African, or Asian, whether expressed by men or women of the second or first Christian millennium, whether European or decisively pre-European.

The purpose is not to survey the bewildering voices of dissent, but to identify and set forth the cohesive central tradition of the general consent of believers to apostolic teaching. The focus is to set forth the sound layers of argument that have been traditionally employed in presenting the most commonly held points of biblical teaching—especially as classically interpreted by the leading teachers of the first five centuries. We should be doggedly pledged to irrelevance when relevance implies a corrupt indebtedness to modernity. What is deemed most relevant in theology is often moldy in a few days.

In the midst of studying the unchanging God, one morning I woke up from a curious dream. The scene was in a New Haven cemetery, where I accidentally stumbled over my own tombstone. I was confronted by this bemusing epitaph: "He made no new contribution to theology."

I woke up feeling deeply reassured, for I have been trying to follow the strict mandate of Irenaeus "not to invent new doctrine." No concept was more deplored by the early ecumenical councils than the notion that theology's task was to "innovate" *(neoterizein)*. That implied some imagined creative addition to the apostolic teaching and thus something "other than" *(heteros)* the received doctrine *(doxa)*, "the baptism into which we have been baptized."

What the ancient church teachers *least* wished for a theology was that it would be "fresh" or "self-expressive" or an embellishment of purely private inspirations, as if these might stand as some "decisive improvement" on the apostolic teaching.

Yet from the first day I thought of becoming a theologian I have been earnestly taught and admonished that my most urgent task was to "think creatively" so as to make "some new contribution" to theology. Nothing at Yale was drummed into my head more firmly than that the theology I would seek would be my own, and my uniqueness would imprint it. I had to summon great effort to resist the repeated reinforcements of my best education in order to overcome the constant temptation to novelty. How relieved I was to see such an intriguing epitaph prefigured in a dream—"He made no new contribution to theology." Evangelicals must resist this constant temptation to novelty.

Our third task in rebuilding after modernity is to *reacquaint ourselves with the classical Christian writers of our faith.* I have found the late seventeenth century to be a reliable dividing line for finding texts in the orthodox tradition, which are not corrupted by modernity.

The apostolic criterion is not whether something is old or new. The criterion is whether it is truthful.

By the classical Christian faith (or ancient ecumenical orthodoxy), I mean the Christian consensus of the first millennium. It must be asked here, What is the standard of orthodoxy in our postmodern world? In brief, it is that faith to which Vincent of Lérins pointed in the concise phrase "that which has been everywhere and always and by everyone believed." It is the faith generally shared by all Christians, especially as defined in the crucial early periods of Christian doctrinal definition.

Lancelot Andrewes, a sixteenth-century Anglican divine, states the answer as memorably as anyone, with a five-finger exercise: "One canon, two Testaments, three creeds [the Apostles,' Nicene, and Athanasian], four [ecumenical] councils, and five centuries along with the Fathers of that period," by which he meant the great doctors of the first five centuries: Athanasius, Basil, Gregory of Nazianzus, and John Chrysostom in the East; and Ambrose, Augustine, Jerome, and Gregory the Great in the West.

Old is not better. Old can be worse. The apostolic criterion is not whether something is old or new. The criterion is whether it is truthful—truthful in the sense of true to the apostolic testimony to God's revelation, the truth personally incarnate in Jesus Christ. There was a great suspicion of novelty in the first five centuries.

Now, modernity has turned that around and said the opposite: If anything is old we reject it. Novelty has become a criterion for truth. So there is as great a phobic response to anything antiquarian in modern consciousness as there was a resistance to novelty in classical Christian consciousness. Although one may take either of these too far, our culture errs in the direction of the idolatry of the new. Believers perennially need and have a right to a living tradition of preaching, worship, and discipline.

THE WINTER TEMPERAMENT

Having sown the wind, we are now reaping the whirlwind of inter-personal alienation and discontent. We have looked to the modern academic and clinical centers and media bureaucracies to tell the church what it is supposed to be doing and what its values are, only to find that "if one blind man leads a blind man, both will fall into a pit" (Matthew 15:14). At the height of our supposed powers, we modern people "stumble [at midday] as if it were twilight; among the strong, we are like the dead" (Isaiah 59:10). We behold a once-fruitful land that, contrary to all our expectations, has become an interpersonal wilderness.

Sometimes it seems that only a few may survive the desolations of modernity. Yet Peter recalled in the New Testament that "God waited patiently in the days of Noah while the ark was being built. In it only a few people, eight in all, were saved through water" (1 Peter 3:20). Even as the remnant that survived the destruction of Rome were the sons and daughters of the Christian martyrs of the second and third centuries, so the remnant that survives modernity may have to go through (God help us) trial by fire.

Waning modernity is a winter season for the classical Christian faith. Spring will come, but only to those who have survived the winter. There is indeed a joy in the Christian life that comes from discipline, a laughter that echoes even under winter's heaviest snows, a happiness that Christians know to be grounded in God's own joy over creation. But it is never easily won or sustained without effort. The season of late modernity is a winter season—it is time to conserve the essentials as we await the spring thaw. As they say, sunshine peaks through wee holes.

203

Afterword
GOD'S IMPOSSIBLE PEOPLE

Will we see a massive breaking with the idols of our age? Are revival and reformation conceivable today? Is it realistic to work for the restoration of the integrity and effectiveness of faith under modern conditions? Is it possible to recover an evangelicalism defined primarily by the gospel—an evangelicalism shaped and united by God's truth more than by lesser loyalties or the "accidents" of history and society?

Only God knows what is in His mind for our future. Only He can fully answer those questions. But to all who wonder if we motley modern disciples are equal to the challenge of our day, here is a concluding meditation on one prerequisite of faith and obedience as we face up to the challenge of modernity—radical nonconformity to the world as a fruit of our love for Jesus Christ.

AN IMPOSSIBLE GOD, AN IMPOSSIBLE PEOPLE

The story is told of Pompey, the great Roman general and fellow-triumvir with Julius Caesar, entering Jerusalem in the first century B.C. He insisted on being shown the sacred, inner chamber of the Jerusalem synagogue because he wanted to see the Jewish representation of their god. He had heard malicious gossip that the Jews never allowed their god to be seen in public because what they really worshiped was a donkey's head.

Pompey, of course, found nothing. The inner sanctum, like the Holy of Holies in the Tabernacle and in Solomon's Temple before it, was empty. There was no graven image of God. But Pompey's reaction was striking—he was infuriated and stunned with disbelief. As Gnaeus Pompeius Magnus, he could invade Jerusalem and carry Jews back to Rome, but he could not lay his hands on the Jewish God for his Roman pantheon. What was unrepresentable also was unassimilable. Such a God was intolerable to Pompey. The God of the Jews was an utterly impossible God.

Pompey was right. He who is, beside whom there is no other—the God of Abraham, Isaac, and Jacob, who is also the God and Father of Jesus Christ—is an impossible God. Later, the grandeur of imperial Rome was to collapse. In its place marched the impossible followers of this impossible God. And, through the centuries, both the Jews and Christians have exhibited this distinguishing mark: In becoming what they worship, they have known the difference of God make such a difference in them that they have become impossible too.

In the eleventh century A.D., for example, the Christian prophet and reformer Peter Damian was so fiercely committed to truth and principle that he was nicknamed "The Impossible Man." Unclassifiable, unmalleable, unassimilable, such people of faith have been so shaped by truth as to appear uncompromising to all other pressures, molds, and seductions. That is the power of true faith.

> *To say that there is one God and no god but God is not simply an article in a creed. It is an overpowering, brain-hammering, heart-stopping truth that is a command to love the only one worthy of our entire and unswerving allegiance.*

Such a faith, and such a truth-shaped social logic of obedience, is a prerequisite for overcoming modernity. The formal name for this truth is "radical monotheism." But it is false to view it as formal, abstract orthodoxy, as if that made the difference. To say that there is one God and no god but God is not the conclusion of a syllogism nor simply an article in a creed. It is an overpowering, brain-hammering, heart-stopping truth that is a command to love the only one worthy of our entire and unswerving allegiance.

A central consequence of the vision of such an impossible God is God-centered relativizing: God and His truth call into question all opinions, customs, loyalties, and claims that differ from their own. Therefore idolatry is out of the question. Friedrich Nietzsche saw more of the truth of the gospel as he rejected it than many Christians do as they accept it. He called monotheism "monototheism" because of its unyielding opposition to idolatry. "Almost two thousand years," he cried in *The Antichrist,* "and not a single new god."[1]

We evangelicals need that truth. We are rightly fearful of undue relativism, but are wrong to resort to undue absolutism. We forget that God alone is absolute, so all that is not God is relative. Simone Weil wrote, "The essential truth to be known concerning this universe is that it is absolutely devoid of finality. Nothing in the way of finality can be ascribed to it except through a lie or a mistake."[2] Unconditional obedience to God therefore means unconditional refusal to give God's place to anyone and anything else. Thus those who confess one God are those who are ready to criticize everything else—nation, class, race, party, power, wealth, ideology, science, government, church—whenever it threatens to usurp the place of God. After all, there is no Other.

Five features define God's impossible people. They are the characteristics of the practice of radical nonconformity that follows from this radical monotheism. All are needed today as we confront the idols of modernity out of our love for Christ.

A PEOPLE WITHOUT RIGHTS

To hold that there is one God, and no god but God, is—first—to feel the force of the moral demand of God and His truth over His followers. Contrary to every impulse of modern thinking and emotion, we are not our own. America is a rights-rich society dedicated to the pursuit of "I for me by myself." In such a society, the disciple of Jesus Christ has no rights—only duties.

The old Jewish folk saying "It's hard to be a Jew" was a product of theology before it was a product of history. The "chosenness" at the heart of Jewishness includes compulsion. The same is true for all who follow Jesus. His lordship requires no less. The call to believe (as obedience to the truth) includes the call to break (being in the world but not of it) and the call to behave (being holy as God is holy). As William Perkins, the great sixteenth-century Puritan, put it, "The ground of the nine later commandments is the first." Or Richard Sibbes, "The breach of the First Commandment is the ground of the breach of all the rest."[3] The call is unequivocal. We are to love the Lord our God with all our heart, soul, mind, and strength.

Often this absolute moral demand makes us uncomfortable. It should. Nothing is more alien to the user-friendly, feel-good sentiment that passes for theology in modern evangelicalism. At such times, we need to feel the force of God's warning to Isaiah: "You shall not say 'too hard' of everything that this people call hard; you shall neither dread nor fear that which they fear. It is the Lord of Hosts whom you must count 'hard.' He it is whom you must fear and dread" (Isaiah 8:12-13, NEB).

Down through the ages the gospel's moral demand beat powerfully in the church—usually in a matter-of-fact, no-nonsense way.

The pulse of the moral demand of the gospel only flutters in the evangelical community today. But down through the ages the gospel's moral demand beats powerfully in the church—usually in very matter-of-fact, no-nonsense terms. "God hath called you to Christ's side," wrote Samuel Rutherford from his own troubled times in the seventeenth century, "and the wind is now in Christ's face in this land; and seeing ye are with him, ye cannot expect the lee-side or the sunny side of the brae [hill]."[4]

Christina Rossetti, the nineteenth-century poet, set out this same stern side of the gospel in her poem "Who shall deliver me?" In fact, the closing stanzas show how close she is to the gospel and how far from us, though she was less than one hundred years from us and nineteen hundred from the New Testament.

> God harden me against myself,
> This coward with pathetic voice
> Who craves for ease, and rest, and joy;
>
> Myself, arch-traitor to myself;
> My hollowest friend, my deadliest foe,
> My clog whatever road I go.
>
> Yet One there is can curb myself,
> Can roll the strangling load from me,
> Break off the yoke and set me free.[5]

Only a few years later, Oswald Chambers wrote of the same truth, "The discipline of dismay is essential in the life of discipleship." Whether it was the hard sayings of Jesus or the sternness of His face set toward Jerusalem, "there is an aspect of Jesus that chills the heart of a disciple to the core and makes the whole spiritual life gasp for breath. This strange Being with his face 'set like flint' and his striding determination, strikes terror into me. He is no longer counsellor and comrade, he is taken up with a point of view I know nothing about, and I am amazed at him."[6]

George Macdonald emphasized the same moral demand in writing of the paradox of Christ's "inexorable love." "This life, this kingdom of God, this simplicity of absolute existence, is hard to enter. How hard? As hard as the Master of salvation could find words to express the hardness."[7] God's impossible people, in other words, are not infuriating because they set out to infuriate. Their intransigence is a by-product of their allegiance. If others find them uncomfortable, it is only because they are—they are discomforted by God.

At other times, this moral demand makes God's impossible people what George Orwell called "unclubbable." From families and neighborhoods to nations, Christians know and appreciate the place of human society. But we are never finally at home there. As Balaam prophesied in Numbers 23:9, "I see a people who live apart and do not consider themselves one of the nations." After all, we are a pilgrim people, so our roots are not in a place nor in the present and past but in the call of God. Weil put it this way:

> The city gives us a feeling of being at home.
> We must take the feeling of being at home into exile.
> We must be rooted in the absence of place.[8]

Or at other times, again, the moral demand makes us uncategorizable. Marching to the divine drummer, we are often out of step with others. Condemned to be seen as outsiders, mad, possessed, odd fellows, dangerous, "we are the imposters who speak to the truth . . . the penniless ones who own the world" (2 Corinthians 6:8, 10, NEB). But the same absolute demand is also what makes the impossible people unconquerable. If we are under God, He is over us—and no one else can be. That is why it is no cliché to say that one person with God is a majority. As the psalmist wrote, "If the Lord had not been on our side when men attacked us, when their anger flared against us, they would have swallowed us alive" (Psalm 124:2). Thus, as John Calvin's friend Beza said to the king of France, "May it please you, Sire, to remember. The church is an anvil which has worn out many hammers."

Have we evangelicals lost the moral demand of the gospel?

209

AGAINST THE WORLD, FOR THE WORLD

Second, to hold that there is one God, and no god but God, is to feel the force of the social dualism of God and His truth over against any culture and society. This social dualism runs counter to all natural religion. Within the perspectives of monism, pantheism, or paganism, for example, God is viewed as the totality of the universe, or the great World-All ("One-is-all-and-all-is-one"). The corresponding thrust of such religions is toward union and absorption. With the therapeutic, too, the thrust is toward integration and adjustment.

> *Against all such tendencies,*
> *God and His truth have the*
> *logic of a sword thrust.*

The social dualism, or deliberately forced tension at the heart of the gospel, is the companion truth to the moral demand that is inherent in the gospel. Over against all such natural tendencies, God and His truth have the logic of a sword thrust. The dualism is not ultimate, of course. It is a social and not a metaphysical dualism. There is no war within the godhead and there are no warring gods, as with the Greeks and Zoroastrians. But because of both creation and the Fall, a chasm exists between God and us and between the kingdom of God and the world. God's truth draws lines and demands choices. It is a standing challenge to every status quo. The result is a prophetic social dualism. Jesus Christ as Lord *stands over all* who believe and obey Him; Jesus Christ as Lord *stands over against all* who disbelieve and disobey Him.

This social dualism is inescapable in the Bible. The impossible followers of an impossible God are set off from all other gods—"I am the Lord your God. . . . You shall have no other Gods before me" (Exodus 20:2-3, NEB). They are set off from their own families—"If anyone comes to me and does not hate his father and mother, his wife and children, his brothers and sisters—yes, even his own life—he cannot be my disciple" (Luke 14:26). We can even be set off from our own bodies— "If your hand or your foot causes you to sin, cut it off and throw it away. It is better for you to enter life maimed or crippled than to have two hands or two feet and be thrown into eternal fire" (Matthew 18:8).

To the early church, this social dualism was a fact and a point of pride. The author of the Epistle to Diognetus writes of Christians, "They dwell in all countries, but only as sojourners. As citizens, they share in all things with others and yet endure all things as if they were strangers. Every foreign land is to them as native country, and every land of birth as land of strangers."

Even Nietzsche, for all his hostility to the church, hailed the fact of a culturally fertile tension throughout the Christian centuries and regretted the collapse of that tension. If the lack of tension is the lack of faith in Scripture—the image of an archer's bow gone slack—such lost tension is also a defining feature of Nietzsche's vision of the Last Men and their collapse into mediocrity and banality.

As Nietzsche's prediction of the Last Men underscores, many monistic tendencies in the modern world prevail to make the practice of social dualism difficult—statism, popular culture, New Age religions, and so on. Even the rhetoric of "alternatives," as in alternative schools and alternative communities, has grown hollow.

But Last Men discipleship is not discipleship at all. True discipleship requires tension. For as Jewish thinkers have long pointed out, the tension of social dualism not only results from prophecy, but it reinforces it too. (The Jews, Nietzsche wrote, are "the little people with the great prophets."[9]) Whereas the task of the priest is routine, consolidating, and normalizing, the task of the prophet is radical. By standing outside and over against society, God's impossible people have the distance and the detachment to aid discernment and, where necessary, denunciation in the name of God's truth and justice.

Have we evangelicals lost the social dualism of the gospel?

A THIRST FOR THE FUTURE

Third, to hold that there is one God, and no god but God, is to feel the force of the historical dynamism of God and His truth in relation to history and time. Like the moral demand and the social dualism, historical dynamism is inherent in the gospel. The French writer Ernest Renan said of the Jew what should also be said of true followers of Christ: He or she is a person "torn with discontent and possessed with a passionate thirst for the future."[10]

Historical dynamism means that God's people are impossible once again. They believe passionately in fulfillment and perfection, but not within present time and history. Freedom, justice, peace, healing, growth—all will be complete through Jesus Christ, but not here and not now. In the flow of history, and under the judgment of God, our best achievements are incomplete and our highest are never final. Until heaven there is no complete success, no enduring achievement, no unalloyed joy. Everything in our life as disciples of Christ strains forward and upward, beyond ourselves. There is no easing off, no settling down.

As Reinhold Niebuhr wrote,

> Nothing that is worth doing can be achieved in our lifetime; therefore we must be saved by hope. Nothing which is true or beautiful or good makes complete sense in any immediate context of history; therefore we must be saved by faith. Nothing we do, however virtuous, can be accomplished alone; therefore we are saved by love. No virtuous act is quite as virtuous from the standpoint of our friend or foe as it is from our standpoint. Therefore we must be saved by the final form of love, which is forgiveness.[11]

Much has been written on the "no longer" and the "not yet" in the last generation, but most of it has remained in books. The "born again" movement of the 1970s trumpeted the "no longer," but forgot the "not yet." Christian activism of the 1980s hailed policy after policy as "Christian" and denounced alternatives as wicked, but gave little thought to the worthwhile compromise, the interim achievement, the provisional success, and the importance of the "for the time being" character of it all.

Historical dynamism has taken many shapes in different periods. Sometimes it has been distorted beyond recognition. But it has always pivoted on three great biblical truths that, combined in this way, are absent from human history elsewhere and never successfully copied. First, human history is taken seriously. Contrary to Eastern views of illusion, or Maya, or postmodern Western views of meaninglessness, history in the biblical perspective is never "a tale told by an idiot" as Shakespeare put it. Rather it is the ultimate arena for human significance and destiny. Second, a thirst for fulfillment and yearnings for life and justice are proper because there will be a consummation and completion to history. Third, human hope of an ultimate outcome must be staked on an ultimate but nonhumanist power beyond our own. Historical dynamism is therefore messianic. It depends on the Messiah.

Thus, unlike humanist activism, messianic dynamism means that God's impossible people wait even as they work. They know their need for the Messiah because their best is never enough. But unlike Christian quietism, God's impossible people work even as they wait. What is coming gives strength to all that they are doing. All that they are doing becomes a sign of what is coming—when Jesus Christ returns.

Have we evangelicals lost the historical dynamism of the gospel?

TRUTH DRAWS LINES

Fourth, to hold that there is one God, and no god but God, is to feel the force of the theological discrimination of God and His truth over against all other truth claims and moral judgments. This theological discrimination is the companion truth to the moral demands, the social dualism, and the historical dynmaism in the gospel. We live in a day when clearly our modern culture is no friend to this point. Tolerance has so recoiled from intolerance as to become intolerant itself. Meanwhile, relativism has become the last absolute, the once-permissive have become the new Puritans, and glorying in being open-minded has become closed-minded. Because nothing is true or false, everything is considered equal—except a truth that does not claim that everything else is true.

The ironies and inconsistencies in this modern position are obvious. As the English novelist E. M. Forster wryly observed, "There are two kinds of people in the world—those who say there are two kinds of people in the world and those who do not." But for followers of Christ, this response is not enough. God's people are impossible about truth because God is.

The first duty of those who love God is to say yes to Him. The second is to know when to say no to anything else.

God insists on distinctions and takes differences seriously. If He alone is God, anything else is either created or an illusion. If His word is truth, anything that differs is a lie. If His character is good, anything deficient or opposed is evil. Since God alone is God, the affirmation of who He is includes the denial of what He is not. The first duty of those who love God is to say yes to Him. The second is to know when to say no to anything else.

This theme is stubbornly persistent in the Scriptures. God is not squeamish about distinctions. "I will bring judgment on all the gods of Egypt. I am the Lord. . . . When I see the blood, I will pass over you" (Exodus 12:13). Nor was Jesus any softer. "I did not come to bring peace, but a sword" (Matthew 10:34). The kingdom of Christ versus the kingdom of Satan, life versus death, light versus darkness, heaven versus hell, sheep versus goats—the Bible is unembarrassed about the difference that makes a

213

difference. Whether it was Noah's ark or the wedding reception in Jesus' story, doors were shut and some were in and others were out. As C. S. Lewis wrote in *The Weight of Glory,* the unfathomable terror of Jesus' words "I never knew you. Depart from me" means "we can be both banished from the presence of Him who is present everywhere, and erased from the knowledge of Him who knows all."[12]

The theme also recurs throughout Christian history and is the essence of Protestantism—prototypically in Martin Luther's "Here I stand. So help me God, I can do no other." In America today, however, it is seen as quaint or offensive. Truth claims and moral judgments have been reduced to the subjective, the cognitive is eclipsed by the emotive, and non-judgmentalism and empathy are prized above confrontation. Theological discrimination and standing for truth have become as reprehensible as back-stabbing and name-calling. If someone challenges someone else over a point of truth in America, the challenge is frequently deflected or lost because the one challenged feels "called into question as a person."

We are not only poorer for this loss of discrimination, but less faithful and more stupid too. G.K. Chesterton wrote, "In all the mess of modern thoughtlessness that still calls itself modern thought, there is perhaps nothing so stupendously stupid as the common saying, 'Religion can never depend on minute disputes about doctrine.' It is like saying that life can never depend on minute disputes about medicine." Indeed, he added, "If a theological distinction is a thread, all Western history has hung upon that thread."[13]

Have we evangelicals lost the theological discrimination of the gospel?

DISTURBERS OF THE PEACE

Fifth, to believe that there is one God, and no god but God, is to feel the force of the spiritual disturbance of God and His truth in relation to all other authorities and powers. This spiritual disturbance joins the moral demand, the social dualism, the historical dynamism, and the theological discrimination as a companion truth inherent in the gospel. God's impossible people should always be troublesome. Commitment to His authority entails conflict with any authority that challenges His. Called to follow the royal road of love, they will still leave in their train a divine discontent, and an unavoidable sense of disturbance.

For the Christian, this spiritual disturbance is a direct product of our love for Christ and allegiance to His authority. But we need only to lose our first love or compromise His authority for the tension to disappear. We Christians then quickly become innocuous or, worse still, we are troubled rather than troubling, scandalous rather than disturbing.

For Jews, however, there is no such easy way out. Since "chosenness" is their very identity as a people, they have always believed that their calling as monotheists is to question all the self-idolizing and self-absoluting tendencies in human society. Jacques Maritain, the Catholic philosopher, wrote admiringly of the Jewish people: "Like an activating fervent . . . [Israel] gives the world no peace. It bars slumber. It teaches the world to be discontented and restless as long as the world has not God. It stimulates the movement of history."[14]

Will Herberg, a sociologist and devout Jew, drew the line linking chosenness to the "principle of anti-idolatry" in Jewishness. He argued that:

> We can state it as the inescapable lesson of history that the Jew is the living embodiment of this principle. He is that not only because the principle stems directly from his religious tradition, but also and more fundamentally because any violation of it . . . any tendency to absolutize a man, a nation, a culture, a system or an issue—sooner or later brings with it a threat to his very existence as a Jew, no matter how otherwise well established in society we may be. The Jew, it has been said with considerable insight, is a kind of living litmus paper by which the spiritual health of a society or culture may be judged.[15]

This description rings hollow to many modern Jews. The degree of their assimilation to American culture leaves them far from unadjusted and little inclined to be a disturber of any peace. But are we modern Christians any better? Is not cultural assimilation the chief mark of our Last Men evangelicalism? Could it be said of us that we so assert "a rival king, Jesus" that we have "made trouble the whole world over"? Are we likely to rouse ourselves to tear down the idols that are entrenched in our own churches and our homes?

Jacques Ellul argues that radical nonconformity would allow the Christian church to offer society "sighting points." These are lookout places from which Christians can interpret events according to their true meaning, hold their contemporaries accountable to truth and right and wrong, and exercise a revolutionary, stock-taking role in society—"a continual calling-in-question from inside a given society."[16]

In short, our role is to be disturbers of the peace. Ellul concludes: "If the Church were truly this permanent dissatisfaction at the heart of societies, which she ought to be, she would play a dynamic role, instead of being forever in the funeral procession of the past."[17]

Have we evangelicals lost the spiritual disturbance of the gospel?

THE TEST OF LOVE

Clearly God's impossible people are never troublesome to other authorities unless they are mastered by God's authority. We are only able to call into question to the extent that we ourselves are following the call. We are only able to provide sighting points for the world if we are sighting God ourselves. We can only do any of these things to the degree that we are loving God. Thus the last word on the tearing down of idols and the reformation of evangelicalism is the first one on discipleship: loving the Lord our God with all our hearts, soul, strength, and mind.

For followers of Jesus Christ, breaking with idols and living in truth are finally not a test of orthodoxy, but of love. That is why idolatry is worse than apostasy—it is adultery. Love is the final expression of truth, just as loyalty to truth is the vital test of love. Thus for followers of Christ who have the consuming passion to be His, entirely His, at all costs and forever His, the present cultural captivity of evangelicalism is a scandal and a sorrow that is also a test of love. It can be said of our condition as it was said of the person in the book of Deuteronomy who led others to compromise, "God is testing you through him to discover whether you love the Lord your God with all your heart and soul." May we who call ourselves by the name of the gospel be found true to the gospel by which we are called.

> *Dieu Seul*
> There is one God,
> There is no god but God,
> And there is no rest for any people who rely on any god but God.
> Let God be God.
> *Sola deo gloria.*

NOTES

Chapter 1: The Idol Factory

1. As quoted from Charles H. Spurgeon, *The Treasury of David* (Grand Rapids: Zondervan, 1968), 1: 279.
2. Lance Morrow, "All Right, What Kind of People Are We?" *Time*, 30 July 1984, p. 108.
3. Roger Gould, *Transformations* (New York: Simon & Schuster, 1979), pp. 17-42.
4. Daniel Boorstin, *The Image* (New York: Atheneum, 1961), pp. 15-16.

Chapter 2: Up to Our Steeples in Politics

1. As quoted in George Marsden, *Fundamentalism and American Culture: The Shaping of Twentieth-Century Evangelicalism, 1870-1925* (Oxford, England: Oxford, 1980), p. 188.
2. Sean Wilentz, "God and Man at Lynchburg," *New Republic*, 25 April 1988, p. 30.
3. Steve Bruce, *The Rise and Fall of the New Christian Right* (Oxford, England: Clarendon, 1988), p. 49.
4. Alexis de Tocqueville, *Democracy in America* (New York: Vintage, 1945), 2: 135.
5. Richard John Neuhaus, "The Christian and the Church," in *Transforming Our World*, ed. James M. Boice (Portland, Oreg.: Multnomah, 1988), p. 120.
6. Nathan Glazer, "Toward a New Corcodat?" *This World* 2 (Summer 1982): 112.
7. Bruce, *Rise and Fall*, p. 22.
8. As quoted in Garry Wills, "Evangels of Abortion," *The New York Review of Books*, 15 June 1989, p. 21.
9. Sidney Blumenthal, "The Righteous Empire," *New Republic*, 22 October 1984, p. 24.
10. John Murray, "Common Grace," in *Collected Writings of John Murray* (Edinburgh, Scotland: Banner of Truth, 1978), 2: 112.
11. Louis Berkhof, *Systematic Theology* (Grand Rapids: Eerdmans, 1939), p. 440.

12. Ibid., p. 436.
13. Peter L. Berger, "Different Gospels: The Social Sources of Apostasy," *This World* 17 (Spring 1987): 16.
14. C. S. Lewis, *The Screwtape Letters* (New York: Macmillan, 1977), pp. 115-16.
15. Neuhaus, "The Christian and the Church," p. 123.
16. H. M. Kuitert, *Everything Is Politics but Politics Is not Everything* (Grand Rapids: Eerdmans, 1986), p. 4.
17. Oliver O'Donovan, *Resurrection and Moral Order* (Grand Rapids: Eerdmans, 1986), p. 72.
18. Wilfred M. McClay, "Religion in Politics; Politics in Religion," *Commentary*, October 1988, pp. 48-49.

Chapter 3: Nostalgia for the Lost Empire

1. Dale Vree, "Ideology versus Theology: Case Studies of Liberation Theology and the Christian New Right," in *Christianity Confronts Modernity*, ed. Kevin Perrota et. al. (Ann Arbor, Mich.: Servant, 1981), p. 71.
2. As quoted in Franklin and Betty Parker, "Behind Textbook Censorship," *National Forum*, Fall 1988, p. 37.
3. Robert Wuthnow, *The Restructuring of American Religion* (Princeton, N.J.: Princeton U., 1988), p. 301.
4. Bernard E. Brown, ed., *Great American Political Thinkers* (New York: Avon, 1983), p. 20.
5. Will Herberg, *From Marxism to Judaism* (New York: Markus Wiener, 1989), p. 281.
6. Sidney Ahlstrom, *A Religious History of the American People* (New Haven, Conn.: Yale U., 1972), p. 347.
7. Martin E. Marty, *Righteous Empire* (New York: Dial, 1970), p. 57.
8. Alexis de Tocqueville, *Democracy in America* (New York: Vintage, 1945), 2: 6.
9. William Lee Miller, *The First Liberty* (New York: Knopf, 1985), p. 363.
10. Ibid., p. 361.
11. Hunter Miller, *Treaties and Other International Acts of the United States* (Washington: Government Printing Office, 1930), p. 365.
12. Oswald Chambers, *Devotions for a Deeper Life* (Grand Rapids: Zondervan, 1986), p. 32.
13. Phil McCombs, "On the Eve of the Abortion Battle," *Washington Post*, 22 January 1992, p. C9.
14. Christine Spolar, "Abortion Foes Defiant," *Washington Post*, 21 January 1992, p. B1.
15. James E. Wood, Jr., "Religious Fundamentalism and the New Right," in *Church and State in American History*, ed. John F. Wilson and Donald L. Drakeman (Boston: Beacon, 1987), p. 250.
16. Joel Belz, "The 'Religious New Right': Just Scaring the Enemy Is Not Enough," *World*, 24 November 1990, p. 9.
17. James Davison Hunter, *American Evangelicalism* (New Brunswick, N.J.: Rutgers U., 1983), p. 49.
18. George Gallup in *Religion Watch*, June 1991, p. 4.
19. James Davison Hunter, "Religion, Knowledge and Power in the Modern Age," unpublished manuscript, University of Virginia, 1991.
20. Robert Wuthnow, *The Restructuring of American Religion*, p. 163.
21. Hunter, "Religion, Knowledge, and Power in the Modern Age," p. 18.

22. Robert Booth Fowler, "The Failure of the New Christian Right," p. 9. Unpublished manuscript prepared for the Ethics and Public Policy Center Conference on Evangelicals, Politics, and the Religious New Right, 14-15 November 1990.

23. George M. Marsden, "The Religious Right and American Politics: Past and Future," adapted from "Afterword: Religion, Politics, and the Search for an American Consensus," in *Religion and American Politics*, ed. Mark A. Noll (Oxford, England: Oxford, 1990), p. 9.

24. T.S. Eliot, as quoted in *Context*, 1 December 1991, p. 2.

25. Rebecca Olsen, "Mailbag," *World*, 1 February 1992, p. 22.

26. David John Seel, *Does My Father Know I'm Hurt?* (Wheaton, Ill.: Tyndale, 1971), p. 71.

27. Ibid., p. 33.

28. Ibid.

29. Martin Marty, as quoted in Wood, *Religious Fundamentalism and the New Right*, p. 250.

30. E.J. Dionne, Jr., "Bloom Is Off Religious Right, Scholars At Conference Agree," *Washington Post*, 30 November 1990, p. A3.

31. Henry Fairlie, *The Seven Deadly Sins Today* (Washington: New Republic Books, 1983), p. 49.

Chapter 4: More Victimized Than Thou

1. From a memorial plaque in the National Cathedral, Washington, D.C.

2. As quoted in O. Hobart Mowrer, *The New Group Therapy* (New York: Van Nostrand Reinhold, 1964), p. 7. Present copyright owner unknown.

3. *Time*, 12 August 1991, cover page.

4. David G. Dalin, ed., *From Marxism to Judaism: Collected Essays of Will Herberg*, (New York: Markus Wiener, 1987), p. 218.

5. Charles W. Colson, "From a Moral Majority to a Persecuted Minority," *Christianity Today*, 14 May 1990, p. 80.

6. William Griffin, "CBA in Orlando," *Publishers Weekly*, 16 August 1991, p. 19.

7. Robert K. Dornan, "Blatant Bigotry," *Washington Post*, 10 February 1990, p. A21.

8. Ken Sidey, "Open Season on Christians?" *Christianity Today*, 23 April 1990, p. 36.

9. Richard Zone on "Sixty Minutes," 21 September 1980.

10. Patrick J. Buchanan, "Hollywood's War on Christianity," *Washington Times*, 27 July 1988, p. F3.

11. As quoted in Deirdre Sullivan, "Targeting Souls," *American Demographics*, October 1991, p. 57.

12. Fred Barnes, "Media Issues of the 90s," *World*, 19 May 1990, p. 10.

13. Colman McCarthy, "McNeil/Lehrer: Fair Game," *Washington Post*, 3 June 1990, p. F2.

14. Friedrich Nietzsche, *Thus Spoke Zarathustra*, trans. Walter Kaufmann (London: Penguin, 1978), p. 100.

15. Joseph Farah, "Why Ted Turner Hates Religion," *World*, 16 June 1990, p. 18.

16. Dietrich Bonhoeffer, *The Cost of Discipleship* (London: SCM, 1959), p. 79.

17. Roger Pooley and Philip Seddon, eds., *Lord of the Journey* (London: Collins, 1986), p. 349.

18. Andrew Bonar, ed., *Letters of Samuel Rutherford* (London: Oliphant, 1891), pp. 161-62.

19. Aleksandr Solzhenitsyn, *The Gulag Archipelago 1918-1956*, trans. Thomas P. Whitney (London: Collins and Harvill, 1975), 2: 615-17.
20. In Pooley and Seddon, *Lord of the Journey*, p. 319.

Chapter 5: Leaving Psychology Behind

1. With credit and apologies to *Newsweek* issue of 17 February 1992.
2. Rita Kramer, *Ed School Follies: The Miseducation of America's Teachers* (New York: Free Press, 1991); see also Chester E. Finn, Jr., "Narcissus Goes to School," *Commentary*, June 1990.
3. Gloria Steinem, *Revolution from Within: A Book of Self-Esteem* (Boston: Little Brown, 1992).
4. A. LaPointe, N. A. Mead, and G. Philips, *A World of Difference: An International Assessment of Mathematics and Science* (Princeton, N.J.: Educational Testing Service, 1989), p. 10.
5. This is also the point of columnist Charles Krauthammer in the *New Republic*, June 1990.
6. As quoted in Kramer, *Ed School Follies*. See also p. 210 in the chapter "Self-esteem Has Replaced Understanding as the Goal of Education."
7. Michael J. Lambert, David A. Shapiro, and Allen E. Bergin, "The Effectiveness of Psychotherapy," in *Handbook of Psychotherapy and Behavior Change*, 3d ed., Sol Garfield and Allen Bergin, eds. (New York: Wiley, 1986), p.160.
8. See Miriam Adahan, *EMMET: A Step by Step Guide to Emotional Maturity Established Through Torah* (Jerusalem: Feldheim, 1987). This is a Jewish cognitive psychotherapy based on the Torah, the first five books of the Bible.
9. The False Memory Syndrome Foundation has headquarters at Suite 128, 3508 Market Street, Philadelphia, PA 19104.
10. See J. Orford, *Excessive Appetites: A Psychological View of Addictions* (New York: Wiley, 1985).
11. Stanton Peele, *Diseasing of America: Addiction Treatment Out of Control* (Boston: Houghton Mifflin, 1989).
12. An important recent example of this is David Stoop and James Masteller, *Forgiving Our Parents, Forgiving Ourselves* (Ann Arbor, Mich.: Servant, 1991). The authors state the problem clearly: "Once you realize how deeply you may have been hurt by those in your family, forgiving them may seem like the last thing you want to do. But in fact, forgiveness is crucial to your spiritual and emotional health. It is the key to freedom from the pain of the past" (p. 155).

Chapter 6: America's Last Men and Their Magnificent Talking Cure

1. As quoted in Ernest Becker, *The Denial of Death* (New York: Free Press, 1973), p. 96.
2. As quoted in E. Brooks Holifield, *A History of Pastoral Care in America* (Nashville: Abingdon, 1983), p. 213.
3. Peter L. Berger, *Facing Up to Modernity* (New York: Basic, 1977), p. 32.
4. Robert Coles, *Harvard Diary* (New York: Crossroad, 1989), p. 92.
5. Tim Stafford, "The Hidden Gospel of the 12 Steps," *Christianity Today*, 22 July 1991, p. 14.
6. As quoted in Dave Carew, "Binding up the Brokenhearted," *Bookstore Journal*, August 1991, pp. 34-35.
7. Philip Rieff, *The Feeling Intellect* (Chicago: U. of Chicago, 1990), p. 354.
8. Bernie Zilbergeld, *The Shrinking of America* (Boston: Little Brown, 1983), p. 33.

9. See Chapter 2 of Zilbergeld, *The Shrinking of America.*
10. As quoted in T. J. Jackson Lears, *No Place of Grace* (New York: Pantheon, 1981), p. 54.
11. Coles, *Harvard Diary*, p. 93.
12. As quoted in Robert Nisbet, *Twilight of Authority* (New York: OUP, 1975), p. 139.
13. Rieff, *The Feeling Intellect,* pp. 335, 354.
14. O. Hobart Mowrer, "The New Challenge to Our Churches and Seminaries," *Foundation* 3 (October 1960): 335-47.
15. Coles, *Harvard Diary*, pp. 11-12.
16. Zilbergeld, *Shrinking of America*, p. 11.
17. As quoted in Zilbergeld, *Shrinking of America*, p. 13; Christopher Lasch, *The Culture of Narcissism* (New York: Warner, 1979), p. 103.
18. As quoted in Zilbergeld, *Shrinking of America*, p. 13.
19. Beth Ann Krier, "Everyday Addicts," *The Los Angeles Times*, 29 July 1990, p. E1.
20. Jerry Adler, "Hey, I'm Terrific!" *Newsweek*, 17 February 1992, p. 46.
21. Ibid., p. 51.
22. Ibid., p. 50.
23. Oswald Chambers, *My Utmost for His Highest* (New York: Dodd, Mead, 1935), June 24.
24. Rieff, *Feeling Intellect*, p. 355.
25. Michelle Bearden, *Publishers Weekly*, 10 February 1992, p. 42.
26. See Holifield, *History of Pastoral Care in America.*
27. Philip Rieff, *The Triumph of the Therapeutic* (Chicago: U. of Chicago, 1987), pp. 24-25.
28. As quoted in Zilbergeld, *Shrinking of America*, p. 159.
29. Rieff, *Feeling Intellect*, p. 359.
30. Hans Eysenck, "What's the Truth About Psychoanalysis?" *Readers Digest*, January 1960, p. 40.
31. "Interview with John Bradshaw," *New Age Journal*, August 1991, p. 25.
32. Rieff, *The Feeling Intellect*, p. 365.

Chapter 7: The Grand Inquisitor Lives: Idolatry in Organizations and Management

1. Fyodor Dostoevsky, *The Brothers Karamazov,* trans. Constance Garnett (New York: Random House, 1950), pp. 255-74. Italics added for emphasis.
2. See Robert Knille, *As I Was Saying: A Chesterton Reader* (Grand Rapids: Eerdmans, 1985).

Chapter 8: Sounding Out the Idols of Church Growth

1. See C. Peter Wagner, *Your Church Can Grow* (Glendale, Calif.: Regal, 1976), chapter 1.
2. Leith Anderson, *Dying for Change* (Minneapolis: Bethany House, 1990), p. 17.
3. C.S. Lewis, *George Macdonald: An Anthology* (London: Geoffrey Bles, 1946), p. 27.
4. Peter L. Berger, *A Rumor of Angels* (Garden City, N.Y.: Doubleday, Anchor, 1970), p. 22.
5. Friedrich Nietzsche, *Twilight of the Idols/The Anti-Christ* (London: Penguin, 1968), p. 21.
6. Michelle Bearden, *Publishers Weekly*, 10 February 1991, p. 42.

7. As quoted in Arthur Unger, "Born Again Phenomenon," *Christian Science Monitor* 13 July 1977; *American Demographics*, August 1988, p. 57.

8. Phillip Rieff, *The Feeling Intellect* (Chicago: U. of Chicago), p. 280.

9. As quoted in Lears, *No Place of Grace*, p. 24.

10. As quoted in *Context*, 15 April 1991, p. 4.

11. Robert Kniller, *As I Was Saying: A Chesterton Reader* (Grand Rapids: Eerdmans, 1985), p. 272.

12. See Christopher Lasch, *The Culture of Narcissism* (New York: Warner, 1979) and Ivan Illich, *Disabling Professions* (London: Marion Boyars, 1977).

Chapter 9: The D-Min-ization of the Ministry

1. See the discussion of this literature in David S. Reynolds, *Faith in Fiction: The Emergence of Religious Literature in America* (Cambridge, Mass.: Harvard U., 1981), pp. 169-96. Reynolds's work is chronologically arranged and is wider in scope than works dealing exclusively with ministers. On this narrower theme, see Horton Davies, *A Mirror of the Ministry in Modern Novels* (New York: Oxford, 1959); Grier Nichol, "The Image of the Protestant Minister in the Christian Social Novel," *Church History* 38 (September 1968): 319-34; Gilbert P. Voight, "The Protestant Minister in American Fiction," *The Lutheran Quarterly* 11 (February 1959): 3-13.

2. The difficulty in defining what in general constitutes a profession is addressed well by Morris L. Cogan, "The Problem of Defining a Profession," *Annals of the American Academy of Political and Social Science* 297 (January 1955: 105-11 and his "Toward a Definition of Profession," *Harvard Educational Review* 23 (Winter 1953): 33-50. Regarding the clergy itself, the same issue is addressed by Everett C. Hughes, "Are the Clergy a Profession?" *Theological Education as Professional Education* (Dayton, Ohio: The American Association of Theological Schools, 1969), p. 149-55. Especially useful in defining the nature of a profession have been sociological analyses; see, for example, Talcott Parsons, "Professions," in *International Encyclopedia of the Social Sciences*, ed. David L. Sills (New York: Macmillan and the Free Press, 1969), 12:536-47.

3. There were long and complex discussions about a professional degree like the D.Min long before it was actually born. The American Theological Society had proposed such a degree in 1942, but the response from the seminaries was not positive. In 1950, the attempt was made again, but only seven of one hundred seminaries in the ATS said that they would offer it if it were inaugurated. No action was taken. In the sixties, however, the Committee on Standards for a Professional Doctorate recommended its standards for the degree to the ATS. Unfortunately, the higher standards for which they argued were consistently voted down, notably that two languages other than English should be required and that candidates for the degree should be able to integrate the classical disciplines into their ministry practice. The period between 1970 and 1978 was one of trial for this increasingly popular degree.

   At the end of this time a task force appointed by ATS President David Hubbard examined the degree and reported back on the considerable misgivings that many had about it. These misgivings centered on the fact that they did not believe a doctorate should be given for what was basically continuing education, that many of the students were not of a high caliber academically, that quality control in the degree was deficient, that many of the faculty in the classical disciplines were unwilling to participate because they were suspicious of it, and because the matter of financial viability had prompted many institutions to offer it.

4. The judgment expressed here is a minority view. Those who are active participants in the degree, such as some of the faculty and the administrators of it, register a far more positive view, as do the beneficiaries, such as presidents and the candidates for the degree. However, a significant number of faculty still have deep reservations about the degree because of its lack of clear definition and because of their unease over the economic motives that drive it.

5. See Jackson W. Carroll and Barbara Wheeler, "Study of Doctoral of Ministry Programs," in *Graduates*, p. 3; an unpublished report conducted under the auspices of Auburn Theological Seminary and the Hartford Seminary's Center for Social and Religious Research, 1987.

6. These figures are based upon an analysis of 434 essays that appeared in *Leadership Journal*. The content study, conducted by the author, also found that 80 percent of the essays treated the personal crises and perplexities encountered by the clergy and 13 percent dealt with techniques for managing the church. For an extended analysis, see David F. Wells, "Things Fall Apart," chapter 3 in *No Place for Truth* (Grand Rapids: Eerdmans, 1992).

7. William Adams Brown, *The Education of American Ministers* (New York: Institute of Social and Religious Research, 1934), 1:21.

8. *Church Planning Inventory: Comparative Tabulations; 72 Congregations* (Hartford, Conn.: Hartford Seminary Center for Social and Religious Research, 1986), p. 6.

9. Half of the two hundred sermons were from *Pulpit Digest* from January-February 1981 to March-April 1991; the other half were sermons from *Preaching*, July-August 1985 to January-February 1991. I am grateful to James Singleton, who extended his doctoral research (at Boston University, Cambridge, Mass.) to include this work and who, therefore, provided the foundation for my own judgments.

10. Leonard I. Sweet, "The Modernization of Protestant Religion in America," *Altered Landscapes*, ed. David W. Lotz (Grand Rapids: Eerdmans, 1989), pp. 33-34.

Afterword

1. Friedrich Nietzsche, *Twilight of the Idols/The Anti-Christ* (London: Penguin, 1968), pp. 35, 128, 129.

2. Simone Weil, *Waiting on God* (London: Routledge and Kegan Paul, 1951), p. 122.

3. As quoted in J. Sears McGee, *The Godly Man in Stuart England* (New Haven, Conn.: Yale U., 1976), p. 71.

4. As quoted in A. W. Tozer, *Renewed Day by Day* (Camp Hill, Pa.: Christian Publications, 1980), July 17.

5. William M. Rossetti, ed., *Poems of Christina Rossetti* (London: Macmillan, 1910), pp. 87-88.

6. Oswald Chambers, *My Utmost for His Highest* (New York: Dodd, Mead, 1935), March 15.

7. C.S. Lewis, *George Macdonald: An Anthology* (London: Geoffrey Bles, 1946), p. 44.

8. Simone Weil, *Gravity and Grace* (London: Routledge and Kegan Paul, 1972), p. 34.

9. As quoted in Philip Rieff, *The Feeling Intellect* (Chicago: U. of Chicago, 1990), p. 54.

10. As quoted in David G. Dalin, ed., *From Marxism to Judaism* (New York: Markus Weiner, 1987), p. 279.

11. As quoted in John P. Diggins, *The Lost Soul of American Politics* (New York: Basic, 1984), p. vii.

12. C.S. Lewis, *The Weight of Glory* (Grand Rapids: Eerdmans, 1965), p. 12.

13. Robert Knille, *As I Was Saying: A Chesterton Reader* (Grand Rapids: Eerdmans, 1985), pp. 158-59.

14. As quoted in Dalin, ed., *From Marxism to Judaism*, p. 98.

15. Ibid., p. 34.

16. Jacques Ellul, *The False Presence of the Kingdom* (New York: Seabury, 1972), p. 202.

17. Ibid.